Refiguring
ENGLISH
STUDIES

Refiguring English Studies provides a forum for scholarship on English Studies as a discipline, a profession, and a vocation. To that end, the series publishes historical work that considers the ways in which English Studies has constructed itself and its objects of study; investigations of the relationships among its constituent parts as conceived in both disciplinary and institutional terms; and examinations of the role the discipline has played or should play in the larger society and public policy. In addition, the series seeks to feature studies that, by their form or focus, challenge our notions about how the written "work" of English can or should be done and to feature writings that represent the professional lives of the discipline's members in both traditional and nontraditional settings. The series also includes scholarship that considers the discipline's possible futures or that draws upon work in other disciplines to shed light on developments in English Studies.

Volumes in the Series

Composition and Sustainability
Teaching for a Threatened Generation

DEREK OWENS
St. John's University

National Council of Teachers of English
1111 W. Kenyon Road, Urbana, Illinois 61801-1096

Staff Editor: Tom Tiller
Interior Design: Jenny Jensen Greenleaf
Cover Design and Calligraphy: Barbara Yale-Read
Cover Artwork: Teva M. Hite

NCTE Stock Number: 00376-3050

It is the policy of NCTE in its journals and other publications to provide a forum for the open discussion of ideas concerning the content and the teaching of English and the language arts. Publicity accorded to any particular point of view does not imply endorsement by the Executive Committee, the Board of Directors, or the membership at large, except in announcements of policy, where such endorsement is clearly specified.

Although every attempt is made to ensure accuracy at the time of publication, NCTE cannot guarantee that all published addresses for electronic mail or Web sites are current.

Excerpt from *Gain* by Richard Powers: Copyright © 1998 by Richard Powers. Reprinted by permission of Farrar, Straus and Giroux, LLC.

Library of Congress Cataloging-in-Publication Data

Owens, Derek, 1963–
        Composition and sustainability: teaching for a threatened generation/
        Derek Owens.
             p. cm.—(Refiguring English studies ; ISSN 1073-9637)
        Includes bibliographical references (p.) and index.
        ISBN 0-8141-0037-6
        1. English language—Rhetoric—Study and teaching. 2. Report
        writing—Study and teaching (Higher) I. Title. II. Series.
        PE1404 .O93 2001
        808'.042'071—dc21
                                                              2001045259

ACKNOWLEDGMENTS

Thanks to the editors who played significant roles at various stages in this project (in order of their appearance): acquisitions editors Michael Greer, Zarina Hock, and the ever patient Kurt Austin, as well as Tom Tiller, whose copyediting improved the manuscript considerably. Special thanks to mentor and friend Stephen North. And, although I did my share of grumbling each time the editorial board requested another rewrite or clarification, the fact is that their attentive readings turned this into a much better book.

I also owe much to the following readers: Michael Blitz, Dan Collins, Sid Dobrin, Mark Hurlbert, Paula Mathieu, Jody Swilky, and the anonymous reviewers. Thanks to Don Byrd, Thomas Dean, Scott Denton, Nancy Dunlop, Rona Fried, Al Gini, Charles Jennings, David Matlin, Thom and Eileen Metzger, David Nentwick, Rev. Patrick Primeaux, Randall Roorda, Paul Ryan, Sean Southey, and Michael Spooner for influential feedback. Thanks as well to the students in my fall 1999 graduate composition theory course who read an early version of this manuscript and offered helpful suggestions.

Tom Kelly and Julie Newman, coordinators of an Environmental Literacy Institute seminar that I attended in the summer of 1997, were superb teachers. Conversations with other participants—Kelly Cain, Mary Lou Dolan, Steve Simpson, Lucian Spataro, Scott Turner, Evan Williams, and Tom Wojciechowski—furthered my thinking. Special thanks to Tom Brown, who invited me to attend, free of charge, a course in his Tracking, Wilderness, and Survival School.

St. John's University was generous with research reductions and summer support. The Center for Teaching and Learning funded my stay at the Environmental Literacy Institute. The Reverend David M. O'Connell offered invaluable encouragement

when he was Dean of the college. Stephen Sicari, chair of the English department, did much to promote this project during my bid for tenure.

Thanks to my parents for instilling in me a foundation for preservation and play. Thanks to my sister Renee, whose work as a biologist and a conservationist has always pushed me to try and make my own work as an educator almost as important. Thanks to my son Ryan for providing the impetus to write this book, which began pretty much the day my wife, Teresa Hewitt, learned she was pregnant. Most of all, thanks to Teresa for putting up with my mood swings during the course of this project, and for modeling for me what it means to be a parent and a teacher.

Finally, thanks to my students, whose words and ideas, whose hopes and fears, are at the core of this project. Without their insights, there would have been no book. In meager reciprocation for granting me permission to quote liberally from their papers (all student names are pseudonyms), all royalties I receive for this manuscript will go to community revitalization projects and third-sector organizations in their neighborhoods.

For Ryan,
my students,
and their kids

CONTENTS

PREFACE

I should explain at the outset how I'm interpreting this concept of sustainability. Although I unpack the term in some detail in Chapter 2, a quick summary now will help establish the intentions of the book. Sustainability is an intergenerational concept that means adjusting our current behavior so that it causes the least amount of harm to future generations. Sustainability is also concerned with intragenerational equity: understanding the links between poverty and ecosystem decline. Sustainability means recognizing the short- and long-term environmental, social, psychological, and economic impact of our conspicuous consumption. It means seeking to make conservation and preservation inevitable effects of our daily lifestyles. It means forsaking a great many of the trappings of our consumerist culture in order to live more simply, thereby diminishing the impact of our ecological footprints. It means looking critically at our contemporary behaviors from the perspective of children living generations hence, and modifying those behaviors accordingly.

My objective is to help introduce the concept of sustainability into some of the conversations that occur within English studies, using my work in the composition classroom as an entry point. I hope that this won't be seen as simply a "green" book. That is, I don't want this to be a book written just for an audience of ecocritics, ecocompositionists, environmental educators, and those who situate themselves in various "eco" disciplines. Certainly I look forward to further conversations with scholars and practitioners in these areas, many of whom are more experienced than I am in designing pedagogies and curricula of sustainability. But the people I'm really hoping to make contact with are teachers and students who are living in suburbs and cities, who are unhappy with the status of their neighborhoods and communities, who are frustrated with the nature of their workplaces, and who are worried about their futures and their kids' futures. This book is for educators with a desire to look long-term, educators who understand the need to create opportunities for long-term thinking throughout the entire curriculum.

In the first chapter, I introduce some of the motives and objectives that shape the book. Chapter 2 attempts to extract from the multiple definitions and ambiguities associated with sustainability a useful list of characteristics associated with a pedagogy of sustainability. Chapters 3, 4, and 5 examine the conceptual zones of "place," "work," and "future"—arenas very much related to sustainability—through the filters of my students' writings and published literature from a range of disciplines. The final chapter is the most tentative in the manuscript; it seeks to invoke a range of theoretical and artistic influences under the rubric of a reconstructivist pedagogical ethic. Following the last chapter are three appendixes: the first a catalog of statistics underscoring the gravity of our current situation, the second a complete "assignment packet" used in one of my composition courses, and the third an excerpt from Richard Powers's novel *Gain* that will serve as the last word on the implications of our consumer class.

The bulk of the book is intended to stimulate readers who are not inclined to think about sustainability to consider the extent to which it might play a vital role both in students' lives and in our own curricular objectives. But readers will have to wait until Appendix B before getting a detailed look at my introductory writing classes, and even then I spend little time addressing how I facilitate discussion, promote revision, and assess portfolios, choosing instead to simply highlight a semester's worth of writing assignments. This is partly because I do not think what I do in the classroom is particularly noteworthy. There's the usual workshopping of drafts, as well as small group conferences and one-on-one sessions with students—nothing terribly radical. As far as I'm concerned, what my students say in their essays is more interesting than my own actions in the classroom, which is why Chapters 3, 4, and 5 draw so heavily from their papers. Besides, my emphasis in Appendix B on course assignments rather than on pedagogical strategies reveals the degree to which my own interests lean more toward the design end of the spectrum: choreographing writing opportunities in ways that highlight connections between my students' local concerns and a range of cross-disciplinary literature treating sustainability-oriented issues.

I have two broad goals in writing this book. The primary goal is to bring sustainability further into the conversations that define composition and English studies. Despite a recent surge in ecocomposition and ecocriticism scholarship, the concept of sustainability has yet to factor significantly in English studies. Consider, for example, the 2000 edition of NCTE's *Trends and Issues in Postsecondary English Studies*: race, gender, class, writing assessment, and technology continue to be the expectedly hot topics, while sustainability is noticeably absent. If nothing else, it is my hope that this book might provoke colleagues into considering various roles that sustainability might play in their work as practitioners and researchers. Composition studies, and, indeed, all of English studies, needs to recognize as a field that sustainability is not only equal in importance to race, class, and gender but also entails many of the concerns associated with these rubrics. I am in fact inclined to agree with Mark Dowie, who claims in *Losing Ground* that the future of American environmentalism will grow in large part out of the experiences of those who, as groups, tend to be particularly sympathetic to human rights: women, people of color, poor people, and working-class people. So far in English studies, "the environment" has taken a back seat to race, gender, and class, and this disparity illustrates a lack of awareness that must be addressed, for matters of social justice are largely matters of sustainability as well. My emphasis on sustainability should not be seen as a turf battle over competing interests; rather, it responds to a need to recognize fundamental interconnections between culture, survival, body, and place.

I have grounded this book in the realm of composition instruction not just because that's where I do most of my work, but also because this disciplinary arena is ideal for engaging new undergraduates in conversations about sustainability. Composition instruction offers a means by which new college students might be made aware, albeit in an introductory and rudimentary way, of the concept of sustainability-based thinking and the role it should play throughout and beyond their academic careers. One of my interests is the fact that composition faculty, due to the cross-disciplinary flexibility of their courses and their ability to reach wide numbers of incoming college students, are positioned to help students draw connections between their needs, their desires, their neighborhoods, their majors, and their future careers—all viewed through the lens of sustainability, with writing and conversation serving as the catalysts for discovery. With this potential in mind, I feel that just as those of us in composition have sought to spread our influence throughout the academy with writing-across-the-curriculum (WAC) initiatives, we should begin working collaboratively with colleagues in other disciplines toward establishing a sustainability-across-the-curriculum (SAC) movement. I do little more than suggest this idea in the current volume—to sketch out proposals and strategies for a bona fide SAC campaign will require another book—but this is an idea hovering in the background throughout the current study.

My secondary objective is to write unabashedly for an audience of researchers and practitioners outside the realms of composition and English studies—namely, any postsecondary educator willing to consider the potential impact of sustainability on his or her research and teaching. I am aware that a book with the word "composition" featured prominently in the title and published by a press aimed at an audience of English educators is unlikely to reach many outside those arenas. Admittedly, my tack here is a little awkward: In struggling to reach an intended audience of composition and English faculty on the one hand, and virtually all other faculty on the other, I realize that the end product might look a little unusual to all of the above. Colleagues in composition might well wish I had spent more time documenting the particulars of what I do in a writing course—recapturing student conversations, providing insight into the evolution of their drafts, discussing the nature of their service-learning projects. Readers in other fields might find my reliance on student voices in the middle chapters, and the appendix detailing course assignments, excessive or distracting. Nevertheless, I have stubbornly tried to create a book of at least some interest to all colleagues regardless of what courses they teach. If nothing else, this kind of book illustrates a problem that will have to be overcome as future writers pursue sustainability within their scholarship and teaching. Sustainability-based thinking is inherently holistic, not specialized, and it requires that we make connections transcending disciplinary borders. In contrast, publication in most academic presses and journals typically requires rootedness within specific disciplinary domains: academics are largely expected to write within their niches to members of their own tribes. Yet to focus on sustainability eventually requires one to synthesize a variety of disciplines. I don't know how well my style of bouncing around will satisfy readers in composition or those in realms outside my department. But at the very least it might illustrate a problem that will have to be addressed by publishers and writers as interest in sustainability grows: how to create new opportunities for publication wherein, rather than being required to address only their immediate colleagues within a shared discipline, writers are enabled and encouraged to communicate with broader audiences.

Finally, let me say clearly that this is less a book on how to live sustainably than it is one which seeks to remind us—myself, my students, you—how far we have to go in order to reach that goal. As much as sustainability has become a buzzword in the media, in corporate rhetoric, and in certain academic disciplines, living sustainably is an exceptionally hard sell. It's one thing to use the word in a book title and another to truly live that way. As a middle-class consumer surrounded by middle-class trappings, I cannot say I live a sustainable life. Yes, my wife and I refuse to buy a second car; I insist upon using public transportation to get to work, even though it doubles my commute from one to two hours each way; I try, with mixed results, to boycott the mall and brand-name clothes and gadgets; I compost, Xeriscape (i.e., landscape to minimize water usage and to be environmentally friendly), and attempt small-scale organic gardening; we hang out our laundry except during the coldest months; and my wife and I invest in socially responsible companies promoting alternative energy, choose Working Assets as our long distance carrier, and so on. But none of this is anything to write home about. My gardening is just a hobby, a luxury made possible by my privileged academic lifestyle. So far I lack the willpower to become a vegetarian, and thus can hardly claim to live low on the food chain. My wife and, more often, I myself spoil my son by buying him far too many toys and books. We still spend money in places like Wal-Mart and Home Depot. And we live on a quarter of an acre of land smack-dab in the middle of suburbia, taking up a lot more space than three people really need, especially on a planet where the population has surged past the six billion mark.

My point is that I do not pretend to be a model for sustainability-based reform, either in my living or in my teaching. Rather, my growing interest in sustainability has led me in recent years to fuss with course design in ways that I think are noteworthy, if only in the degree to which they have brought my students' concerns to the fore. More than anything, the course I designed (and continue to design) as a result of immersing myself in the literature of sustainability is presented here as a case study. As our environmental crises become increasingly profound and, indeed, inescapable—as they most certainly will—more teachers will design their courses and structure their research around concepts and goals relating to sustainability. This book seeks to accelerate conversations fundamental to that kind of retooling and refocusing—whether one teaches courses in writing, literature, or any other field.

CHAPTER ONE

Chameleon Vision

Sustainability and English Studies

Hastily defined, *sustainability* means meeting today's needs without jeopardizing the well-being of future generations. Currently the word remains associated with academic disciplines like ecology, environmental studies, ecological economics, and planning, but soon the idea of sustainability will undoubtedly surface in a growing number of other academic departments. As it becomes increasingly impossible to ignore our escalating local and global environmental crises, and as the painful side effects of our consumer culture sink in further, educators in a number of fields will have to make room for sustainability in their teaching and in their research. Just as multiculturalism has shaped education in profound ways during the last two decades, I anticipate that sustainability—as a metaphor, a design problem, a cultural imperative, and a social and ecological necessity—will become one of the new paradigms shaping much of our work as teachers and scholars. If it doesn't, so much the worse for us.

From its inception, this book was written specifically for NCTE's Refiguring English Studies series. The language used to describe the objectives of this series is particularly apt when it comes to sustainability. For example, thinking sustainably requires that we envision ourselves less as autonomous individuals than as collaborators who are not only dependent upon but also literally connected to our local environments in complex ways. Because a curriculum of sustainability would have to be inherently holistic and cross-disciplinary, it would require not that we reject specialization per se but that we stop fetishizing specialization and stigmatizing the "generalist." And since an ethic of sustainability values an understanding of the degree to which we are interconnected with our environs, it acknowledges degrees of interdependency between the "private" and the "public." All of these objectives have echoes in the mission of the Refiguring English Studies series, which, as articulated in NCTE's official series description (see page i of this book), "publishes historical work that considers the ways in which English Studies has constructed itself and its objects of study; investigations of the relationships among its constituent parts as conceived in both disciplinary and institutional terms; and examinations of the role the discipline has played or should play in the larger society and public policy." An investigation of sustainability also forces us to rethink our jobs as professionals in English studies, thereby challenging (again in the words of the Refiguring series description) "our notions about how the written 'work' of English can or should be done." And because sustainability requires us to be profoundly future-oriented—to anticipate the effects of contemporary actions on future conditions—sustainability-related discussions are appropriate for a series promoting "scholarship that considers the discipline's possible futures."

It comes as no surprise, then, that, even though neither the series per se nor any of the books it has published focuses explicitly on sustainability, some of the titles do focus on themes indirectly related to concerns of sustainability. Jed Rasula's *The American Poetry Wax Museum* reveals the degree to which anthologies of American poetry have served as museums and greenhouses containing largely the same limited species, thereby rendering virtually a gamut of alternative and experimental writing commercially extinct. (One could compare reading an anthology of American poetry to buying produce and grain at the average supermarket, where one has little choice but to purchase the same limited varieties of apples, tomatoes, potatoes, and rice over and over again, even though thousands of different varieties of these foods exist.) In *Rhetorics, Poetics, and Cultures: Refiguring College English Studies*, James Berlin emphasizes the significance of both the mediating job that English faculty have as gatekeepers and their transformative role as catalysts for "consciousness formation" (179). Michael Blitz and C. Mark Hurlbert's *Letters for the Living: Teaching Writing in a Violent Age* and Charles M. Anderson and Marian M. MacCurdy's *Writing and*

Healing: Toward an Informed Practice both address the role of English studies, particularly composition, in helping our students—so many of whom are at risk—survive. Where these volumes focus on preserving the welfare of our students, Stephen M. North et al.'s *Refiguring the Ph.D. in English Studies: Writing, Doctoral Education, and the Fusion-Based Curriculum* concludes that the only way left to resolve the crisis facing English studies is for faculty to reinvent their departments by moving outside the safety of their specializations, to bring "outsiders" into the department in order to further revitalize course offerings, and, most important, to let graduate students play a key role in reconstructing the nature of English studies on their own terms. At this early stage in the series, one already finds a preoccupation with extinction, survival, preservation, and reconstruction, all themes at the heart of sustainability.

The time is right for our conversations to address sustainability. Recent publications in composition and rhetoric have been moving in this direction, with examinations of the rhetoric of sustainability (Killingsworth and Palmer), environmental rhetoric (Herndl and Brown), environmental discourse and communication (Cantrill and Oravec), ecofeminism (McAndrew), nature writing and composition (Roorda, *Dramas* and "Sites"), postcolonialism and environmental pedagogy (Stephen Brown), and ecocomposition (Dobrin and Weisser, *Ecocomposition* and *Natural Discourse*; Dobrin and Keller). Yet despite this recent activity, English studies is decades behind other disciplines in recognizing the importance of considering our research and teaching in light of local and global environmental exigencies. There is still a pervasive, if unacknowledged, belief that much of our work ought to focus on the triad of race/class/gender, whereas "environment" remains a category awkwardly associated with largely "white," middle-class values and geographies, and thus confined to the perimeters of our conversations.

Some of this is understandable. Attempts in the mid-1990s to establish ecocriticism and "green" cultural studies as legitimate fields—see *Ecological Literary Criticism: Romantic Imagining and the Biology of Mind* (Kroeber), *Voices in the Wilderness: American Nature Writing and Environmental Politics* (Payne), and *The Ecocriticism Reader* (Glotfelty and Fromm)—were sometimes criticized as too removed from the day-to-day realities of urban and suburban populations: "Nature writing and ecocriticism is a middle-class preserve" some argued, "attracting people who have the leisure and money to go out and enjoy nature" (Winkler A9).[1] But such critiques also reflect a missed opportunity. Instead of responding with impatience to recent eco-minded directions in scholarship as examples of bourgeois scholarship, a more useful direction would have been to further explore the ways in which feminism, multiculturalism, and environmentalism have always been bundled together, as feminist ecologists have repeatedly argued. Unfortunately, much of the literature of critical pedagogy—at least in English studies—has revolved around race, class, and gender without acknowledging that such sites of cultural conflict are so often matters of environmental injustice as well. The "environment," after all, is a rubric that doesn't just include "nature" (which, as suggested by Bill McKibben's *The End of Nature*, is a precarious construct in itself, given the degree to which humans now shape, control, and define "nature") but also suburban sprawl, the workplace, apartment buildings, strip malls, parking lots, highways, and campuses.

Because an understanding of sustainability requires an awareness of the interconnectedness of what are traditionally considered separate academic fields—ecology and economics, architecture and education, planning and sociology, philosophy and marketing, and so on—teachers who work in pedagogical zones where cross-disciplinary inquiry is encouraged have more leeway to design sustainability-focused pedagogies than do those in fields demanding greater specialization. This is where English studies, and especially composition studies, can play an influential role in imagining and developing curricula that promote awareness of sustainability.

I emphasize composition because in some respects I think it lies at the heart of English studies, or at least makes up one or two chambers of that heart. Obviously many who identify themselves with "English studies" proper—whether as literary theorists, cultural critics, historians, or century- or genre-specific scholars—will balk at this characterization. Compositionists like myself are, as Robert Scholes delicately puts it, still perceived as the ones doing "the shitwork" of English studies (35). But writing is at the core of what English majors do, as Stephen North et al. have convincingly demonstrated, and writing courses, obviously, are where so much of this activity takes place in English curricula. Certainly composition courses remain the economic bread and butter of English departments, which rely on these courses to justify their relevance to the institution. But whether one casts composition as the core of English studies or as a necessary entry point into the discipline, I trust many will agree that composition occupies a significant portion of what constitutes English studies. In any case, in a manner reminiscent of James Berlin's consideration of the crisis of English studies from the perspective of someone working in the rhetoric branch of the discipline, I can, as a writing instructor, explore some of the larger global and local environmental crises confronting all of us through the eyes of undergraduates in my writing courses. The main difference here is that instead of focusing on the "crisis" of English studies as it has come to be defined throughout the 1990s, my overriding concern is how English studies, and particularly composition, might respond to a complex web of environmental crises and catastrophes threatening not just students in English courses, but all of society.

The composition instructor enjoys a kind of contextual freedom and disciplinary flexibility unknown to many of his or her colleagues. This is composition's little secret. Certainly writing teachers still suffer from a secondary status compared to their colleagues who specialize in literature, theory, and cultural studies; they are expected to do more work (all those papers, week after week), and without adequate compensation, especially for the serfs (adjuncts and graduate assistants) but also for full-time faculty members whose work in composition makes them less eligible for a variety of grants reserved for those who work in the loftier realms of English studies. But while teaching composition is as labor intensive as any teaching in higher education, the writing instructor has more leverage for encouraging students to explore a variety of themes and experiences than do those who teach in more specialized areas. Not only do compositionists and their students inject material into courses that other colleagues and their students can't address, but also they can orchestrate zones of inquiry that juxtapose eclectic webs of information, inspiration, and provocation, the likes of which can't easily be generated elsewhere in academe. Faculty who teach "disciplin-ized" courses—Advanced Commercial Computing, Basic Ther-modynamics, Introduction to Urban Transport Planning, the Irish Novel, Judicial Process and Behavior, South Asian Society—do their work in classes where students simply have less opportu-nity to talk and write about the kinds of things that students pull into composition courses: date rape, suburban ennui, farm life in Mexico, drive-by shootings, traffic congestion, a grandmother's childhood in Beijing—all subjects which can easily surface within the same classroom, even in the same week. In a course on Milton or macroeconomics, "Milton" and "macroeconomics" have, like interior decorators, already entered the classroom space before the semester has begun, predetermining to some extent the land-scape of the classroom, or at least one's methods of negotiating that landscape, no matter how much that conceptual nucleus gets deconstructed and contested throughout the course. While no course is a tabula rasa—like any classroom environment, the ter-ritory of the writing workspace is shaped by a host of ideological impulses swirling around the professor, the institution, the stu-dents, the local region, and other involved parties—students in composition classes play an obviously greater role in that inte-rior decorating, and the conversations cannot help but be more variegated and more unexpected—and often riskier—than in so many other classrooms beholden to the parameters of some pre-determined subject.

Because of this flexibility, and because most students take these courses during the first year of college, the inherently cross-disciplinary composition course can serve as an introductory arena where students begin to view their personal and academic needs and desires through the lens of sustainability. In this sense, we can envision composition studies as environmental studies—not as an offshoot of ecology but as the study of one's immediate and future environs (city blocks, mall parking lots, backyards, office cubicles, apartment buildings, crowded highways) so that stu-dents might explore how their identities have been composed by such places and vice versa. This approach conceives the writing workspace as a place for students to explore what they consider right and what wrong about where they work and where they live; a site for thinking about the cultures and families that matter to them, and how to preserve the stories and the languages that belong to them; and an arena for thinking about one's needs and desires (and the fundamental differences between these two concepts) in conjunction with possible future careers. Composition studies can thus be reconceptualized as a disciplinary vehicle that, in developing the intellectual and cultural arts of writing, reading, and talking, promotes sustainability-conscious thinking. And, in cases where the fruits of such courses—the students' writings—are published in print or online journals, books, and newsletters, the composition classroom offers a means by which student testimonies can catch the attention of other faculty, administrators, and even the public. In this way, composition becomes a different kind of "service" discipline, serving as a reminder of the conditions of our students' neighborhoods, jobs, and cultures, as well as an indication of their hopes and fears for the future. Composition would then serve students by providing a writing workspace where they could grow as writers and readers, and it would also serve the larger academic and public realms by making available student testimonies about their environments.

For me the challenge becomes how to create a classroom environment where students have the freedom to pursue writing projects that matter to them, and yet where, as an instructor, I not only remain energized by their questions and pursuits but also consider the ongoing conversations to be of paramount importance to my students' short- and long-term survival. If the writing teacher has the power to make students write and read about practically anything, what then are the most important things for them to write and read? Of all the information available to them, what is absolutely crucial to their intellectual, spiritual, economic, and physical survival? Of all the possible writing assignments one can come up with, which ones will have the greatest effect on their lives? From this perspective the writing classroom becomes a course in local, necessary knowledge—a thumbnail sketch revealing not only what that teacher deems important for students of writing, but also what the teacher and students consider most important, period.

Chameleon Vision

If this book were to have a mascot, it might be the chameleon, for two reasons. The more obvious reason is that the chameleon's unique skin enables it to blend in with its surroundings, although, apparently, these color changes have less to do with camouflage than with communicating with other chameleons and indicating the animal's body temperature and health. Still, the image of the chameleon "becoming one" with its local environment is an attractive one for a book like this, which argues that learning how to live sustainably ought to be our primary cultural concern and, as such, must play a central role within our curricula. Fluctuating external conditions trigger within the chameleon the release of hormones that in turn modify magical things in its remarkable skin called chromatophores, thereby allowing the animal to harmonize with its surroundings. We, on the other hand, take our environs for granted, and our ignorance is killing us: physically, emotionally, culturally, economically. Clearly we need to pay more attention to how external or "outside" conditions are never really completely outside us at all, but inextricably woven into our own health and behavior. If we could turn chameleon, and our bodies reflected the status of our watersheds, energy resources, topsoil, climate changes, food supplies, transportation systems, workplaces, neighborhoods, community networks, and global markets, what would we see looking back at us in the mirror?

The other reason for invoking the chameleon is its spectacular kind of eyes, which are even more entrancing than its shifting color. A chameleon's independently rotating eyes allow it to look in two directions at once. The effect is both mesmerizing and a little creepy, as if two separate brains were housed inside that tiny head, each one operating its own little periscope. Does the animal see in split-screen? Or are the separate images somehow fused? Other creatures possess equally bizarre visual equipment—for example, the cluster eyes of spiders; the compound eyes of various insects; and the divided eyes of the Anableps fish, which enable it to see simultaneously above and below the waterline—but the mechanically separate eyes of the chameleon, when not working in tandem to zero in on an unsuspecting bug, can literally look forward and backward at the same time. To me they invoke a metaphor for gazing simultaneously into two very different futures.

Increasingly I find myself thinking in chameleon vision. One "eye" belongs to that of the father, the husband, the teacher. It is an optimistic eye preoccupied with figuring out ways of enriching the lives of my family and my students. It is driven less by naïveté (I hope) than by hopeful pragmatism. This eye is unabashedly committed to imagining and creating, as awkward as this sounds, something like a better future for the people it encounters on a daily basis—family, friends, and students. While this eye is fully aware of the seriousness of our various environmental crises, it seeks to maintain a constructive optimism in the face of such news. Clearly it's an eye the likes of which informs other recent titles: Alan AtKisson's *Believing Cassandra: An Optimist Looks at a Pessimist's World*; Paul Hawken's *The Ecology of Commerce: A Declaration of Sustainability*; Hawken's subsequent book *Natural Capitalism: Creating the Next Industrial Revolution*, written with Amory Lovins and L. Hunter Lovins; and even, despite the title, Mark Dowie's *Losing Ground: American Environmentalism at the Close of the Twentieth Century*.

The second eye, though, is a more pessimistic eye, a nervous and increasingly frightened eye—not so much cynical (I hope) as darkly pragmatic. It is an eye which, the more it regards current trends, arrives at unsettling conclusions that literally cause me to lie awake some nights and fear for my son's future. Plenty of other writers view their work through this eye as well: Robert Kaplan's *The Coming Anarchy: Shattering the Dreams of the Post Cold War*; Eugene Linden's *The Future in Plain Sight: Nine Clues to the Coming Instability*; and Graham Lyons, Evonne Moore, and Joseph Wayne Smith's *Is the End Nigh? Internationalism, Global Chaos and the Destruction of the Earth*. Even scholars committed to building a sustainable society have moments when their fears are revealed: Edward and Jean Stead, in the closing of their otherwise optimistic *Management for a Small Planet*, admit that "the idea that economic man will ever willingly surrender his quest for castles and gold so that people he will never know can have a comfortable place to live in a safe society with clean air to breath [sic], adequate soil for food, clean water to drink, and the opportunity for creative self-expression is essentially ludicrous within the current framework of the materialistic, ego-centered, growth-oriented, mechanical, mental models that are currently driving human thought processes" (238).

Perhaps I should have written this as two books contained within the same binding, like a child's flip-over book. One side would have been written from the optimistic eye; turn the book upside down and flip it over, and there would be the darker version. Neither story would take precedence over the other: in the center of the book would be a blank page, where the reader would be expected to synthesize the two halves on his or her own terms. Does one view both futures in split-screen? Fuse them together? As sensible as a structure like this seems to me, editors and readers would surely have found it too gimmicky, unbefitting for a book aimed at an audience of teachers and academics who understandably expect the works they read to have been written by authors who have made up their minds. And so I have settled for writing mostly in the first eye. The result is a largely optimistic book written from the point of view of a teacher who needs to believe that there is still time for academics to address sustainability within their courses and institutions in order to help effect necessary change.

This might be the riskiest claim in the entire book. There are many who will argue—and on my "dark eye" days I am one of them—that change happens far too slowly in academe for it to ever have any profound impact on something so enormous as creating a sustainable culture. For one thing, colleges and universities, even when we take into consideration the growing number that have made major strides in greening their campuses, are poor models of behavior. Studies like Sara Hammond Creighton's *Greening the Ivory Tower: Improving the Environmental Track Record of Universities, Colleges, and Other Institutions* are of obvious importance, for they show us how conscientious institutions like Tufts University, Brown University, Ball State University, Georgetown University, the University of Vermont, and the University of Wisconsin serve as models for innovative and systemic environmental stewardship (see too Eagan and Orr's *The Campus and Environmental Responsibility*; Filho's *Sustainability and University Life*; Keniry's *Ecodemia*; and April Smith's *Campus Ecology*). But most academic institutions still lack the vision and the commitment to convert their operations into sustainable ones. Academic institutions everywhere are undermining their own missions by eliminating tenure-track faculty lines. When administrations are so hell-bent on cutting corners by replacing long-term, full-time faculty with part-time faculty, how serious could they possibly be when it comes to fostering ongoing environmental stewardship on campus—especially when the success of such stewardship depends in large part on the presence of an active, committed, and institutionally supported full-time faculty?

But the problems are considerably larger than academia's failure at taking sustainability seriously. There is ample evidence to support the belief that our various global environmental crises are of such enormity, and that so much damage has occurred already, that sustainability itself might be a romantic if not impossible concept. Before I explain my own reasons for holding onto the concept of sustainability, and my decision as an educator to continue viewing my work through a largely optimistic lens, it's important to pause and consider some of the reasons why such optimism is in conflict with available evidence.

The Sad Lens: Synthesizing Bad News

Were this like a number of titles in environmental education, sustainable business, and ecological economics, this is the part of the book where I would insert a litany of statistics illustrating the depths of our environmental crises. Part preamble and part elegy comprised of what Herman Daly and John Cobb call "wild facts" (1), such lists are common if not obligatory in much environmentally oriented literature. These gloomy inventories of global bad news attempt to grab one's attention and establish motive, justifying the inevitable sense of urgency running throughout the remaining argument. But while a desire to stir the audience with startling statistics highlighting the horrors of contemporary ecocide is understandable, these preambles can come across more as requiem than as call to action. We have all heard bad news like this before, and, even though the bad news keeps getting worse, we become immune to cited examples of worldwide environmental devastation. Not that it isn't necessary to make these invocations, if only for testimonial purposes; I too have collected my own catalog of "wild facts" and assembled them in Appendix A, if for no other reason than to catalog the kind of information that prompted me to write this book. For now, though, I will limit myself to three examples that should illustrate why, when we look into the future, things can look very bad.

1. For approaching twenty years, the Worldwatch Institute has released its annual State of the World progress reports. In the *State of the World 1989*, reference was made to the upcoming 1990s as a "turnaround decade," citing scientists who believed that the future of the environment would depend on what would and would not happen in the 1990s (Brown et al. 192). The *State of the World 1989* concludes with this: "By the end of the next decade, the die will pretty well be cast. As the world enters the twenty-first century, the community of nations either will have rallied and turned back the threatening trends, or environmental deterioration and social disintegration will be feeding on each other" (194). Later, in a 1991 publication, Lester Brown, director of the Worldwatch Institute, wrote, "If all these trends I've been describing are still going on at the end of the next decade [the 1990s], then I think the social disintegration and environmental deterioration will be feeding on each other on a growing scale" ("Battle" 182). Words like this might remind some of the incendiary rhetoric associated with more radical environmental organizations, like Earth First! But Lester Brown's work as a global educator is widely respected. The language of the Worldwatch Institute's annual planetary checkups in the widely translated State of the World reports has been praised for its "studious omission of overt scare tactics like the lurid apocalyptic narratives we have seen in the popular press" (Killingsworth and Palmer 264).

Nor was Brown alone in making such claims. Others argued that we were looking ahead to likely "overshoot and collapse" (i.e., to the point where populations increase beyond their region's carrying capacity, which results in "correction factors" such as disease, war, and extinction). Among the world's poorest nations there would be continued hyperbolic population growth, resulting in depletion of already strained resources beyond natural limits and leading in turn to widespread starvation, while the rest of us could expect to witness "decline: first, in the intangible qualities of life (like peace, quiet, access to fresh air, drinkable streams and unspoiled landscapes), [and] later in material standards (i.e. per capita availability of consumer goods and services)" (Randers 23). David Orr expressed the same message this way: "The decisions about how or whether life will be lived in the next century are being made now. We have a decade or two in which we must make unprecedented changes in the way we relate to each other and to nature" (*Ecological Literacy* 3).

The implications of such deadlines are particularly humbling for teachers. Because time is so short, one might conclude that those of us charged with teaching the next generation how to live sustainably are inconsequential. Here is yet another of Lester Brown's claims, stated after a lecture: "We don't have time to train a generation of teachers, who would train a generation of students, who a generation later will become decision-makers. That's not an option any more. The changes have to come within a matter of years among those of us who are already making decisions" ("Battle" 186).

Everyone knows by now that the turnaround decade didn't. In fact, it did quite the opposite. Beginning in 1994, the 1990s witnessed a sustained period of go-go growth that didn't stop until March 2000, thus constituting the longest expansion ever on record. A great many benefited from this extraordinary productivity: we saw the lowest unemployment in generations, an increase in real wage growth, significantly increased business investments, and the meteoric rise of the stock market. But when looked at from the point of reigning in our use of limited resources and adopting simpler lifestyles in accordance with the goals of sustainability, the exuberant growth of the 1990s was exactly the opposite of what organizations like the Worldwatch Institute were hoping to see. The situation in 1989 was dire enough; by the end of the 1990s it was profoundly worse.

2. In 1992 the Union of Concerned Scientists issued a document titled "World Scientists' Warning to Humanity" that opened with these words: "Human beings and the natural world are on a collision course. Human activities inflict harsh and often irreversible damage on the environment and on critical resources. If not

COMPOSITION AND SUSTAINABILITY

checked, many of our current practices put at serious risk the future that we wish for human society and the plant and animal kingdoms, and may so alter the living world that it will be unable to sustain life in the manner that we know. Fundamental changes are urgent if we are to avoid the collision our present course will bring about."

More than fifteen hundred academics signed this document: chemists, physicists, geologists, epidemiologists, computer scientists, biochemists, meteorologists, agricultural scientists, mathematicians, astronomers, geneticists, pediatricians, economists, oceanographers, engineers, psychologists, ecologists, endocrinologists, anthropologists, geophysicists, limnologists, oncologists, neurologists, neurobiologists, physiologists, botanists, entomologists, embryologists, hematologists, physicians, and zoologists. Many of these were Nobel laureates.[2] While lists of names and an impressive array of methodically reasoned arguments by authorities certainly don't prove that civilization as we know it might indeed end shortly—Gregory Bateson reminds us that "science never proves anything" (*Mind and Nature* 27–30)—the concern expressed in such a document is profound. (One finds a similar sense of fear running through more recent public documents, such as *GEO-1*, the United Nations Environment Programme's Global State of the Environment Report 1997.)

When fifteen hundred scientists publicly express their collective fear that our consumer society, if left unchecked, is doomed, this is news. When the ensuing seven years after the release of the report bring record-setting levels of worldwide material production and economic expansion—far beyond current levels at the time this document was written—it is even bigger news.

3. In 1997 Jay Hanson, a retired systems analyst living in Hawaii, started building a Web site: www.dieoff.org. It is an archive of more than 150 articles and essays, most of them reprints of articles and book chapters that Hanson has collected under such categories as economic theory, population, climate change, carrying capacity, and sustainability. Perhaps the most important piece of Hanson's site is a compilation of papers catalogued under the heading "fossilgate." According to the experts in petroleum geology whose work Hanson has reprinted (Colin Campbell,

Brian Fleay, Jean Laherrère, Walter Youngquist, and others), the most pressing issue facing humanity, more pressing even than climate change or population growth, is an impending oil crisis that will lead to nothing less than global economic decline. Based on findings gathered in the 1990s—most notably in Colin Campbell's *The Coming Oil Crisis* and Campbell and Laherrère's landmark article in *Scientific American*, "The End of Cheap Oil"—world petroleum output is expected to peak sometime late in the first decade of this century, after which the cost of extracting oil will continue to rise, and rise, and rise, in turn triggering chronic global economic decline. The issue is not that the world will run out of oil, but rather that the world will run out of *cheap* oil, which of course drives the global economy. Once we have used more than half of available reserves—which, according to current research, could happen anywhere between 2005 and 2010 (and production of cheap oil outside the Persian Gulf is already peaking in 2000–2001 [see Fleay])—we enter a radically new world, one where none of us can ever again take fossil fuel for granted. Nor will we be able to simply convert en masse to alternative energy resources, as the research, development, and dissemination of alternative energy technologies such as fuel cells, photovoltaics, and wind turbines will for some time continue to rely on fossil fuel. As I write this, the implications of the impending oil crisis are being considered on two active discussion lists, "energyresources" and "runningonempty," both of which are offshoots of Hanson's dieoff site.[3] At energyresources, one finds petroleum geologists, engineers, systems analysts, and ecologists examining recent research and news reports about the impending oil crisis; the discussions at runningonempty revolve around strategies for alerting an as of yet uninterested media, as well as suggestions for surviving after the crisis hits.

Of course, apocalyptic and dystopian dreams thrive on the Internet, from Y2K survival sites, which appear now as virtual relics from a forgotten age, to goofy organizations like the Earth Changes movement, which believes that polar shifts will soon cause the continents to alter and much of civilization to fall into the sea (according to their prophecies, Long Island, where I live, should already have disappeared under water). But Hanson's dieoff site, despite its initial sensationalism (several graphic photographs of dead infants practically dare visitors to stay away), is a compendium of information originally written by scholars for peer-reviewed journals and presses. What's most amazing about the dieoff site is that, despite the recent appearance of other sources of related material—see, for example, www.hubbertpeak.com (M. King Hubbert, a petroleum geologist, created a bell curve forecasting petroleum production and depletion)—almost no one, as of this writing, seems interested in discussing this information. Neither the mainstream nor the alternative media, and neither politicians nor academics, seem aware of the possibility of global economic decline beginning in less than ten years. Sooner or later, though, if these scientists are right, the end of cheap oil will alter our lives in ways that few of us are ready to comprehend.

By this point some readers will be wondering why I have put such stock in arguments about coming environmental catastrophes without acknowledging dissenting views, of which there are many. The reason that I will not spend time in this book giving equal due to those on the flip side of other so-called environmental debates is this: the arguments I have read by greenhouse skeptics and environmental critics are for the most part unsupported arguments, and not infrequently outright lies, by writers who cannot publish in peer-reviewed arenas, and whose work is largely funded by political interest groups wishing to discredit environmental organizations for their own political gain. In some cases the conservative political agenda shaping such work is obvious, as in Peter Huber's *Hard Green: Saving the Environment from the Environmentalists: A Conservative Manifesto*, an example of the kind of unsubstantiated "research" frequently found in such anti-environmental "correctives" (Huber is a senior fellow at the Manhattan Institute, as well as a columnist for *Forbes*). Sometimes such "alternative" environmental critiques are thinly disguised examples of "greenwashing"; thus Jonathan H. Adler's progressively titled *Environmentalism at the Crossroads: Green Activism in America* is in fact written by someone who works for the Competitive Enterprise Institute, an anti-environmental think tank. In *Facts, Not Fear: A Parent's Guide to Teaching Children about the Environment* by Michael Sanera and Jane S. Shaw, one notices that the introduction is written by Marilyn Quayle. As

Brian Tokar reminds us in *Earth for Sale: Reclaiming Ecology in the Age of Corporate Greenwash*, it was of course Quayle's infamous husband who, in overseeing the Council on Competitiveness when he was Vice President, sought to remove wetlands protections in twenty-nine states, change the Clean Air Act to enable utilities to remain in control of their own air emissions permits, halt a ban on incineration of lead batteries, eliminate proposed quality control standards for medical labs, and subvert biotechnology regulations (63–64). Some of the anti-environmentalist propaganda available is blatantly absurd, like Norman Myers and Julian L. Simon's *Scarcity or Abundance: A Debate on the Environment*, in which the authors state that "we now have in our hands . . . the technology to feed, clothe, and supply energy to an ever-growing population for the next 7 billion years," an obviously groundless claim that is nevertheless taken seriously and painstakingly refuted in Paul and Anne Ehrlich's examination of the anti-science rhetoric of "wise use" policies, "greenscamming," and "brownslashing" (*Betrayal* 66–67, 100–104).[4]

Still, lies such as those proffered by writers like Dixy Lee Ray and Lou Guzzo are frequently cited.[5] In *Environmental Overkill: Whatever Happened to Common Sense?* Ray and Guzzo claim that "for every assertion made by a reputable scientific expert that the world is warming up, there is another one from an equally qualified scientist who says that it is not" (13). It is important to realize the depth of this particular untruth. In 1995 several thousand scientists on the Intergovernmental Panel on Climate Change (IPCC) concluded that global warming—climate change, as it is more accurately known—is not just a theory but a fact; in 2000 the IPCC went so far as to conclude that much of this climate change is the result of the burning of fossil fuels (Revkin, "Shift"). On the other side of the issue, there are approximately two dozen frequently cited greenhouse skeptics who maintain that evidence of climate change is inconclusive. Thus the ratio of those who view climate change as fact to those who do not is more than 100 to 1. What's more, some of the more vocal opponents of climate change—those whom writers like Ray and Guzzo tend to cite—have been funded by the petroleum industry, the same trillion-dollar industry that once circulated a "scientific petition" formatted to resemble a reprint from the journal for the National Academy of Sciences and that not only opposed the global climate change accord but also proclaimed that increased levels in carbon dioxide are beneficial (Park). The questionable research marshaled by such skeptics has been discredited by other scientists as scientifically unfit to appear in peer-reviewed journals, as documented in Ross Gelbspan's *The Heat Is On: The High Stakes Battle over Earth's Threatened Climate* (2002).[6]

The evidence that we are in dire straits when it comes to rapidly diminishing energy resources, climate change, mass extinctions, topsoil depletion, rising sprawl and development, and environmental injustice is embarrassingly and overwhelmingly obvious. (For more evidence, see Appendix A.)

The Optimistic Eye: Visualizing Path B

Given the news currently available, then, why have I devoted such time to writing a book aimed at sparking awareness when, after reading conversations like those on the runningonempty discussion list, it would seem that the more important teaching these days is happening not in academia but in places like Tom Brown's Tracking, Nature, and Wilderness Survival School or do-it-yourself sustainable home design schools such as the Earthwood Building School (Roy)? I don't have an easy answer to this. To be sure—and this will probably sound irresponsible to more than a few readers—there are days when I think that introductory courses in biointensive gardening, permaculture, off-grid living, and techniques for community networking would be a far more effective use of time than the majority of core college courses currently being taught, including those in English departments.

So why all this time spent on gathering student testimonies to fuel an argument for sustainability-focused curricular reform? Because, as corny and self-serving as it might sound, I don't want to let my students (or my son) down. I still feel a responsibility to try and figure out this problem of how to imagine and design a sustainable culture, and how to let those goals take form, directly and indirectly, within one's classes and throughout the curriculum. There really is no other choice. The remaining options

—to leave sustainability up to other courses and other disciplines because it's "not our business," or to refuse to design a pedagogy of sustainability since things already look so bleak, and, after all, what can just one English instructor possibly do anyway?—are pure cynicism, that is, expressions of what Peter Sloterdijk calls "enlightened false consciousness" (5). And, in the end, such gestures are uninteresting, because they are so predictable. Perhaps the most radical decision that educators can make, then, both pedagogically and artistically, is to remain convinced that they and their students can literally reconstruct their local worlds for the better.

In *Earth at a Crossroads: Paths to a Sustainable Future*, Hartmut Bossel creates two future scenarios: "Path A," the route we will take if current trends persist, and "Path B," a vision of a sustainable world. In the Path A scenario,

> the curricula of the transnational college industry are dominated by the developing "global culture" with major foundations in Anglo-American culture and tradition, and the values of competitive, globalized society. The contributions of other cultures disappear from these curricula and the libraries, and are eventually forgotten. . . . As curricula (and cultures) are standardized world-wide, there is little incentive for studying in other regions. First-hand knowledge of other countries, cultures, and languages becomes rare. Second-hand knowledge, as interpreted by the information industry, determines personal experience and development. . . .
>
> The educational system degenerates to a supplier of professional training, where educational content is determined by the commercial interests of business and industry. This system does not educate for excellence of scientific or cultural achievements. The level of general education declines as professional specialization and subjects of trivial culture dominate. (124–25)

The sustainable Path B scenario is radically different. Local cultures are emphasized within the curriculum. Intercultural student exchange is facilitated in ways that lead "to an understanding of the dynamics of change and development, and of the significance of diversity and sustainability," and the curriculum is inherently interdisciplinary, flexible, and directed toward individual student needs (136). Bossel advocates the following choice:

I think the correct conclusions under current conditions are: (a) "Ecological and social sustainability of human society face serious and increasing threats," and (b) "We have the means and the obligation to turn things around and get on a sustainable path while we still can." With such an attitude, you look at the situation realistically and do your part to change it. (305)

Bossel's Path B is the obvious choice; ultimately, his conclusion must be our own as well.

Chapter Two

Sustainability

*Sustainability and sustainable development often present
themselves as the most influential concepts in the environmental agenda because they stand for new thinking,
and they have been echoed and re-echoed in many contexts, specialist and political, scientific and economic,
global and local. But "newness" is not a simple idea:
what is new in one context is familiar elsewhere; and a
successful concept recurs so often that it ages quickly and
has to be actively renewed.*

George Myerson and Yvonne Rydin,
The Language of Environment: A New Rhetoric

The terms "sustainable" and "sustainability" started surfac-
ing with growing regularity in the early 1980s. As Albert
Bartlett writes in a historical analysis of the term, "'Sustainability'
has become big-time," and "University centers and professional
organizations have sprung up using the word 'sustainable' as a
prominent part of their names" (6). The terms are used in an
increasing number of disciplines—not just ecology and environmental studies but also economics, planning, architecture, management, and, to a lesser extent, education and art. As a result,
some of these disciplines have changed in fundamental ways:
environmental science is now considered an "interdiscipline"
(Sloep)[1], and the relatively new discipline of ecological economics is structured almost entirely around the concept of
sustainability. Yet there are many academic disciplines—like
English studies—that have yet to explore the implications this
concept might have for their content and practice. As we explore
the possibilities for developing English curricula that engage

sustainability, we need to examine the conflicting definitions embedded within this concept, particularly the contradictory ways in which it has been employed.

Considering the more than two pages of definitions for the root "sustain" found in the *Oxford English Dictionary,* it's not surprising that "sustainability" has been used in a variety of often conflicting contexts. Some of these definitions—e.g., "to give support to a person's conduct," "to cause to continue in a certain state," "to keep up without intermission," "to provide for the upkeep of (an institution, establishment, estate, etc.)"—are at odds with what many consider to be the essence of "strong definitions" of sustainability (explained below), since it is precisely our consumer addictions and our upkeep of growth-driven institutions that work against the goal of forging a sustainable culture.

The word "sustainability"—often used interchangeably, and thus confusingly, with "sustainable development"—attracted significant attention when it appeared in a 1987 report by the United Nations World Commission on Environment and Development (also called the Brundtland Commission), published under the title *Our Common Future* (World Commission). The report stated that "humanity has the ability to make development sustainable— to ensure that it meets the needs of the present without compromising the ability of future generations to meet their own needs" (8)—which, as Stead and Stead point out, is a rephrasing of a Kenyan proverb: "We didn't inherit the Earth from our parents; we borrowed it from our children" (134). As sustainability started to figure prominently in the language of international policy, due in large part to the Brundtland Report, the term appeared in a number of principal documents generated by ensuing international summits: the 1992 Rio Earth Summit (United Nations Conference on Environment and Development, or UNCED), which led to the UN Commission on Sustainable Development; the 1993 World Conference on Human Rights in Vienna; the 1994 International Conference on Population and Development in Cairo; the 1995 World Summit on Social Development in Copenhagen; the 1996 Second UN Conference on Human Settlements in Istanbul; the 1997 World Food Summit in Rome; and the second UN Conference on Environment and Development in New York in 1997.

In some of the earlier arguments for sustainability, like Lester Brown's 1981 *Building a Sustainable Society*, the term is never explicitly defined, indicating a confidence on the part of the author that the intended audience is already familiar enough with the concept. In Brown's book, sustainability is characterized in terms of the obstacles facing those who would create a sustainable society: soil erosion, deterioration of biological systems, population increase, and oil reserve depletion, all of which will require "fundamental economic and social changes, a wholesale alteration of economic priorities and population policies" (8), if we are to create a sustainable society. Actually, Brown's closest approach to defining sustainability in this early book can be found in the dedication: "To Brian and Brenda—and generations to come." For despite the multiple definitions of sustainability, most are predicated on an ethos of intergenerational justice.[2]

This ethos marks, for example, Markandya and Pearce's definition of sustainability: "The central idea behind sustainability is the protection of the natural resource base for future generations" (270).[3] Herman Daly and John Cobb describe this mode of living as "justice extended to the future" (146). Elsewhere sustainability has been equated with "permanent livability," where present and future generations have equal access to the same natural resources (Pearce 59), and with the quest for "enoughness" (Stead and Stead 61–63). Indeed, as Holmberg and Sandbrook have written, "The notion of intergenerational equity lies at the core of the concept of sustainable development. While there is no solid definition to go by, development that does not meet the criteria of intergenerational equity must be bad development" (91). Hence the frequent comparison between sustainable thinking and the Iroquois Confederacy's (probably romanticized [see Krech]) practice of projecting the consequences of specific actions seven generations into the future before undertaking significant decisions. At least one writer has claimed that looking ahead should go even further than seven generations (Chianese 530)—no small task, given that as humans we generally "don't include future generations within our moral horizon because we tend to lose the concept of 'ours' after great grandchildren" (Daly, "Economic Growth Debate" 127).

Alan Gilpin, in his *Dictionary of Environment and Sustainable Development*, offers the following definition of sustainable development:

> Development that provides economic, social, and environmental benefits in the long term, having regard to the needs of living and future generations. . . . Sustainable development considers both the living and non-living resource base with regard for conservation and the advantages and disadvantages of alternative courses of action for future generations. It allows the use of depletable resources in an efficient manner, with an eye to the substitution of other resources in due course. Sustainable development calls for much more emphasis on conserving natural systems and the resource base on which all development depends; a greater regard for equity within society at present and between rich and poor nations, with particular regard to the world's poor; and a planning-horizon that goes well beyond the needs and aspirations of those alive today. It requires an integration of environmental, social, and economic considerations in decision-making. (206)

Not surprisingly, as the term gained in popularity, "sustainable development" began appearing as a political and corporate cliché (Myerson and Rydin 100–103). In *One World, Ready or Not: The Manic Logic of Global Capitalism*, William Greider writes that the phrase "carries revolutionary implications, but sounds so wholesome that almost everybody can endorse it. Every enlightened politician now supports the goal of sustainable development; so does every leading corporation and financial institution that is sensitive to popular opinion. Meanwhile, the global system plunges forward along its usual path, building toward some sort of epic showdown with nature" (448–49).[4] Nor do ecological economists uniformly agree with definitions of sustainability promoted by the development regimes. Even though the Brundtland Report's definition is the one most frequently quoted, critics like Robert Goodland have faulted the report's claim that a five- to ten-fold increase in world industrial output would be necessary in order to reach a level of sustainable growth—the idea was to make less developed countries more developed, though in fact this would also have moved them further from economic sustainability—since, according to Goodland's calculations, current growth in throughput (the process whereby energy and matter from natural resources, i.e., "sources," get used by us and eventually end up as pollution and wastes, or "sinks") is already at unsustainable levels (16). Herman Daly goes even further, arguing that sustainable growth (as opposed to development) is impossible ("Sustainable Growth"); he also reminds us that, due to inevitable long-term loss of energy and matter through entropy, even the steady-state economy he promotes could not last forever ("Postscript" 378–79).

Some of the confusion associated with the term *sustainability* is due to its evolution from what were originally strictly biological associations to its currently larger social and economic implications (Dixon and Fallon 94). For sustainability

> has two components. One is economic sustainability—the ability of an economic system to continue operating at some level of output. The other is ecosystem sustainability referring not to an absolutely unchanged ecosystem equilibrium but to . . . ecosystem resilience . . . [which] refers to the bounce-back capacity which allows ecosystems to recover from short-term damage or disruption. True sustainability must include both components. (Harris 98)

When sustainability is considered in only the former sense, it is often viewed as *weak* sustainability, a concept associated with neoclassical economic thinking and promoted by "cornucopians" who tend to view sustainability as a locally isolated and controllable phenomenon: "A good example would be depletion of soil fertility through erosion, with attendant substitution of mechanization, irrigation, and fertilizer to give equal or higher yields" (Harris 98). Here sustainability is a modifier of growth, and, in this sense, it is often appropriated by companies, advertising executives, and politicians as a sound bite meaning little more than "keeping the economy growing" or sustaining profits.

Strong sustainability, on the other hand, "gives priority to ecosystem resilience, and does not accept human-made capital accumulation as an adequate substitute for natural capital depletion" (Harris 98). Myerson and Rydin further subdivide strong sustainability into three categories, ranging from moderate to extreme. The first category refers to support for marginal change in current development practices, a "social choice" position which "sees a degree of conflict between environmental protection and economic goals as inevitable, but optimistically argues that trade-offs between these two goals can be managed so as to achieve an optimal balance and an overall maximum level of welfare" (104–5). A second, stronger stance is the "new economics" position, which argues for more substantial change and is associated with a more radical redistribution of resources, "allowing a more com-munity-orientated, bottom-up approach, and resulting in new patterns of production and consumption that would reduce the current conflict between environmental production and economic activity" (105). The third stance—the "strongest" of the three positions, and the one I embrace as the most important—is a "limits to growth" perspective, which "involves full, precaution-ary protection of ecosystems and maintenance of all 'natural capi-tal'" (103). Proponents for a steady-state economy, like Herman Daly, can be found at this end of the spectrum; they argue for maintaining constant stocks of people and physical wealth in a state where throughput should be as low as possible (Daly, "The Steady-State Economy" 325). This third and strongest of the strong definitions of sustainability links the term closely with the concept of limits, harking back to the influential 1972 book *Limits to Growth* (Meadows, Meadows, Randers, and Behrens), which in many respects initiated all subsequent conversations about sustainability.

Ronald Engel writes that

> there is nothing inherent in the term "sustainable development" to keep it from becoming the name for an alternative post-mod-ern social paradigm and a new moral conception of world order. "Sustainable," by definition, means not only indefinitely pro-longed, but nourishing, as the Earth is nourishing to life, and as a healthy natural environment is nourishing for the self-actualiz-ing of persons and communities. The word "development" need not be restricted to economic activity, much less to the kind of economic activity that now dominates the world, but can mean the evolution, unfolding, growth, and fulfillment of any and all aspects of life. Thus "sustainable development," in the broadest

sense, may be defined as the kind of human activity that nourishes and perpetuates the historical fulfillment of the whole community of life on Earth. ("Introduction" 10–11)

Similarly, in painting their own version of the weak-to-strong spectrum of definitions of *sustainability*, Richard Clugston and Thomas Rogers of the Center for Respect of Life and Environment describe the stronger definition as defined by personal, spiritual growth: a mixture of humility, recognition of limits, and an awareness of natural systems as "circuits of aliveness." Clugston and Rogers, however, implicitly regard all living systems as ecologically nonhierarchical, an approach that some have argued is indefensible.[5] A more successful approach to defining sustainability might be to adopt the six fundamental values embedded in the concept, as clarified by Stead and Stead: wholeness, posterity, smallness, community, quality, and spiritual fulfillment (132–46). Despite these differences, however, Engel, Clugston and Rogers, and Stead and Stead all present a holistic interpretation of sustainability that can be useful to educators who agree that we have a responsibility to design a pedagogical ethic informed by the need to think and act sustainably.

I will argue that such a pedagogical ethic must be grounded in the following six tenets:

1. A sustainable society cannot be created without sustainability-conscious curricula.

A variety of calls have been made for curricula that engage the concerns of sustainability. Ted Trainer makes a case for a new kind of curriculum for training people to become citizens of a new conserver society (166–77). Gregory Smith argues for a curriculum that promotes interdependent living, where courses in "conflict resolution, ecological principles, peace studies, group dynamics, systems theory, global environmental trends, and multicultural studies" are standard (94). Paul Ryan has developed the "Earthscore Curriculum," which is "an experiential, interdisciplinary way of developing an ecology of mind, that is, patterns of thinking in keeping with ecological patterns" (*Video Mind* 302–07). Some have called for new curricula that include, among other things, studying sustainable indigenous cultures;

understanding the complex relationships between soil, vegetation, and climate, as well as the complexities inherent in principles of energy flow and dissipation; and developing an awareness of the implications of radical differences in socioeconomic expectations between the North and the South (Clark 76). In addition, according to David Orr, conventional understandings of what a core curriculum should address are all wrong. He argues that no one should be permitted to graduate from any institution of higher education without a basic understanding of

- the laws of thermodynamics,
- the basic principles of ecology,
- carrying capacity,
- energetics,
- least-cost, end-use analysis,
- limits of technology,
- appropriate scale,
- sustainable agriculture and forestry,
- steady-state economics, and
- environmental ethics. (*Earth in Mind* 14)

"I would add to this list of analytical and academic things," Orr continues, "practical things necessary to the art of living well in a place: growing food; building shelter; using solar energy; and a knowledge of local soils, flora, fauna, and the local watershed" (14).

In light of such calls for curricular reform, no academic department can claim that it is above, beyond, or outside such concerns. All departments want to stay in business; they want to attract a stable number of majors and defend their relevance in the eyes of the institution and the student body. But to what degree can one remain interested in sustaining one's own niche while remaining uninterested in sustainability? How long can any canon of information or methodological practices remain supported in academic disciplines if the problem of sustainability goes ignored? It stands to reason that a sustainable culture cannot exist unless sustainability features prominently throughout the curriculum.

2. A pedagogy of sustainability would call attention to "social traps" of unsustainability, leading teachers and students to begin imagining means by which to avoid them.

Costanza and Daly define a social trap as "any situation in which the short-run, local reinforcements guiding individual behavior are inconsistent with the long-run, global best interest of the individual and society" (57). When fashion, consumer addictions, laziness, and social insecurity induce all of us—students and faculty alike—to fall into social traps of unsustainability, then a curriculum that does not provide the tools and the time to identify and critique the implications of such traps becomes a trap in itself. To address this cycle requires recognizing the degree to which social traps infiltrate our institutions. As Thomas Prugh puts it:

> The goals of long-term global ecological and economic health and sustainability will often be more critical than local, short-term goals for economic growth or the goals of private interests. But our institutions and incentive structures are set up to address primarily these short-term, private interests. And since people, companies and countries consistently pursue private self-interests and frequently are not checked by the institutions, they thus tend to undermine the larger goals. That is, our institutions and incentive structures set social traps. (115)

The elimination of such social traps must come about, Prugh argues, through intervention—through, moreover, a mechanism that is already a commonplace in the primary and secondary schools that already assume responsibility for making students aware of the long-term consequences of short-term behavior such as smoking, drinking, drug use, and unprotected sex (115). Consequently a sustainable pedagogy would be inherently interventionist: it would recognize that our consumer culture fosters unsustainable behavior, and that the educator's job, on some level, is to disrupt the assumptions implicit within that culture.

3. A pedagogy of sustainability should be antigrowth and pro-development.

Herman Daly provides an effective means of distinguishing between these two terms.

> *To grow* means "to increase naturally in size by the addition of material through assimilation or accretion." *To develop* means "to expand or realize the potentialities of; to bring gradually to a fuller, greater, or better state." When something grows it gets bigger. When something develops it gets different. The earth ecosystem develops (evolves), but does not grow. Its subsystem, the economy, must eventually stop growing, but can continue to develop. The term "sustainable development" therefore makes sense for the economy, but only if it is understood as "development without growth." ("Sustainable Growth" 267–68)

Development has become a bad word for many, but battles between the "developers" of housing complexes, shopping malls, parking lots, and golf courses on one hand and advocates for open space on the other are really battles about irresponsible growth.[6]

We are conditioned to equate growth with goodness. But the GNP (gross national product) and GDP (gross domestic product) don't register the toll that growth takes on natural capital.[7] For example, the *Exxon Valdez* spill resulted in billions of dollars being spent on cleanup, compensation, and litigation—all contributing to the GNP—but of course "net total welfare would surely have been higher if the ship had missed the reef" (Prugh 84–85).[8] If we were to begin imagining a pedagogy that emphasized development rather than growth, we might be left with an emphasis not on the accumulation of data but on the development of student ideas; an emphasis not on a minimum number of credit hours necessary to graduate but on the ability to articulate a developing synthesis treating varied subject matter; and so on.

4. A pedagogy of sustainability would promote an ethic of sustainability.

Environmental debates tend to get presented as tugs-of-war between human-centered individualists on the conservative end and ecosystem-centered holists on the "green" end. The former are seen as privileging human welfare over nonhuman species; the latter, "ecosystem rights" above human rights. Not only does such oversimplification distort the needs and motives of those on both sides, but also, according to Kristin Shrader-Frechette, neither extreme can lead to sustainability. Instead she argues for what she calls "hierarchical holism," in which priority-ranking systems are used to determine our duties, rights, and responsibilities in relation to the quest for sustainability. For example, we might argue that "strong human rights (such as the right to bodily security)" come first, with priority then going to "environmental and biocentric goals," followed by "weak human rights (such as rights to property)" (69).[9]

At the heart of such a system is the distinction between needs and desires. A pedagogy of sustainability would create contexts in which students and faculty define, rank, and ultimately redefine our needs and desires. What does one "need" in order to develop intellectually, socially, physically, spiritually? What will it take to fulfill those needs, and at what cost? The exploration of a needs-versus-desires dialectic would inevitably result in a pedagogy that condemns luxury lifestyles as well as consumption for the sake of consumption. "The basic needs of the present should always come first, but luxuries of the present generation should not. Future generations cannot act in present markets, so our present economic actions should show a moral concern for the future" (Daly, "Economic Growth" 127). Arguably, then, every student who graduates from an institution and remains committed to living an indefensible consumer lifestyle—fancy cars, multiple credit cards, extensive brand-name wardrobes, expensive gadgets—constitutes a failure for that institution.

5. A pedagogy of sustainability would reject many conventional notions of work and labor, recognizing the need to reinvent the nature of business and work as a fundamental part of creating a sustainable society.

Paul Hawken, from *The Ecology of Commerce: A Declaration of Sustainability*:

> The word "sustainability" can be defined in terms of carrying capacity of the ecosystem, and described with input-output models of energy and resource consumption. Sustainability is an economic state where the demands placed upon the environment by people and commerce can be met without reducing the capacity of the environment to provide for future generations. It can also be expressed in the simple terms of an economic golden rule for

the restorative economy: Leave the world better than you found it, take no more than you need, try not to harm life or the environment, make amends if you do. Sustainability means that your service or product does not compete in the marketplace in terms of its superior image, power, speed, packaging, etc. Instead, your business must deliver clothing, objects, food, or services to the customer in a way that reduces consumption, energy use, distribution costs, economic concentration, soil erosion, atmospheric pollution, and other forms of environmental damage. (139)

As teachers, we want our students to get "good jobs." But most of those "good jobs" are unsustainable. In fact, as Hawken reminds us, our very notion of business must be radically reinvented if it is to become sustainable. "The ultimate purpose of business is not, or should not be, simply to make money. Nor is it merely a system of making and selling things. The promise of business is to increase the general well-being of humankind through service, a creative invention and ethical philosophy" (1). If teachers fail to give students the means by which they might come to reevaluate their job expectations and their assumptions about work, then in the long view teachers are arguably doing more harm than good when their labors result in students entering and perpetuating unsustainable careers.

6. The daily operations of the college campus must reflect the ethic of sustainability promoted within the curriculum.
  Eric Zencey, from "The Rootless Professors":

How many college professors (excluding hydrologists and geographers, who may be assumed to have a professional interest) can describe the watershed in which they live? The absolute necessity of water to life is well known; ninety-some percent of the body is water; yet most academics have no idea whence theirs comes or where it goes when its incorporative service is done. From the vantage of cosmopolitan transcendence, even something as large as a watershed can seem a parochial detail. This learned ignorance, felt as a *worthy* ignorance, is a significant root of our culture's ongoing environmental crisis. (Zencey 16)

Zencey's criticism reminds us that the curriculum is directly related to the daily operations of the local college community: food acquisition, preparation, and disposal; maintenance of buildings and grounds; purchasing for labs, departments, offices, and classrooms; energy expenditure; and so on. If a college's daily operations work against sustainability, as most do, then the institution's very existence will undermine and compete with any attempts to foster curricula of sustainability rather than work toward the goal of building a sustainable culture.

In 1997 I attended a two-week-long Environmental Literacy Institute at Tufts University, sponsored by University Leaders for a Sustainable Future. Prior to arriving, all participants were asked to complete a "Campus Profile." The intention was to make us aware of how little most educators know about crucial aspects of their workplace. It worked: we arrived rather humbled at how much we didn't know, not to mention how difficult it was to find answers to some of the following questions:

1. In what water shed(s) is your campus situated?

2. In what city, town, or municipality is your campus located?

3. Name the following officials representing the community your campus is a part of: (a) City Council; (b) State Senate and Congressional Representatives; (c) Federal Senate and Congressional Representatives

4. (a) Where does the energy for electricity on your campus come from? (b) What is the fuel source? (c) Who is in charge of energy management?

5. (a) Where does the water on your campus come from? (b) Where does it go when it leaves? (c) Who is in charge of water management?

6. (a) Where does the majority of food from your campus come from? (b) Where does it go when it leaves? (c) Who is in charge of food management?

7. (a) What are the major materials used (i.e., construction, office, laboratory, etc.) on your campus? (b) Where do they come from? (c) Where do they go when they leave? (d) Who is in charge of purchasing and disposal?

8. What problems does your university impose on the environment?

9. What would you identify as your current administration's top three policy issues?

For those of us concerned with creating a sustainable curriculum, we can begin by first understanding the extent of our institutional ignorance when it comes to sustainability. This can be done very quickly by taking the "Sustainability Assessment Questionnaire (SAQ) for Colleges and Universities" (available from University Leaders for a Sustainable Future, and downloadable from ULSF's Web site: www.ulsf.org). The SAQ asks a series of questions aimed at assessing an institution's commitment, or lack thereof, to sustainability—the presence of sustainability within curriculum, scholarship, faculty and staff development and rewards, outreach and service, and institutional mission and structure. One of the goals of such questionnaires, of course, is to make us aware of our failures as educators in teaching for sustainability. In an age when so many faculty members and administrators are obsessed with various assessment mechanisms, we need first to step back and honestly confront our collective failure as educators in building a sustainable culture.

A second step for reconceiving our courses and curricula in light of sustainability is to explore the findings of other sustainability-minded scholars and organizations. For instance, in 1997 the President's Council on Sustainable Development established the Public Linkage, Dialogue, and Education Task Force, which issued a report titled "From Classroom to Community and Beyond: Educating for a Sustainable Future." The report lists the following three objectives for sustainability-minded education:

> Ensure that awareness, knowledge, and understanding of sustainability become part of the mainstream consciousness, both nationally and internationally. . . .

> Engage key domestic constituencies in a dialogue about sustainability to produce consensus. . . .

> Foster the skills, attitudes, motivation, and values that will redirect action to sustainable practices and produce the commitment to work individually and collectively toward a sustainable world.

The report goes on to emphasize that sustainable education must entail *collaboration* ("colleges and universities should work with other schools and communities . . . to deliver information, identify questions for research, and provide direct services to help solve community problems"), *cross-disciplinary connection making* ("connections among all subject areas, as well as geographic and cultural relationships [thereby offering] an opportunity to strengthen [individual disciplines] by demonstrating vital interrelationships"), and *relevance* ("learning citizenship skills and understanding that citizens have the power to shape their lives and their communities in light of their vision of a healthy and prosperous future").

Finally, the third and most challenging step is to take the existing information on sustainability and begin inventing ways of applying this information to our work as teachers and scholars so as to invite collaboration and exchange between faculty and students. In using sustainability as a design principle for rebuilding my entry-level writing courses—an overview of which is provided in Appendix B—I have become increasingly aware of my students' concerns about where they live, where they work, and what their futures might or might not hold. Their insights, coupled with relevant literature on sustainability, will occupy the next three chapters.

CHAPTER THREE

Place

*After all anybody is as their land and air is. Anybody is
as the sky is low or high, the air heavy or clear and anybody is as there is wind or no wind there. It is that which
makes them and the arts they make and the work they
do and the way they eat and the way they drink and the
way they learn and everything.*

GERTRUDE STEIN, "Landscape"

Where do I live? Where do you live? What passes for living
where we live? You can work with colleagues for years,
talk to hundreds of students on an annual basis, and yet never
really know what many of these peoples' apartments, houses,
yards, streets, blocks, developments, and neighborhoods look,
feel, and sound like. What impact does this detachment have on
one's teaching? One's profession? One's students?[1] Academic discourse can be such a placeless discourse: the constant flow of
monographs and articles and papers, so many composed as if by
disembodied entities detached from any specific locale. How might
it affect our reading of such texts if we could see photographs of
the scholars' homes or videotapes of their neighborhoods, or if
we had insight into their feelings about where they lived?

For four years I have begun my writing courses by having
students make written and photographic portraits of where they
live. I do this because students can speak with authority about
how their neighborhoods make them feel, because students are
genuinely interested in learning about each other's communities
(partly because it alleviates some of the anonymity college students typically feel, especially at a predominantly commuter campus like mine), and because an awareness of sustainability cannot

exist without a developing awareness of the conditions and limitations of one's immediate environment. I begin this chapter, then, by doing what I ask my students to do. When a friend read a draft of this chapter, he replied that while he found my "place portrait" interesting (in part, no doubt, because he too lives on Long Island), he wondered whether most readers would "give a rat's ass" about my account of this uneventful splotch of suburbia. I'm inclined to wonder this too. Still, my intention here is not to reflect upon my local surroundings as a means of providing local color for narrative effect. My point, rather, is that we need to recognize—even with the landscape of published academic discourse—that who we are and what we have to say is in so many ways interwoven, directly and indirectly, consciously and unconsciously, with our local environs.

Where I'm Writing From

> Where the hell is Ronkonkomano?
> A CHARACTER IN THE FILM
> *200 CIGARETTES*

I am writing this book at the corner of Lake Promenade and Second Street in the hamlet of Lake Ronkonkoma, in the township of Brookhaven (the largest in New York state), which is located in Suffolk County, a chunk of land that forms the eastern half of Long Island. My house is in the exact center of this island. In 1994 I got a job at St. John's University, which is located in Queens, on the western half of the island, but we moved farther out east because my wife's family is here—her parents, her sisters' families, her aunt and uncle, her cousins—most of them less than five minutes away. Close extended families are always something to celebrate, but such tribal islands are crucial when you live in the middle of a sea of suburban sprawl.[2]

Sixty thousand years ago a mile-high glacier called the Wisconsinan bulldozed its way in slow motion down through Canada and New England and didn't stop until it reached just about where I'm sitting right now. Warmer temperatures caused it to melt and retreat, leaving behind the detritus (mud, sand, gravel, boulders) that geologists now call the Ronkonkoma Terminal Moraine, a line of glacier droppings (including rocks, called "erratics" or "messengers," sheared off of the tops of northern mountains) that extends all the way to Montauk Point, the easternmost tip of New York State. A few thousand years later the very same glacier came back and did it all over again, dumping another string of debris stretching the entire length of the island, this one running from Brooklyn to Orient Point, the northern fork of the island. When the ice began to melt, the land "began to rebound the way a small boat bobs back up when people step out of it" (Isachsen et al. 177). As the ice retreated, mammoth chunks broke loose, got buried, and eventually melted within the ground, forming kettle holes. One of the largest is Lake Ronkonkoma, the freshwater lake that is a fifteen-minute walk from where I sit. Eventually—perhaps as recently as six thousand years ago—Long Island evolved into its present-day shape, making it, geologically speaking, a baby compared with the rest of the state.

The variety of ecosystems caused by the proximity of outwash and moraines led to hardwood forests, salt marshes, and even prairies (a geological anomaly now thought to be the result of periodic burning by American Indians), which, combined, supported an unusual diversity of flora and fauna. Five thousand years ago, the first humans settled in the area—Archaic American Indians of the Orient phase, followed by American Indians of the Woodland phase. These were the first people to clear forests for agricultural purposes. Contact with Europeans occurred five hundred years ago, and, just two centuries later, most of the American Indian population had disappeared or blended with European ethnicities as a result of factors including genocide, slavery, alcoholism, smallpox, and intermarriage. In the seventeenth century, the four American Indian communities around Lake Ronkonkoma were conned into relinquishing water rights (Curtis 5) to settlers who, from the beginning, had a hard time pronouncing, let alone spelling, the name of the area (local historical documents include, for example, references to "Ronconkomy Plains" and "Rocconkkemy Pond").[3] Three separate townships now abut the lake, and the lack of coordination between the localities has contributed to the lake's steady decline since the 1950s.

By 1850 the Long Island Rail Road (LIRR) had already spanned the length of Long Island, making wealthy New Yorkers aware of the lake and turning the area into a "millionaire's playground" around the turn of the nineteenth century. Mansions sprouted around the perimeter of the lake, along with dozens of hotels, lodges, and beach pavilions. Postcards from this period show men lounging in flannel bathing suits and children climbing two-story-tall water slides or scampering like mice in giant water wheels. Summer dances were held on Saturday nights in the halls bordering the lake; in winter, scooters and iceboats raced across the ice. During prohibition, houses of prostitution and speakeasies popped up in the surrounding woods, and one could buy "needle beer" that made one's fingers tingle (Curtis 100). During the 1920s, anti-Catholic sentiment helped create an active Ku Klux Klan presence: one conductor on the Long Island Rail Road actually sold KKK outfits on the Greenport line (Curtis 134).[1]

In the 1940s, MacArthur Airport opened two miles away from the Lake. (Our house is situated along one of the flight paths; you can almost make out the passengers in the windows of the Southwest jets that pass overhead.) An auction sale catalog from 1937 advertised the selling of two hundred lots near the lake, emphasizing the easy commute from this "gem of Long Island" to Penn Station via twenty-four daily trains. The population surged as summer cottages were converted for year-round living. (My own single-story, two-bedroom home, while not large by middle-class Long Island standards, started out as a bungalow, and has been added onto three or four times in the last four decades.) A local historian writes that "many new developments appeared, and unfortunately some of the promoters emphasized cheapness rather than quality which attracted some buyers who were less desirable," and that "the crowning blow to the town" came when a significant woodland stretch was sold to developers (Curtis 148). Development continued. Lakeside pavilions were sold, and those left abandoned were burned. In the 1960s and 1970s "unrestricted dumping of fill over the banks of the lake destroyed many trees and left unsightly yellow gashes here and there on the east side of the lake": "Large sections of the Great Swamp were filled in and the once beautiful lake was becoming an eye sore." In 1975 the entire lake was closed for three days due to pollution from storm drains carrying runoff into the water (Curtis 161).

Today Lake Ronkonkoma is a working- and middle-class suburb, indistinguishable from a hundred other suburbs on the island, most of them spilling into each other so that one's sense of boundaries comes not from any visual sense of "village limits" but from proximity to highways and strip malls. (In his stand-up days, the comedian Jerry Seinfeld, who grew up half an hour away in Massapequa, joked that the town's name was Indian for "near the mall.")

If you walk out my front door and view the neighborhood, you will see streets that are safe and quiet, except on occasional summer days when neighborhood kids and sometimes their fathers race motorcycles, looking furtively at intersections for signs of cops. Up to 25 percent of the homes in the area are rentals converted into two or more illegal apartments. Despite the fact that when the house next door was rented out the new tenants found the basement littered with vials and syringes, obvious drug activity in the neighborhood is virtually nonexistent, save for an occasional teenager shuffling down the street smoking a joint, or a pipe tossed into the bushes. An abandoned shopping cart across the street is evidence of the "sober house" up the street, a home containing eight apartments (all legal, surprisingly) rented out to men trying to get back on their feet. These men are some of the more visible members of the community, walking (their drivers' licenses have been revoked) six blocks to a minimarket for groceries. Because these men are not permitted to have overnight guests, on a few occasions women have spent the night sleeping in cars outside our house.

Like much of suburbia in Suffolk County, the streets here have no sidewalks, just sandy shoulders. The side streets are often very wide—so wide in fact that five, possibly even six, cars could park side by side across the width of the street and still not touch the lawns on either side.

It has been established . . . that suburban streets all over America ought to be as wide as two-lane country highways, regardless of whether this promotes driving at excessive speeds where children play, or destroys the spatial relationship between the houses on the street. Back in the 1950s, when these formulas were devised, the width of residential streets was tied closely to the idea of a probable nuclear war with the Russians. And in the aftermath of a war, it was believed, wide streets would make it easier to clean up the mess with heavy equipment. (Kunstler 113–14)[5]

If you walk five blocks north from our house you will come to a service road that runs parallel to the Long Island Expressway (LIE), with its (increasingly slow-moving) current of 24/7 traffic. At night the hiss of cars in the distance spills in through our bedroom skylight.

In 1998 they started widening the highway, extending the HOV lanes. Although HOV stands for "high occupancy vehicle," in this case two people—even if that second person is a baby—are considered "high occupancy." The HOV lanes have been added to decrease congestion by encouraging carpooling. Traffic, even out here, ninety minutes from Manhattan—off peak—is thick: on weekdays as early as 6:30 A.M. the westbound lane of the LIE can crawl at 15 m.p.h. But studies show the HOV lanes to be ineffective. In a car culture like Long Island's, people are reluctant to carpool (the newspapers occasionally report stories of drivers getting caught in HOV lanes with mannequins sitting next to them or cabbage patch dolls in baby seats), and, even when they do, the time it takes to navigate the crowded secondary highways to pick up one's passengers requires people to get up that much earlier.

So you think traffic on Long Island is bad now? Stick around.
In a mere 22 years, it will be unbearable unless something is done.
That's the prediction of a team of consultants hired by the state Department of Transportation.
Their study, released by the department last week, makes it clear that existing and planned HOV lanes on the Long Island Express way aren't going to solve anything. . . . The forecasters say that by 2020, the amount of time Long Islanders are delayed in traffic will nearly double. The 1,091 miles of congested lanes

during the morning rush will increase by a whopping 75 percent. And it will take longer to get where we're going; the average travel speed during morning and evening rush hours will decrease by 17 percent.

. . . The big problem is that Long Island's highway system is close to overflowing already, according to the experts. Even a small increase in the number of cars on the road can cause big problems. (Adcock)

Yet construction of the new lanes continues. By the time they are finished, the LIE will be twelve lanes wide in places: the outside shoulder, three lanes of traffic, an on-off lane for entering and leaving the HOV lane, and the HOV lane itself—times two. (See Figure 1 for a construction photo.)

If you want to walk more than five blocks north from my house you will have to walk under the LIE, which means crossing a busy service road. Continue for another five blocks and you will find yourself looking at Lake Ronkonkoma. Although the lake is described as "the jewel" of the community, there is no boardwalk, sidewalk, or even pathway encircling the lake—just a perimeter road (dangerous to walk on due to lack of shoulders), scattered homes in some areas, a restaurant, low-income apartments, and a trailer park. There are three beaches, but each resides in one of the three localities bordering the lake, so residents are permitted to use only one of them. (See Figure 2.)

If you walk several blocks east or west from my house you will arrive at busy four-lane streets (seven-lane, if you count the wide shoulders and the center turning lanes), which serve as effective pedestrian barriers, boxing in and thereby defining the parameters of our little "neighborhood." Both roads were widened in the last decade. One street has a light that sometimes changes color before you can reach the other side; the other is an artery connecting the expressway to the Long Island Rail Road and, beyond that, Veteran's Highway. I am reluctant to take walks with my son in this direction because the traffic on Ronkonkoma Avenue is constant and fast-moving (I was nearly run over early one morning while walking to the train station). On the other hand, living so close to the Ronkonkoma LIRR station (see Figures 3 and 4) is helpful since I take the train to work. (My daily commute is almost two hours, each way: a fifteen-minute walk

FIGURE 1. May 14, 1998, 3:55 P.M. Looking down at HOV lane
construction on the Long Island Expressway from the Ronkonkoma
Avenue overpass between exits 59 and 60, about forty-five miles from
Manhattan. "The Long Island Expressway was built without rapid
transit—and without provision for rapid transit in the future. And as each
section of the superhighway opened [beginning in 1955], it was
jammed—with traffic jams of immense dimensions. [Robert Moses']
dream became a nightmare—an enduring, year-after-year nightmare—for
tens of thousands of other men. Year by year, the huge road bulled its
way eastward, through Queens, across Nassau County, deeper and deeper
into Suffolk; it would take fifteen years to build it out to Riverhead. And
as each section opened, as each piece of Moses' largest road-building
achievement fell into place, the congestion grew worse. The Long Island
Expressway's designed daily capacity was 80,000 vehicles. By 1963, it
was carrying 132,000 vehicles per day, a load that jammed the expressway even at 'off' hours—during the rush hours, the expressway was solid
with cars, congealed with them, chaos solidified. The drivers trapped on it
nicknamed Moses' longest road 'the world's longest parking lot.'" (Caro,
Power Broker 949)

to the train station, a one-hour train ride to Jamaica, Queens, a
fifteen-minute wait for the Q30 or Q31 bus, and another twenty-
to twenty-five-minute ride to campus.)

If you choose to walk south from my house you can go only
two blocks before coming to a wooded acre of (for the moment)[6]
undeveloped land, which ends at the railroad tracks. A tall fence

Photo by Derek Owens

FIGURE 2. A view of Lake Ronkonkoma (obstructed by low-income housing).

prevents one from crossing the tracks, which are electrified and will cause third-degree burns and possibly death if one touches the third rail. It is in this wooded plot of land that in the late summer of 1997 I found, hidden amid the black oaks and scrub pines, the remains of a campsite.

They had been living in two ripped tents, the smaller one erected inside the larger one, apparently in an attempt to keep out rain and mosquitoes. Filthy clothes and broken furniture were strewn everywhere. From the smell of the cheese and chopped meat left in a plastic foam cooler, and the remains of a cat coated with maggots and wrapped in a blanket, the site had been abandoned for several weeks. (See Figure 5.) The next day I made an attempt to clean it up but only got so far as to fill a half a dozen garbage bags before I grew too disgusted and gave up. In the process, I found a shoebox of old photographs and a diary. The two squatters had been teenage girls who had taken to living back here in this tiny patch of woods, subsisting for a time by cashing in on a stepfather's social security checks. I wondered what had caused them to leave so suddenly.

FIGURES 3 AND 4. **Abandoned stores and empty lots at the Ronkonkoma train station.** In 1995 a new multimillion-dollar train station was built here, this being the busiest LIRR hub east of Queens. But the new station has not led to the revitalization of local businesses. A billboard in the center of an empty lot next to the train station promises future stores as early as 1997, but as of 2001 the lot remains empty.

Photo by Derek Owens

FIGURE 5. **Squatters in suburbia.**

Despite the filth they left behind, part of me admired them. In Ronkonkoma, like most suburbs, teenagers, along with elderly persons, are the ones most victimized by the absence of a public commons, of meeting places, of coffee shops or bookstores or independent movie theaters or parks. As a result, many teenagers skulk around in small bands, knocking over fences, stealing the occasional mailbox, and parking at night in the dark beneath shot-out streetlights to hang out, get stoned, or have sex (twice I've found used condoms on the shoulder outside our house, and, once, a discarded early pregnancy test kit in the bushes).

As a teenager I visited my old suburban chums back on Long Island from time to time and I did not envy their lot in life. By puberty, they had entered a kind of coma. There was so little for them to do in Northwood, and hardly any worthwhile destination reachable by bike or foot, for now all the surrounding territory was composed of similar one-dimensional housing developments punctuated at intervals by equally boring shopping plazas. Since they had no public gathering places, teens congregated in furtive little holes—bedrooms and basements—to smoke pot and imitate the rock and roll bands who played on

the radio. Otherwise, teen life there was reduced to waiting for
that transforming moment of becoming a licensed driver. (Kunstler
14)

One writer has suggested, not completely tongue in cheek,
that it is the sameness of the Long Island landscape, perfected
early on in that famous suburb of Levittown, that makes Nassau
and Suffolk county produce more than their share of kidnappers,
serial killers, snipers, teenage killers, spouse murderers, and other
dangerous individuals. In "Long Island, Babylon," Ron
Rosenbaum implies that the inability to situate oneself psycho-
logically or physically within a specific space distinguishable from
other spaces leads to psychosis. Moreover, Rosenbaum sees the
percolation of antisocial behavior on Long Island as a harbinger
for the rest of the country:

> Long Island, after all, was supposed to be the future *before* the
> future. We always had a head start on the life cycle of suburban
> baby-boom culture because we were the first-born burbs of the
> baby boom; a burbland created almost all at once, very fast and
> virtually ex nihilo, right after the war, a self-contained social or-
> ganism. An organism whose sociobiological clock started tick-
> ing a little earlier than subsequent burbs, and whose shrill alarms
> now seem to signal that it has raced through its mature stage and
> is now rocketing headlong into the social-organism equivalent of
> senile dementia. (628)

Others have called attention to what some see as a dispropor-
tionate number of famous crimes associated with Nassau and
Suffolk county (Demoretcky; Jensen; Wacker). Two weeks after
the April 1999 high school massacre in Colorado, an article appeared in the *New York Times* speculating about the role of suburban sprawl in fostering the kind of environment where such
tragedies occur: "At a time when the renegade sprawl of suburbs
themselves is being intensely scrutinized, the troubling vision of
a nation re-pioneered in vast tracts of disconnected communities
has produced uneasy discussion about the psychological disori-
entation they might house" (Hamilton, "Suburban Design" F1).

At least the two squatters near my house had made, for a
piece of their summer, a hovel of their own away from others'

eyes, tucked away by the tracks in a copse of trees sandwiched between the Quality Muffler Shop and a dirt parking lot owned by the LIRR. As disgusted with them as I was for having defiled that place, I am more ashamed of the planners and architects and developers, and their backers, who have bequeathed to other people's children what James Kunstler calls "a landscape of scary places, the geography of nowhere, that has simply ceased to be a credible human habitat" (15). If their community leaders had exhibited no imagination in designing neighborhoods and had polluted the environs with industrial parks and strip malls, one could hardly criticize these girls for desecrating their own hidden home, which was, after all, distinctly *their* mess, and not a copy of a copy of someone else's idea of what a home or neighborhood should look like. Embarrassing as it was, this pathetic campsite had become, for a few weeks, their space, an island constructed in the center of an island marked by unchecked sprawl.

Where My Students Are Writing From

To be sure, much of my discontent here on Long Island is the result of growing up within walking distance of rivers and woods in upstate New York; my childhood was spent wandering up and down the Chemung River in "Mark Twain Country." And obviously there are good and even great things I have not mentioned about Long Island: being a ninety-minute train ride away from Manhattan, and just twenty minutes away from ferries to Fire Island; the pine barrens farther east and the still relatively undeveloped landscape of the north fork, with its farms and wineries; the beaches, of course. There are activities in nearby Connetquot State Park, and a growing number of film festivals in Nassau and Suffolk county. For the most part, the neighborhoods around here, albeit nondescript, are peaceful, safe, and pleasant.

But it's hard for me to keep from focusing on the darker side of living here: the "tens of thousands" of aging fuel tanks (the primary source of home heating in Nassau and Suffolk counties) buried in back yards throughout the island, many of them leaking (Fagin, "No-Win"); the 41,901 gasoline and oil spills in Nassau, Suffolk, and Queens as of April 1998 ("Spills of the

Island"); the fact that M.T.B.E. (methyl tertiary butane ether), a toxic and possibly carcinogenic gasoline additive, is "rapidly moving through the region's groundwater, penetrating drinking water supplies" (Rather, "Contaminant" LI1); the presence of the Brookhaven National Laboratory a few miles away from here, which surrounding residents have for years suspected to be the cause of suspicious cancers in their neighborhoods (Nelson); the fact that baby teeth collected on Long Island over a three year period as part of the "Tooth Fairy Project" show high levels of the radioactive carcinogen strontium-90 (Rather, "Babies' Teeth"); a history of graft and governmental corruption throughout the rest of the township of Brookhaven, sometimes referred to as Crookhaven, which much of the public seems to take in stride (Halbfinger, "Scandal"); predicted increases in mosquito-borne diseases and coastal flooding, especially on the south shore, due to an expected annual rise in temperatures over the coming decades—an April 1999 *Newsday* article features maps of coastal neighborhoods that might be gone in fifty years due to rising sea levels (Fagin, "Trouble"); a recent study indicating that commuters like "most of the 18,000 people who ride in [to Penn Station on the LIRR] every morning from Ronkonkoma" are, because of their lengthy commute, sleep-deprived (Halbfinger, "I've Been Sleeping"). And then there is the continued loss of open space due to the constant building of new homes, new malls, and new industrial parks, and, at the same time, the absence of parks, pedestrian centers, commons—the "good places" that people go out of their way to be in.

But what also bothers me about my frustrations over where I live is my guilt when I consider that in the eyes of my students I have made it: to many of them this is "the country," the land of suburban milk and honey that they dream of moving to and dying in when their ships come in. For where I live is so much better than where many of them do. When I get off the train at eleven o'clock at night and walk the half-mile home, the streets are safe and pleasant. Although our house was burglarized not too long ago, this happens everywhere, and there is little crime to speak of in the immediate neighborhood. The fact is, we're very lucky to have a quarter of an acre of property—far more land than most Americans have—which offers us ample space for my experiments in vegetable gardening, a tree house, half a dozen enormous maples and oaks, a number of small perennial gardens, and plenty of yard for Ryan and his cousins and friends to enjoy. If the surrounding area is not exactly what I would consider a "good place," at least we've managed to make our private compound compensate to some degree. My son thrives in our backyard, which at age three he actually referred to as "paradise" (although if he were fifteen, too old for backyard romping but too young too drive, he might characterize his home a little differently). Were my students to see how I lived, I imagine some would be amused or disgusted by their spoiled professor's whiny portrait of his neighborhood.

After reading their papers over the years, I've come to realize that many of my students are not happy with where they live. Most live in Queens, Brooklyn, the Bronx, or Nassau county, and more often than not they are disappointed, discouraged, and bored with—and, not infrequently, scared of—their places. This is not to say they never have fun, or that they feel their hangouts and street-corner gatherings have no redeeming qualities. But when I ask students to write about where they live, what I get are sketches of homes and buildings and blocks marked not by joy but by monotony, restlessness, violence, and neglect.

A number of my students who live in New York City were once country kids who in some ways have never fully gotten used to living in the city.

> I lived on a farm [in Korea] with my grandmother during the first seven years of my life. . . . [T]he adults and the children usually gathered around the front lounge eating meals, telling stories, and resting from work. . . . Living on the farm allowed me to realize that the most important and valuable things about living are to appreciate neighbors. . . . In Brooklyn, most of my neighbors . . . are too busy performing their own life. They have to run their businesses and take care of family problems. It is too much for them. . . . We are losing beauty of life such as forgiveness of each other, belief in each other, and loving each other. . . . My family and I now . . . operate within the new way of living without feeling guilt. The result, "I am just like them."
>
> EUN HEE

This morning I looked out from my terrace [onto Jamaica Avenue in Queens] at the bus stop. Of course because of the season, there are many who are cold, and have been waiting for that Queens bus to come for at least twenty minutes. . . . My surroundings are totally different from my parents' surroundings at my age, especially my father's. He was brought up on a huge estate and farmland. They had horses and all kinds of other animals. Tons of trees, different sizes and bearing different fruits. An endless walk if you were up to it. I only know this from my visits to Guyana, and from pictures I've seen. . . . I wish we could have traded our "places".

CHARISSE

It seems like it was yesterday when [in Ecuador] I used to chase the chickens and the ducks of the farm, when I used to ride my bicycle along the riverside, when I used to take those never-ending baths in the river or just to run across the corn and soy fields. . . . My grandfather colonized these territories around the 1916's. These were fertile fields, apt for stockbreeding and banana production. He dedicated his entire life to his farm that one day would belong to his sons and daughters. . . . Fifteen years have passed by. My grandmother still lives in Quevedo. Our family is trying to maintain those values that kept us once together, preserve our family roots. . . . [M]y heart still longs for those good days when I used to be woken up by the noisy but enchanting trilling of the rooster.

VIOLETTA

When I look back to my childhood and see that special place of mine, I feel sad and melancholy that I do not have it any more. I lived there my first five years and they were fantastic. It was a very small community (only thirty to forty houses) call Lemons . . . located about four to five hours away from the capital of Guatemala.

. . . All the people from this community were very close to each other. If a person had an economical problem everybody would get together and help them solve their problem. All the kids were also united when it was time to play. . . .

Nowadays [in Brooklyn] people do not care about their neighbors, not at all. They do not care about their sufferings, they are egotistic and indifferent to each other. . . . [W]here I grew up in Guatemala was like a little reproduction of the biblical Eden. . . . People were always helping you and giving you their support when you needed it. They were like an extension of your own family. I would like to go back someday and live there the rest of my life. If God gives me the opportunity to do it, I am sure I will in the future.

CLARA

Some of my students are refugees, having recently emigrated from war-ravaged countries.

I want to write about growing up in Tbilisi Georgia. . . . Recollecting my childhood I see the faces of my friends I grew up with: boys and girls, Georgians and Russians, Armenians and Jews, Ossetians and Azerbaijanians. . . . Every family lived its life, had its own problems, but these problems were often resolved by mutual efforts, people were together for better or for worse. They pulled together in hardship and joy—they arranged weddings and family occasions: and when misery or disaster knocked at the door, you could always count on your neighbor or friend, you could always lean on somebody's shoulder. . . . [A]ll of a sudden everything turned upside down and vanished in the past.

War!!! Blood and tears, black mourning clothes of mothers and sisters who lost their sons and beloved ones, exhausted, gloomy faces of men, fears and misery in every family, disaster in every heart. . . . But what is the most scary, is vicious and bloody instinct in the eyes of youngsters! Nothing is sacred any more. There is anarchy and chaos all over. Once you cross the border between life and death, there is no way back to your childhood. You can't hide behind your mother's skirt and she, your mother, can't protect you any longer, because she might be assaulted or even be murdered in Abkhazia or Svanetia by one of your contemporaries. Tooth for tooth, eye for eye, blood for blood. . . .

ANNA

If I was to choose one place that means something to me it would have to be the basement of my house [back in Bosnia]. Remembering these times sometimes requires a lot of emotional courage. . . . [T]hose six walls of concrete provided protection necessary for my family. . . . In the month that war began, we used it as a shelter against grenades. Mom brought some blankets to cover the floor against the cold, and huddled us together in one corner listening to the grumbling that went on outside. You couldn't tell if it was day or night, but I remember staring at the ceiling while everyone slept. I was looking, I guess, for an explanation, and as if the ceiling had the answers I spoke out loud, conversed with it. Eventually I would fall asleep without my answers. I didn't mind sometimes; some things are better left unsaid. . . . Even though it's just walls, it protects you when you need it. I guess you don't know what you have until you're cornered and hopeless.

MARTA

My students also comment on excessive development in their neighborhoods.

The developments that are supposed to be going underway in Nassau [County] are attempts to just eat up land and destroy our environment. It's what I like to call "Lego City." Remember as kids when we used to play with those Lego pieces? We used to build cities, cars, spaceships, etc. The whole city built of Lego was the only place your Lego men would live in—no progression, no mobilization. It was safe to say that your little people had their lives planned out since the moment they came out of the box. . . . In Nassau they are creating something called the Hub, which is just one huge Lego City. This is meant to lessen traffic and make the motorists comfortable so they can get to work on time. I hate this concept that people live to work, I always thought that it was to live to live life. Instead we are wasting our lives suffering just to be able to pay the rent.

OSCAR

I grew up on a beautiful island in Greece called Chalkis. My hometown had a dazzling beauty that I just can't describe. It was like a paradise God created for himself. . . . My house was right across from the sea. One of my favorite things to do was to stand on my balcony and watch the enchanting view with my field glasses. . . .

The place I used to love is not the same any more. . . . Enormous forestland used to cover the place all over! . . . There were olive trees and fig trees all around. Now, all you can see are dark, empty spaces. People set fires in order to buy these lands and make profit off of them. The street which was once closed to automobiles and open only to pedestrians is now full of vehicles. The noise is unbearable. The atmosphere is not clear anymore. I take my field glasses now but I can't see on the other side even when it's sunny. . . . When I'm thinking of Chalkis now—and I'm doing this quite often actually—I feel really sad. I don't want to live to see the day when I won't have the will to go back there.

ANGELA

They write about traffic congestion and commuting difficulties.

I have been living on Linden Blvd. right off Flatbush Ave. for two years now. I hate it. Whenever it is possible I find some reason to be away from that place. . . . The streets are not safe to walk on, they are designed solely for the purpose of the drivers, without caring about the people that live and pass through these places. Even the buildings look identical. . . . I am disgusted by my neighborhood and its surrounding area. It is not a place for people to live in with all that hustle and bustle going on. Whenever I am in my neighborhood I either stay inside or I go out to escape the place.

NATALIE

Traffic congestion is an especially horrible problem that exists in my neighborhood. Early morning rush hour, midday and afternoon rush hour are the worst times to be on the streets, not to mention a busy Saturday. Sundays are moderately quiet since this is the rest day to get ready for the madhouse you are sure to encounter the next morning.

Crossing the street is no easy feat to accomplish. You have to be constantly on the lookout. The streets are always packed and everyone is out for themselves. The dollar vans [private commuter vans that compete with public transportation services] stop in the middle of the street to pick up a passenger, while holding up traffic or nearly causing an accident. People drive crazily cutting people off any chance that they get, no one wants to slow down to let anyone cross the street even when the sign says WALK . . . . It is not uncommon to hear profanity being shouted to other drivers, or to see people giving each other the finger. . . . The constant flow of traffic that passes through the neighborhood is not that great on the roads either. There are many rough spots and potholes all over.[7]

ROXANNE

They write of the boredom and monotony in their communities.

I live in the most boring neighborhood in the entire United States of America! Nothing ever happens on my block [in Queens] or in the surrounding areas. You can go outside at 10:00 A.M. and stay out until 5:00 P.M. and not see anybody or see anything happen. . . .

My block has 36 houses on it. Every house looks the same. If we did not have addresses, you could never tell which family lived in which house. . . . The only people that can have any type of fun are the licensed drivers. Even with a license, we do not really have that much fun. The friends of mine that have licenses either go to school, work, or both. They have little, if any, free time. Even the licensed drivers have boring lives in my neighborhood.

Anybody with at least half of a social life and a normal personality should not even visit my neighborhood! My block and its surrounding areas can take the life out of even the most exuberant person. There is no real hope of any sort of life ever coming to this area. If I had the opportunity, I would leave here. This is not the place for any child to grow up in.

Ross

When I think about Jewel Park, the word "hate" comes to mind . . . . You see, many people I know, including myself, complain about hanging out at the park, and yet, we still end up hanging out there. It's a chance for many young Filipinos to all hang out together [but] there is never a day that passes without a fight. Jewel Park has taught me that this so-called "flip [Filipino] scene" that I am a part of is not all that it is cracked up to be. . . . The bad memories outweigh the good ones. Then again, if we had no Jewel Park, where would we go to talk?

RACHAEL

If you were to take a walk down [my] block you would be looking at apartment buildings about four stories high, with fences surrounding them and a flight of steps leading up to the front doors. The only difference you would notice is the color of the buildings. I think there should be some kind of difference rather than making everything so similar and dreary. When I go out I like to be able to look around and take in the different sites, but in a neighborhood such as mine that is impossible. Everywhere you turn you would be confronted with the exact same things, no matter what direction you turn to. . . . I'm much better staying inside where I can move from room to room which at least holds a different picture in each. . . .

JOANNE

Many of my students are all too familiar with poor living conditions and dirty apartment buildings.

I live in the southern part of Manhattan in an apartment building beside the East River. . . . The lounge is gloomy when it rains. The hallways of each floor are lighted with insufficient fluorescent light bulbs. . . . Once, two robbers hid behind the staircase door; when they saw my neighbor open the door to her apartment, they pushed her in and stuck a gun at her. This is why living near the staircase can be dangerous. . . . In this neighborhood there are all sorts of sad things happening. Teenagers getting pregnant, people getting shot once in a while, and kidnappers kidnapping children are the things that my parents do not want us to get influenced by. . . .

ZHU

I live in Flushing right off Parson Boulevard, which is very commercial. The traffic makes it annoying to get anywhere around my neighborhood. And added to that is the annoying people all around screaming at you to move or cursing at you cause you took their parking place. I can honestly say that there are no nice people in my neighborhood. The next thing that's not good about my house is the building itself. It's always dirty, or the elevator doesn't work, or it smells. My building always has some kind of garbage smell roaming around the halls which really stinks. What makes it worse is that if you're in the hallway waiting for the elevator the smell follows you around like it sticks to you on your clothes your hair etc. Next we have the garbage lying around the hallways or we have dogs pee on the floor in the middle of the hall so it's gross to see. You would think with all the money the tenants pay for rent they could clean the hallways and the entrance. And last but not least the elevators are always broken. I really can't blame all this on the owners of the building or the super, the tenants are also to blame. They just don't care and they make it hard for those tenants who do care.

WINSOME

Many of my students know too well how poverty can turn urban neighborhoods into unsafe zones.

With the increasing gang related crimes, people fear to go and just walk around Chinatown. I, personally, witnessed two crime situations in Chinatown when I was helping my mom when she was a vendor. I was standing there folding some clothes when I heard a loud noise. Thinking that it was just some sort of firecracker, I did not really look around or care too much about it until I saw this guy limping on the street. He fell and I saw blood on his upper thigh. After seeing that, I feared to go to Chinatown and help my mom out and I was scared to see that she had to work on such dangerous streets. . . . I saw another person get shot. . . . like four times and the last one in his head.

SUE

The crime rate has gone up in my neighborhood [in Brooklyn]. I was never scared of walking around the streets late at night, now I am petrified. It is scary when you constantly have to be paranoid and watch your back. This happens in a lot of places around us, but this makes me a more defensive person. When I come home late at night, I always have my key ready, I lock up the car and run with full speed to the front door. It is so hard to trust people. There are so many negative qualities in my personality that have been brought out by the changes of the neighborhood.

I used to see myself as a light-hearted person, not really worrying too much. Now, I do not open up to meeting new people. I find it very hard to trust people. This all started after I was mugged on the train. I had a knife put to my neck. This was one of the most horrifying things that ever happened to me. Because of this I will never be the same, I look at people so much differently. The attitude I have now is everyone is out for themselves not caring about anyone. This is a really negative attitude but, I do not know how to change it.

PAULINA

As for my neighborhood [in Brownsville, Brooklyn], my two biggest complaints are that of its violence and its state of underdevelopment. As for the violence, I don't mean like I hear gun shots every night (although it happens more than I'd like). I mean mostly robberies and gang violence. Many people close to me have been robbed either in or close to my building. These people include my mother, sister and best friend who have all been robbed on separate occasions. All of them at either gun or knife point. And all too often, you hear the tales of "this one" or "that one" and what happened to them last night while they were on their way to "wherever." I have to constantly look over my shoulder and to both of my sides when walking from the train station in the evenings. As far as the gang violence, that's something pretty new, that started out small and harmless, if you can call it that, and has grown into an outrageous problem. I'm sorry, but one shouldn't have to worry about what colors they're wearing when they're in their own neighborhood or anyone else's. But we do. If you wear the colors of one gang in another gang's "territory," you become a blind target for any amount of things to happen to you.

NANETTE

My students write of places dominated by boredom, drugs, and poverty.

On the corner of 50th St. and 4th Ave. a small store stands. Santiago's is a street corner bodega in the Sunset Park section of Brooklyn. A dumpster and a pay phone surround the store, a dumpster to drink your drink after purchasing it from Mr. Santiago himself, and a pay phone where you can return your beeps while you were getting drunk or high. This is a corner where every imaginable temptation is put upon you. I should know, I spent two of my high school years atop that very dumpster.

Mr. Santiago didn't care whether you were twenty-one or twelve, if you had the cash in hand you got what you wanted, beer, cigarettes, anything. . . . If you got caught by the cops drinking or smoking you would blame it on Juan. Juan was a made-up person that we blamed everything on. Then there's a person by the name of Angel, his name was really Erik but we called him Angel, because to all the drug addicts they thought of him as God. Like an umbrella salesman he stood by the telephone waiting for any business to come his way. From crack to glue he had everything, and to many of us he was kind of like a big brother.

This corner gave most of us kids a sense of security and a closeness that only a father or a mother would give to their son. If it wasn't Angel looking after us, it would be each other. I can remember Christmas, as poor as everyone was each of us would get what we wanted, whether it was Nintendo or a leather jacket we got it. Even Mr. Santiago would give out free sodas and cheese doodles. . . .

[Whenever you travel out of the neighborhood] you envy the places you see because your economic status holds you prisoner in the neighborhood you don't want to live in.

Luis

Sometimes students express pride in neighborhoods they depict in very negative ways, which might sound hypocritical were it not that this is the only neighborhood they have.

Where I live now the streets smell like urine and there are cracks in the sidewalk. There is graffiti everywhere. It is boring most of the time because there is nothing to do. The people are rude and impolite, and have bad attitudes. Most of them are junkies and are just rotting away. My neighborhood looks like an old abandoned western town.

I live in Coney Island in a small area called Brighton Beach. The D train is right behind my house, so it is pretty noisy. . . . The neighborhood looks like it's decaying. It has potholes, wild grass growing out of the sidewalks, crack pipes and condoms all over the streets. The street that I live on is the infamous Oceanview Avenue, where the ladies of the night come out to do their jobs. About three to four ladies work the block every night from twelve a.m. to five a.m. The houses across the street are no more than fifteen steps away. Each house is no more than five feet away from each other, which makes the neighborhood look tightly packed.

It does have its good sides. There is plenty of public transportation, grocery stores, and clothing stores. But it seems that things are getting worse as I get older. . . . Things have changed. Instead of saying hello people say "do you have a problem?" or "do you need some weed?" But as I walk down Oceanview Avenue, I feel that I am with the street because it is where I come from. . . . There is a bond between the people [in this neighborhood] that is unbreakable. There were times when I was starving and people would offer to buy me food. I do not think it would bother me if I could not find anything good about my neighborhood. Regardless, I love it because it is where I was born and raised. . . . I would not want it to change for anything in the world.

RAVI

In one of the slum streets of the Bronx, stands a six story high building that is painted in gray and orange. That's the one I call home. About four other buildings stand adjacent to mine. In three of the corners there is a Bodega and in one corner there is a laundromat. The artificial trees that were placed in front of every other building are either without leaves or no longer existing. . . . Teenagers and drugs rule the streets. As you enter my block you see a lot of teenagers standing in the corner stores and in the buildings. Their hobbies are to use drugs, sell drugs, stay out late, drag race, make rap music, and protect their lives from their enemies. You see them hiding out in your building whenever the cops are around the neighborhood. They influence younger children into dealing drugs. All I am describing is what I see and have always seen since I have lived here. Stereotypes of the Bronx are cruel and sometimes false; my intentions are not to add to these stereotypes.

My neighborhood could be better. You are not really living in fear because of what could happen to you when you step out the door, but I'm not saying you are safe either. My streets are full of low life teenagers that are making their life off dealing with drugs. . . . Then again, half of these youngsters don't know any better because they grew up in the streets and refuse to surpass this corrupt life.

[And yet] I would feel awkward if I moved away to a better neighborhood. There have been times that I've gone on vacation to places that are truly amazing in respect to the atmosphere. Yet I can't get used to these places. For example, I visited Florida one summer and I just couldn't see myself living there for the rest of my life. It was beautiful. It was safe. It was boring. It was not home! My neighborhood has more negative qualities than positive ones, but I don't think it's that bad because it could be worse. I would not like to live here for the rest of my life, but where would I go? and would it still be home?

SANDRA

They tell of lives and communities shaped around work.

I live in Elmont, "the gateway to Nassau county." It is part of the great wall of China dividing Queens from the "innocence" of Long Island. It is a sea of suburbia, littered from wall to wall with two story houses and garages. . . . My town serves for the most part as a resting stop for many working, middle-class people on their way to and from work. You might say that they live there, but I don't equate "living" with working all day then coming home to rest before returning to work in the morning and going to and from the city for work. . . . There is too much to do. Too much work not enough time. Why do Americans choose to live like this? This cannot be the "American Dream." The "American Dream" is like Bigfoot, people have heard of it and claim to have seen it, but no hard evidence of it exists.

RICHARD

They write about the crime in their neighborhoods.

I presently live in Fresh Meadow, Queens, an urban neighborhood with one family houses. Most houses are landscaped with beautiful flowers and shaped bushes on the front lawn. . . . At night the neighborhood gets really dark and each block only has one street light which is right in front of my house. This is bad because many times there are burglars who try to break in houses where there are bushes covering the windows and try to break in through there. If your house is not protected by an alarm system, motion light, or an attack dog be ready to see your house vandalized or the steering wheel of your car stolen. That has happened to my house two times. The neighborhood may be peaceful and pretty to the eye of the beholder but at night prowlers use that to their advantage. My garage has been broken into . . . which caused my father to tint the windows so people wouldn't be able to see inside. Almost every house is protected by a different alarm system and if not they might probably be equipped with flood lights which make a person feel like they have been spotted by a police helicopter.

ELLEN

I grew up on New York's crime side of Brownsville, Brooklyn. My family and I lived in the 289 projects building on Blake St. I lived there for nine years. I wish I could have grown up in a much better environment, but I didn't have any control over that. Brownsville is the type of neighborhood that people have nightmares about. When I was growing up I constantly saw drugs being sold, teenagers gambling in the hallways of my building, drunks passed out on the front steps. I could never forget the time that my dad and I saw a lady getting robbed. I was about seven years old. My dad was walking me to school one day at seven o'clock in the morning. We heard a loud scream and ran to the next floor. We saw the back of the man who took the lady's pocketbook. What happened on that morning was on my mind all day. That night before I went to sleep I thought about my life in the projects. I wanted to get out and move away, anywhere. I knew if I didn't I'd end up dead or selling drugs. See people in the projects have no motive to move out, so very few people move out. So I thought that this was the place I was going to spend the rest of my life. When I was a kid I had the attitude that school didn't matter, my goals in life didn't matter because I'm going to end up dying in the projects anyway. Brownsville's school was the worst, teachers passed kids easily and I was one of those kids. There were many bad values that came out of living in Brooklyn.

JORGE

They write of communities suffering from abandonment and neglect.

If you were to drive through Hempstead today you would see something totally different. You would see large abandoned buildings with weathered bricks falling apart, appearing to almost barely hold up this massive architecture, obviously not maintained. The doors which were once actively revolving doors are now boarded up and matted with graffiti tags. During the summer when you drive by you are sure to see a small forest of weeds growing out of the cracks which have formed in the desolate parking lots. A few letters still remain of what used to read,

"Abraham & Strauss," now Abr-ha- & -trauss. It has done some good being that now these letters are the home of a few birds' nests. . . .

DAN

The dream of my parents brought them to a nice area called Cliffside Park, New Jersey. In the early 1970's and throughout the mid 1980's, Cliffside Park was a town that had character. It was clean, the people were nice, trouble was rare and only good things could be said about the town. It was your average town, average people lived here, and now it has changed because greed entered everyone's mind. . . .

When I played little league baseball, the field was well manicured. Now, the grass is sometimes so high, when the baseball hits the infield it slows down so much that it can't make it to the outfield. The tennis courts are cracking, sometimes no nets are put up, or the net is broken. You find broken glass or rocks on the field. There are two manholes on the field which are covered by Astroturf. . . .

My overall person is defined by my environment, but to what exact extent, I'm not sure of. When I was younger, I was a hard working individual, now, I feel like an aging veteran who has lost a step or two. Something is not right, because I am only twenty-one years old.

WALTER

They write of communities that lack a sense of community.

My town [in Brooklyn] is very small. In my block, it has just two big, white buildings. People might think that it is very pleasurable to live here. Yes, it looks clean and nice, but I can not feel anything from it. It is just like one big matchbox. My neighbors and me, we are living in a box. . . .

My place has some serious problems. First, we have lack of communication with each other. . . . All my neighbors hate noise. They close their doors and windows just like their minds. . . . [T]hey close their minds everyday, and do not want get involved with anything that happens. We are too busy to care about our own problems. We have a robber in our building but my neighbors or even myself do not recognize him because we do not know each other's faces.

ESTHER

I have lived on 91st Road in Queens Village for almost fifteen years. . . . I can look around and say that our block is growing with the times. . . . The beauty of the block has also been taken away. Favorite trees of mine have been torn down by the city. . . .

I remember the first couple of days after I moved to 91st Road and earned the title "Mayor of the Block." I must have been about four then and would walk up and down the block and introduce myself to any new face I saw. I remember playing house, tag, red light/green light, spud and ice cream parlor in the street. . . . Now you have to worry about not being killed when crossing the street.

As I grew older I started seeing that many families were leaving for summer homes on Long Island. The block became lonely at times and my friends and I would put on shows for the neighbors. We would practice on the front lawn between two bayberry bushes that my neighbor said everyone used to have. We would dance and put on skits and when it was all over we would get candy and listen to [an elderly neighbor] tell stories about the neighborhood as it once was.

Now at eighteen years I sit less and less on my steps. I see that that sense of unity will never be the same and is shamefully forgotten.

Rosa

Even my affluent students, who live in what many would consider desirable areas, can find their places wanting in fundamental ways.

My neighborhood [in Nassau county] is extremely quiet. You never yearn to get away because there is never anything to escape from. In the morning we awaken to the beautiful sounds of the birds singing. No one is ever bothered or annoyed by others. It is a very safe environment, in which everyone always has their privacy and it is never threatened. On a warm evening you could sit in the yard and the only sound you will hear are the crickets, which totally relaxes you. It is overall a tranquil environment which seems ideal to the outsider.

Although my neighborhood is peaceful, alongside of this comes solitude, which at times can be frustrating. Loneliness is not rare in such an environment. Many times I feel as if I live in no man's land. There are never any people in the streets or outside their homes which makes me feel as if I am the only person alive for miles and miles around. I can never seek help or comfort from my surrounding society, due to my fear of rejection. I shut people out due to my belief that they show no concern for anyone other than themselves. . . .

Angela

Boredom and Hyperboredom

Of course, not all of my students' accounts are tinged with frustration. In every class there are those who write about how fortunate they are to live where they do. One student writes of how her neighborhood block association provides a rich and supportive community, making her home at 89th Avenue in Hollis (Queens) so desirable that she can't imagine living anywhere else. Another student loves her home in New Hyde Park so much that she talked her father out of selling it. Another complains about the negative stereotypes she hears about Brooklyn, none of which match the reality of her community in Gravesend, where the houses are kept neat and attractive and the neighbors shovel each other's walks in winter: "I do not think I would change anything," she writes of her neighborhood. "It has everything I think a good neighborhood should have." Another creates an idyllic portrait of Broad Channel, an urban village in Jamaica Bay, near the Jamaica Bay Wildlife Refuge and Rockaway Beach. Some of my students live in gated communities, which they tend to adore for their security, privacy, recreational facilities, and peace and quiet. Increasingly, now that our university has built dormitories and is attracting a growing number of students from all over the country, students will sometimes write about suburban and rural homes near woods and creeks and wildlife. Not surprisingly, my students who like their neighborhoods so much they never want to leave write of places with three recurring characteristics: a mixed-use community (homes, business, and services all in close proximity, usually in walking distance) with low crime and good public transportation. These students emphasize the presence of restaurants, stores, schools, parks, and easy access to bus and subway lines that can take them into Manhattan in thirty to forty-five minutes: "I have everything I need here," many of them write.

But while many students are happy with where they live, in my four years of reading these portraits I have seen the majority of my students express dissatisfaction and frustration with their communities. And while, as the preceding excerpts reveal, some of my students are nervous and fearful in what they call "active" (high-crime) neighborhoods, the majority who express discontent are not so much afraid—I doubt that more than ten to twenty percent of the students in any of my classes live in areas where gangs and robberies are a concern—as they are bored. This connection between place and boredom is worth examining more closely, especially if, as I suspect is the case, it is the majority of our students who are bored with where they live.

While the following excerpt from one of my student's papers is more extreme than most I receive, particularly in its cavalier account of racism, vandalism, and violence, I don't think the omnipresent boredom running throughout the piece is unique to this person's experience. In this passage, which I quote at length, Mike tells of how he and his fellow high school students in southern Nassau county would spend their weekends hanging out at a strip mall parking lot, clustered around an all-night convenience store.

> [The strip mall] was a chain of five stores including an I-Hop [International House of Pancakes] and a Philly Cheese Steak located in the center of a rather enormous parking lot that always seemed a bit unnecessary for such a small grouping of establishments. On weekend nights the site attracted large numbers of teenagers from the local Oceanside school district that had been designated as a hang-out for years. While I attended the high school, the numbers late on a Saturday night would swell to well over three hundred kids in the parking lot alone with absolutely nothing to do. It must be an intriguing sight to the common passerby on their way to Long Beach, witnessing over three hundred high school students gathered in the parking lot of the last commercial enclave before the bridge to Long Island's barrier islands. It wasn't like there was some major attraction there. One would think that 16 and 17-year-old kids would want to do something interesting. All during the school week kids would promise themselves that they would not end up at 24 [an all-night store], but there they would be, sitting on someone's car eating a cream cheese bagel.
>
> . . . The situation was one of boredom. . . . No one ever wanted to be there, but in the end you would be there. Kids would always complain about how pathetic the site was but from as far back as I can remember there would always be at least fifty plus kids there every late weekend night. Often it would be the same kids that claimed to loathe it, myself included. The place intrigued me so much because it attracts the entire high school no matter who you were. It was not an isolated hang-out for one group, but the hang-out for the entire school. It wasn't the place

where kids would spend their whole night but it was where they would be at the end of the night. After a typical night of over-drinking and busted parties it was the place to go when it was all over. By one AM the place was full and would remain that way for another two hours. . . .

It was with striking consistency that the weekend always went down in this fashion. If you ever heard the stereotype that Long Island kids spend their high school years getting drunk and high, well that's not so far from the truth from where I stand anyway. . . .

When we did arrive at 24 we did precisely what we intended to do, get sober fast. That's where we got our bagels that helped absorb the alcohol in our systems. There were ample dark allies behind the store chain for urinating and vomiting. . . . The place represented many of the negative things that youth can be brought to when they have nothing to do. I watched people too drunk to stand on all fours vomiting up their insides for hours on the pavements. I saw my friend lose his scholarship to Cortland on a drug bust and I saw fistfights that were over parking spaces. The entire situation was a breeding ground for bickering amongst one another. Why did the night go wrong, whose fault is it we're here, stay away from my girlfriend, get off my car. We argued about such stupid things. One would be surprised how often these quarrels led to actual violence among "friends."

. . . I remember when the clerk at the steakhouse was hitting on my friend's girlfriend in Spanish so we trashed the place. . . . Now many of these kids are drunk, but they are also hopelessly ignorant white kids who just look for an excuse for more mischief. At any rate . . . the all county linebacker/tight end that was her boyfriend immediately exchanged words with the clerk, and we encouraged him. After all most of the crowd had left by then and we were just looking for something to do anyway. Naturally the half sober ones knew to leave before real trouble started. . . . Trash cans were flying. Garbage was to become the most effective weapon against the evil cheese steak guy. The fact that he was Hispanic made it even worse. The first thing we did was to immediately empty the five trash cans on the tiled floor of the poor man's establishment. The smell was not pleasant. Alarmed, the man threatened us, and once again in Spanish no less. The poor guy really started to panic when we threw the cans themselves at him, and then our empty 40 bottles. When the glass started a-breakin' this guy really started a-shakin'. By now the man was terrified, hiding in the corner of the kitchen room clenching what I perceived to be a small wooden club of sorts, praying for the arrival of the Nassau PD. As a final touch to an eventful evening, my enraged football friend jabs at the window with a solid blow. . . .

The only explanation I could give as to why people would want to hang out in a stupid parking lot by the hundred, would simply be because there is nothing to do on this stupid island. When you're under 18 your choices are limited to begin with. Oceanside doesn't even have a decent movie theater in a population of over 40,000 denizens. It's all houses on the fringe and all stores in the center of town.

. . . Perhaps my biggest gripe with 24 is that . . . I managed to waste so much time there doing nothing that I could consider special to me.

There's a lot to unpack in a narrative like this. Mike's contempt for his peers, his community, and himself makes me wonder to what extent poorly designed neighborhoods become catalysts for self-hatred. And the racism and xenophobia in Mike's conflicted narrative recall how both played a role in the original construction of suburbia. What stands out to me most, though, is Mike's implicit awareness of the degree to which boredom is a condition of place. Or, more precisely, how bad places—places that are not pedestrian-centered, that lack accessible public transportation and affordable housing, that do not include a mixture of retail, housing, entertainment, and light industrial spaces as well as parks and open public spaces—create the conditions for extreme boredom. And the most vulnerable inhabitants are always people in their teens and twenties.

Ray Oldenburg finds that suburban ennui arises most clearly in the behavior of city-dwelling adolescents who find themselves visiting the suburbs:

[T]he visiting teenager in the subdivision soon acts like an animal in a cage. . . . There is no place to which they can escape and join their own kind. There is nothing for them to do on their own. There is nothing in the surroundings but the houses of strangers and nobody on the streets. Adults make a more successful adjustment, largely because they demand less. But few at any age find vitality in the housing developments. David Riesman . . . once attempted to describe the import of suburbia upon most of those who live there. "There would seem," he wrote, "to be an aimlessness, a pervasive low-keyed unpleasure." The word he

seemed averse to using is boring. A teenager would not have had
to struggle for the right phrasing. (6)

This phenomenon might actually be something much worse
than boredom, something Seán Desmond Healy calls hyperboredom.
In *Boredom, Self, and Culture* Healy distinguishes between the
two. Boredom is the kind of temporary restlessness that everyone experiences on occasion—kids on rainy Saturdays, people
waiting in line, students suffering through lectures on MLA style.
But Healy describes hyperboredom as "an aberration peculiar to
mankind," something "comparable to an agonizing and chronically painful disease" (10, 28). In a state of hyperboredom, "all
people, objects, relations, and activities are permanently, and it
seems unaccountably, stripped of interest, and . . . the search for
anything of interest itself appears utterly uninteresting, worth-
less, or totally ineffective" (44). "Hyperboredom is the escalating apprehension of the void; the nihilism of the masses; the largely
unconscious, unacknowledged sense that the bottom has fallen
out of the world" (92).

At the root of hyperboredom is the misconception that self
and world are separate, and as long as a "self/world dichotomy
is maintained," hyperboredom isn't going to go away (Healy 65).
As Maturana and Varela have written, "every act of knowing
brings forth a world" (*Tree of Knowledge* 26); action and cognition are always interembedded and inseparable. But hyperboredom
happens when we forget this—or, more precisely, when we spend
our lives living in places that were designed without our needs in
mind: our need to feel attached to a place; our need to be able to
find economic, cultural, and spiritual sustenance without driving
long distances; our need to see what is good about ourselves reflected in the places we spend our lives in.

When humans were more preoccupied with the daily need to
survive, hyperboredom did not exist: "With one's nose close to
the soil . . . there is no room for hyperboredom. There is no alternative, no other realm of possibility; every grain of rice, every
drop of water, every drain or saving of energy has meaning, significance, importance. Life may be appallingly hard, often boring, but never hyperboring" (Healy 65–66). A hyperbored culture
on the other hand no longer finds its local physical universe com-

pelling—and, so long as the self is understood to be detached from that universe, attempts at cultivating self-worth and finding meaning within one's home territories are going to be thwarted.

The violence, boredom, and depression running through my students' narratives are never removed from the formal conditions of their local environments. In a "town" like Mike's, where the residential areas are kept separate from commercial zones, where one must rely on cars since cheap, efficient, and frequent public transportation is nonexistent, and where opportunities for people his age to creatively express and entertain themselves are almost nil, the resultant hyperboredom, or cynicism, or ennui—call it what you will—is not something these kids created but something they inherited. Certainly Mike's disgust with himself at the close of his essay is understandable—by his own admission he did squander a healthy chunk of his high school years. But more tragic is the degree to which what passes for community is no more than a gathering of mildly desperate individuals where mindlessness and misery become inevitable. Middle class kids living in the suburbs self-medicate and purge after-hours in the no-places of strip mall parking lots. Urban kids experience the same thing, only the threat of violence and the level of desperation for so many of them can be considerably higher, due in no small part to the fact that people in such communities are prevented from owning property—for, if the sense of displacement underlying the malaise in Mike's world is palpable, how much more so for people who don't even have twenty square feet of backyard to work with, and who can only design their interior spaces in accordance with apartment regulations and building codes.

Educators have a responsibility to help students resist the cynicism and hyperboredom of contemporary, consumer culture by discovering the kind of self-worth that comes from being amazed at one's local worlds. But to do this we must first learn all we can about the environments our students live in, day after day, and give them opportunities to testify about what is wrong and what is good about those worlds, what they think should and shouldn't be changed, and we must provide them with a vocabulary with which they might critique their environments and develop an awareness of what exactly it is about one's environment that can make a person miserable, bored, angry, tired, scared, depressed. Without this fundamental awareness of why places are the way they are, and why they have these effects upon us, it will be difficult to imagine ways of reconstructing them.

An Out of Place Profession

In one of her lectures, Gertrude Stein said that Americans "are abstract and cruel," having "no close contact with the earth such as most Europeans have. Their materialism is not the materialism of existence, of possession, it is the materialism of action and abstraction" (72). If abstraction and cruelty are closely related, then the academy fosters its own peculiar brand of meanness. For while place surely matters in the academy, it tends to do so in the form of various real estate battles associated with the acquisition and preservation of institutional power. The local places that students and staff and faculty go home to after leaving the university behind remain largely invisible, supposedly unrelated to the activity of the academy, despite mission statement rhetoric about serving community and helping students become responsible citizens. "Place" and "placement" are important academic issues—but place as power, as access, and always as defined in the academy's terms.

Students take placement tests so that they can be placed into programs that either stigmatize or reward them and which, in the case of the former, one might eventually place out of. In some institutions like mine, a limited number of slots are reserved for those students in "honors" programs, who have access to "honors" classes. While a "developmental writing" course and an "honors composition" course can be held back to back within the exact same classroom, the intellectual property value of that room fluctuates accordingly. The irony is that, regardless of the course taught, the room itself is drab and uninteresting. At their worst, such classrooms are advertising arenas: when I was a graduate student at a state university, the only decorative elements in the classrooms I taught in were advertisements for Citibank charge cards and discount flights to Cancún, turning the classroom spaces into advertising environments used (for free) by corporations.

Faculty status can also be interpreted in terms of real estate, as academic rank is all about moving upwards into professional gated communities protected by tenure. An academic department is rarely a unified tribe but more often a piece of institutional property zoned for three different working classes. Increasingly, the majority of department members—adjuncts and graduate TAs—live in migrant camps, sharing office space semester by semester and having no voting rights in matters affecting the status of their positions in the departmental plantation. Junior faculty get to live in the main house, enjoying to some extent the fruits of the migrant laborers, but they too are still boarders, signing year-long leases. Senior faculty are permanent residents, some of whom have considerable say in determining which junior faculty must be forced out and which can be admitted to the upstairs level. But again the irony is that the actual physical spaces inhabited by the faculty are not much different; the migrant workers are crowded together in their offices in ways full-time faculty are not, but the offices are mostly still the same size, and everyone is subject to the environmental conditions of the building—which, if they are anything like the one I work in, fall short of meeting OSHA health regulations.

Institutional power and prestige are clearly matters of place. Administrators and faculty continually jostle for more desirable campus real estate, always at a premium, and they are ever aware of the status (or lack thereof) that comes with office location. Academic labor is a matter of place, as those at the top of the administrative food chain get the largest and most lavish offices, while adjuncts and staff get the windowless cubicles. At a predominantly commuter campus like mine, transportation is a daily struggle over place: on the way to and from work students, faculty, staff, and administrators fight their way through traffic, competing for a better space in a faster lane on the expressway, and, until recently when a new parking garage was added, if they arrived on campus too late in the day (i.e. after 8:30 A.M.), all except those with reserved parking spots often had to literally wait in lines for parking spaces, sometimes for as long as fifteen minutes. Those who use mass transit spend their time standing on crowded buses and trains.

Yet, while place matters in the abstract as an agent for preserving and denying power, an even larger problem is the fact that the significance of place does not factor into the design of either the campus or the university's various curricula. College campuses—even the ones with sprawling lawns, the obligatory ivy, immaculate landscaping—evolve with little or no attention paid to ways in which the architecture and landscape reflect or instill cohesiveness among different departments and offices. And curriculum, which at least in theory is the intellectual glue of the academic institution, is ethereal, abstract, and detached from the local universe of surrounding neighborhoods, from the students' and employees' neighborhoods, and from the campus itself.

In *Place and Placelessness* Edward Relph, referring to the placelessness one finds in the development of suburban and urban fringe, defines "subtopia" as "a set of apparently randomly located points and areas, each of which serves a single purpose and each of which is isolated from its setting, linked only by roads which are themselves isolated from the surrounding townscape except for the adjacent strips of other-directed buildings" (109). This is exactly what we have in the college campus, where departments, libraries, and administrative offices are arranged without any logical connection to each other. The result is an arbitrarily designed campus instead of a network of offices and meeting places arranged to further cross-disciplinary communication and collaboration.

More problematic than the physical layout of any campus are our placeless curricula, the existence of which Eric Zencey traces to the academy's insistence on hiring only members of a cosmopolitan professoriate. In his essay "The Rootless Professors," Zencey attacks the academy for promoting an insidious antilocalism, with dire effects.

> As citizens of the *cosmo polis*, the mythical "world city," professors are expected to owe no allegiance to geographical territory; we're supposed to belong to the boundless world of books and ideas and eternal truths, not the infinitely particular world of watersheds, growing seasons, and ecological niches. Most pro-

fessors get their jobs through national searches, and while we may have our preferences for specific regions of the country, most of us are living wherever we could find work. (15)

Faculty are deemed best suited to their jobs when they are aliens and strangers who, Clint Eastwood–like, ride into the university from parts unknown, from places deemed exotic because they are anywhere but "here." Though the majority of American college students attend institutions in their home states, they are taught, by and large, by cosmopolites, a class of transient exotics. "Because professors tend to be rootless, they are systematically ignorant of a key aspect of an integrated life, the life that is, after all, a primary goal of a good liberal arts education. They are woefully ignorant of the values of connectedness to place" (Zencey 16).

In response Zencey calls for a shift toward "rooted education," which would require an end to the academy's discrimination against locals, allowing them instead a greater role in the shaping of curricula, as well as turning the landscapes and communities surrounding the campus into laboratories, and enabling faculty to make a concentrated effort to work within regional organizations as forums for discussing "a curriculum rooted in locale . . . rather than being a political alternative to or a pale reflection of the agenda of the national organizations" (19). This approach is not to be confused with "multicultural inclusiveness," which "tends to perpetuate a politics of placeless identity rather than a politics of rootedness in place" (17). Indeed, the academy's embrace of multiculturalism is often distinctly anti-indigenous. In *Victims of Progress* John Bodley argues that what indigenous peoples share first and foremost is an identification with the land that is fundamentally different from that understood by consumer peoples. Bodley quotes a member of an indigenous tribe: "What most unites us is the defense of our land. The land has never been merchandise for us, as it is with capitalism, but it is the support for our cultural universe" (167). In contrast, industrial civilizations are "cultures of consumption" where "'standard of living' [is measured] in terms of levels of material consumption" (4). In other words, the basis of "indigenous culture" is a cultivated knowledge of the facticity of the local physical universe. Implicit within that culture is a stewardship of "the land," maintaining a balance of bioregional relationships. The academy, in contrast, seeks cultural and ethnic diversification separate from identification with any local landscape. How could the inherently anti-indigenous university promote cross-cultural awareness when place has been taken out of the equation?

Unfortunately Zencey's insightful critique is too simplistic—would that the problem before us were just a matter of turning more towards local talent and incorporating local communities into the curriculum. But in recent years the academy has indicated that it is not just against local scholars but against full-time faculty in general. With this in mind, the irony of Zencey's critique is that, given the outsourcing of full-time positions to part-time adjuncts, we now have more local instructors than ever before. The influence of such faculty on shaping the curriculum in any substantive way is minimal at best, however, since these are people whom the university has failed to invest in by paying them decent salaries or giving them benefits, let alone private offices with phones and computers. Because their influence cannot extend beyond the (overcrowded) classes they teach—adjuncts and TAs almost never serve on committees and, given their semester-by-semester status, have no long-term impact on curricular reform—whatever local talent exists in the academy is not just severely uncompensated for its labor, but largely untapped, ignored, and unsupported.

I know that when I have my students investigate the places where they live, and explore why their homes make them feel the way they do, I am not necessarily helping them lead sustainable lives, nor am I doing much to counteract the university's dismissal of the local. After all, there are more than eighteen thousand students in my university alone, and only twenty-five in each of my writing courses, where we spend just three or four weeks writing and discussing the places that matter to them. I know that such written testimonies need to be conducted within a continual, cross-disciplinary investigation into the relationships between self and place, far beyond my own attempts at giving students opportunities to imagine better communities (see the "Eutopia" assignment sequence in my course assignment packet in Appendix B). What I've done is admittedly simple and hardly unique: creating a space where students write and share stories about where they live, a space where they might come to see ways in which their needs and desires reflect the condition of those communities, and, hopefully, begin to think of their local environments not as separate, incidental landscapes but as extensions of themselves. (And for those students who choose a service-learning option—see "Service-Learning Project" in Appendix B—there are opportunities for them to further realize the role they can play in the ongoing construction of those communities.)

Yet for all its simplicity, I'm convinced that this kind of inquiry into one's local surroundings is precisely the kind of exercise that has to happen in a variety of courses, within and outside of English studies, if we are ever to begin thinking of ourselves within the context of sustainability. As educators we pride ourselves on teaching something called critical thinking, but often at the cost of promoting local thinking. "Higher" learning aims upward, away from the mundane, the everyday, the provincial. We see this represented literally in the number of colleges and universities intentionally built on hills rising above surrounding communities. What we need more of is *lower* learning, thinking that keeps bringing us back to the local conditions of the communities that we and our students return to once we leave the classroom.

In *The Power of Place: How Our Surroundings Shape Our Thoughts, Emotions, and Actions*, Winifred Gallagher documents how geomagnetic fields and tectonic strains might account for the blackouts, electrical disruptions, and mass sightings typically associated with UFO experiences and with religious visions reported at sacred sites (79–98). Unfortunately, people find unimaginative stories about alien visitations more captivating than the mystery of strange geophysical forces beneath their feet. Similarly, I don't think it's too much of a stretch to call a sizeable portion of academic publications, removed as they are from "local matters," cerebral distant cousins of the Elvis-on-a-UFO discourse published in tabloids. Ellen Cushman levels a related critique, directed particularly at scholars of cultural studies whose work never makes any visceral impact within the populations of local at-risk neighborhoods:

I'm not asking for composition teachers to march into the homes, churches, community centers, and schools of their community. I'm not asking for us to become social workers either. I am asking for a deeper consideration of the civic purpose of our positions in the academy, of what we do with our knowledge, for whom, and by what means. I am asking for a shift in our critical focus away from our own navels, Madonna, and cereal boxes to the ways in which we can begin to locate ourselves within the democratic process of everyday teaching and learning in our neighborhoods. (12)

What Cushman is asking of us—to self-consciously locate ourselves within the local worlds of our students' neighborhoods and explore ways of making them more livable—is an essential component of a pedagogy of sustainability. The composition classroom lends itself remarkably well to sharing and exploring such narratives. When students tell stories about the failings and the attributes of their neighborhoods, and the psychological, economic, cultural, and spiritual effects these places have on them, the classroom arena has the potential to become decidedly local. Such classroom spaces let students know that the status of their communities is not something beyond the proper domain of the academy, but a vital part of the curriculum. Certainly, telling tales about one's town or neighborhood and what's good or bad about it is only a first step towards fulfilling the objectives of a sustainable pedagogy. Ideally such introspection and critique would evolve into extended service-learning and research projects throughout the curriculum, aimed at sustainable renewal and community revitalization. But a first step is to create sustained classroom spaces where students can think critically about the past, present, and future of their communities, and where we not only listen to these narratives but also imagine ways in which our pedagogies and curricula can facilitate the redesigning, the revitalization, and the preservation of these local environments.

CHAPTER FOUR

Work

*Our epoch has been called the century of work. It is in
fact the century of pain, misery and corruption.*
PAUL LAFARGUE, *The Right to Be Lazy*

In *Teaching Composition as a Social Process*, Bruce
McComiskey writes: "Most writing teachers agree that their
courses prepare students for 'life' in the 'real world,' but few
teachers have theorized what sort of 'life' they wish for their students, and even fewer describe the condition of this 'real world.'
Yet, these are crucial tasks that those in academia cannot ignore"
(113). But the conditions of this "real world"—which, to a large
extent, is another way of saying "the world of work"—are rarely
confronted and critiqued anywhere in the curriculum. Considering our career centers, business curricula, and job fairs, as well as
the language of mission statements about creating future leaders
and professionals, such a claim might seem misplaced. But when
we explore the facts about work, or, more precisely, the nature of
what I call "workpain," the academy seems to be in a state of
disinterest and denial. This turning away is evident in English
studies, which continues to take money from increasing numbers
of graduate students who, after being exploited as cheap labor
while training as scholars, critics, and would-be professors, are
paid back with advanced degrees that, in an age of academic
downsizing, are of questionable value. Much of the "crisis" in
English studies comes down to our failure to help the students
who pay our salaries get decent work. But even in the sciences
and technology-oriented disciplines—academic arenas with better track records in placing their students in "desirable" careers—
scant attention is paid to the miserable reality that too often passes

for work and what it does to our students, colleagues, families, and friends. If educators have a responsibility to prepare students for the workplace as it currently exists, then we have an even greater responsibility to provide contexts where students might critique and reinvent the idea of work so that it is no longer a four-letter word but something spiritually fulfilling, supportive of more free time, environmentally defensible, and, most important of all, sustainable.

Characterizing work as a four-letter word might seem extreme to readers of this book, since as academics we not only presumably make a living from our passions but enjoy flexible work schedules that the majority of employees, blue- and white-collar alike, will never experience. But by "work" I do not mean labor on one's own terms: building a house, writing a book, planting a garden, designing a course, or other activity akin to adult play. Nor do I mean forms of hard labor with obvious rejuvenating benefits, especially labor that brings one in contact with the earth (Hasselstrom), or even the arguably necessary experience of nothingness and drudgery that is an inevitable part of the human experience, what Matthew Fox calls the *via negativa* of work.

While Fox rightly distinguishes between work and jobs, where the latter is defined as just a means of getting by while the former should be our raison d'etre, here I'm using "work" the way people do when one says, "I have to go to work tomorrow"—that is, what one does for pay on a regular (or, for many, irregular) basis. In his call for a ludic revolution to end the suffering that is work, Bob Black defines work as "forced labor" or "compulsory production" (18), and this is the context within which I use the word here, a context that is operative even for those of us who are grateful to have jobs, and for the even luckier few who truly love our jobs. Just as John Taylor Gatto lists the seven hateful "lessons" teachers inevitably impose upon students—confusion, hierarchical ranking, indifference, emotional and intellectual dependency, provisional self-esteem, and constant surveillance—we can list four grim realities of work at the beginning of the twenty-first century. The first three realities pertain to the suffering of the individual worker and can be referred to collectively by the term "workpain": work never ends, work hurts, and work doesn't pay like it used to. The fourth reality pertains to the suffering of future generations due to a business ethic designed to perpetuate our existence within a consumptive economy that works against sustainability. Since we are, as McComiskey writes, in the business of preparing our students for the real world (of work), we should first explore why so much of what passes for work is miserable, discouraging, and irresponsibly unsustainable.

What's Wrong with Work

Work Never Ends

> "Birth, school, work, death."
>
> THE GODFATHERS, title lyric to a post-punk song

Americans now work more hours than ever before. A 1999 International Labor Organization study found that Americans are working more hours annually while those in most other industrialized countries are working fewer hours. "This trend has given Americans the dubious distinction of moving into first place in the number of hours worked each year (1,966), surpassing even the Japanese by about 70 hours. On average, Americans work 350 hours more per year (that's almost nine full work weeks) than Europeans" (Greenhouse WK1). Apparently we are working more hours than many people did in "primitive" and preindustrial societies. In some hunting and gathering societies, people worked only 15 to 20 hours a week, spending the rest of the time in "socializing, partying, playing, storytelling, and artistic or religious activities" (Brandt 301). In ancient Rome the nonenslaved citizenry enjoyed around 175 public festivals each year (Brandt 301); medieval serfs averaged under 20 hours of work per week, with more than 150 days off each year (Schor, *Overworked* 43–48; Durning 47–48). In 1883, writing from prison, Paul Lafargue states in his manifesto *The Right to Be Lazy* that fifteenth-century church law guaranteed French laborers "ninety rest days, fifty-two Sundays and thirty-eight holidays, during which he was strictly forbidden to work" (44). In his manifesto "The Abolition of Work," Bob Black refers to the

Kapauku of West Irian, who work only every other day, with each day of rest designed to "regain the lost power and health" spent in working (23).

Al Gini culls the following statistics from the Department of Labor: blue and white collar workers average 50 hours a week; middle and upper-management work 58–65 hours a week. Americans work eight weeks more per year than the Germans and French, and eleven weeks more than the Swiss. In *The Overworked American* Juliet Schor calculates that by the 1980s Americans were working 163 hours more than they had twenty years prior—one whole extra month of work per year—a figure which still did not include the amount of time women and caregivers spent doing housework and raising kids (29). More than a quarter of all full-time workers clock over 49 hours each week (Rifkin, *End of Work* 223). Americans have received increasingly less paid time off, while Europeans have steadily gained (Schor, *Overworked* 32); Canadians get three weeks off after two or three years on the job, and in Germany, France, and Scandinavian countries, most workers get five or six weeks off (Brandt 301; Dolnick). More recent calculations show that the average American worker now works 140 hours more per year than in 1982, and while the median income of American households increased in the mid-1990s, the extra money was the result of second jobs and longer hours, not higher pay; seven million Americans now work at two or more jobs (Madrick 139).

> Fathers and mothers, sons and daughters are working longer hours for roughly the same hourly pay. It is not higher wages but extra time on the job that is the main source of the rising household income. That is a precarious affluence. When the economy weakens, as it inevitably will, the extra work can disappear abruptly, as it did in the aftermath of the last recession. Raises are harder to reverse. (Uchitelle, "More Work, Less Pay" 4)

By now, everyone knows what a lie it was that new technologies would deliver workers from longer hours. Just the opposite has happened: "With pagers, cell phones, and laptop computers, all time becomes work time" (Aronowitz et al. 35). In fact, "increasingly the distinction between work and life has blurred": "Live to work, or work to live? With pagers, cellular phones, laptops and electronic mail, it's increasingly live to work, any-time, anywhere" (Bryant). Meanwhile, "technology has equipped us with 'conveniences' like microwave ovens and frozen dinners that merely enable us to adopt a similar frantic pace in our home lives so we can cope with more hours at paid work" (Brandt 300).

And commuting time, which must be included in any tally of one's working hours, since it is hardly free time, has increased since 1975 to an extra three days per year (Schor, *Overworked* 33). For those who do not have access to safe and efficient mass transportation—which includes the majority of Americans, who now live in the suburbs—a considerable amount of time (at least for middle-class residents) must be spent in driving some distance to grocery stores and, for those with families, chauffeuring kids to athletic events, friends' homes, parties, malls, and movie theaters. Although one doesn't get paid for it, time clocked in the car can scarcely be called leisure time—which has fallen by forty-seven hours a year (Schor, *Overworked* 36).

Once upon a time there was a shorter-hour movement in this country, spearheaded in large part by the Kellogg Company, which in 1932 trimmed its workweek to thirty hours in order to put hundreds more employees on payroll while raising the (male) hourly minimum wage to compensate for the lost hours (Rifkin, *End of Work* 26–27). Amazingly progressive even by today's standards, Kellogg wanted its workers to have more leisure time

> so they could renew their commitments to family and community and explore their own personal freedom. The company introduced a number of innovations at the plant and in the community to advance the leisure ethic, including the erection of a gymnasium and recreation hall, an outdoor athletic park, a recreation park, employee garden plots, day-care facilities, and a nature center to allow its employees to enjoy the beauty of the Michigan countryside. (Rifkin, *End of Work* 27)

That same year, more than half of American industrial employers cut back hours. A bill was passed in the Senate the following year mandating a thirty-hour week, and it was expected to pass in the House, until it was defeated by President Roosevelt and influential representatives of the business community (Rifkin, *End of Work* 28–29; Hunnicutt). Since then, the shorter-hours movement has remained dormant in this country, and, in fact, in the second half of the century, free time has decreased. Yet countries including France, Italy, Germany, Sweden, and even Japan have woken up to the human need for more time off from work, symbolized in the Italian trade union slogan translated as "Work Less, and Everyone Works" (Rifkin, *End of Work* 224; Brandt 301). But corporate America seems committed to working its employees to the bone: Rifkin cites a survey where three hundred business leaders were asked their opinion on a shorter work week, and not a single CEO responded favorably (*End of Work* 227)—this, despite findings that average Americans are willing to give up almost 5 percent of their wages for more free time (Rifkin, *End of Work* 233).

One of the most disturbing findings is that, perversely, more Americans *want* to spend more time at work. Arlie Hochschild's research indicates that working parents aren't just working longer hours out of financial necessity, but because the workplace is sometimes less stressful than the home, especially for mothers, who still shoulder the bulk of household chores and child-rearing activities. Not only have people become accommodated to work, but, at some point, workplace and household have for many people traded places.

> Increasing numbers of women are discovering a great male secret—that work can be an escape from the pressures of home, pressures that the changing nature of work itself are only intensifying. Neither men nor women are going to take up "family friendly" policies, whether corporate or governmental, as long as the current realities of work and home remain as they are. For a substantial number of time-bound parents, the stripped-down home and the neighborhood devoid of community are simply losing out to the pull of the workplace. (84)

The real losers in this battle, Hochschild concludes, are children, whose parents are increasingly absent from home. Kids end up spending more time with baby-sitters, more time alone in the house, and, one might presume, more time watching television or getting into trouble—and, through it all, internalizing the message that work comes before family. One study shows that in 1986 parents spent ten to twelve hours fewer per week with their kids than they did in 1960 (Rifkin, *End of Work* 234). And for those unfortunate enough to own cars, the hours spent bridge-and-tunneling to and from work can add up to the equivalent of a second part-time job (Gross).

Bob Black argues that the abuse of the worker spills over into the family:

> It's not too misleading to call our system democracy or capitalism or—better still—industrialism, but its real names are factory fascism and office oligarchy. Anybody who says these people are "free" is lying or stupid. You are what you do. If you do boring, stupid, monotonous work, chances are you'll end up boring, stupid and monotonous. Work is a much better explanation for the creeping cretinization all around us than even such significant moronizing mechanisms as television and education. People who are regimented all their lives, handed off to work from school and bracketed by the family in the beginning and the nursing home at the end, are habituated to hierarchy and psychologically enslaved. Their aptitude for autonomy is so atrophied that their fear of freedom is among their few rationally grounded phobias. Their obedience training at work caries over into the families they start, thus reproducing the system in more ways than one, and into politics, culture and everything else. Once you drain the vitality from people at work, they'll likely submit to hierarchy and expertise in everything. They're used to it. (Black 21–22)

Work Hurts

Work Is Hell.
—*Newsweek* cover, August 12, 1996

In 1995 there were seventeen work fatalities each day, one-sixth of which were related to "workplace violence," which also happens to be the leading cause of job-related death for women. In addition to the 1,610 fatalities that year, 3.6 million Americans are disabled because of work (Nordheimer). And work does a job on us indirectly as well:

> Even if you aren't killed or crippled while actually working, you very well might be while going to work, looking for work, or trying to forget about work. The vast majority of victims of the automobile are either doing one of these work-obligatory

activities or else fall afoul of those who do them. To this aug-
mented body-count must be added the victims of auto-industrial
pollution and work-induced alcoholism and drug addiction.
(Black 27)

"Workers apparently feel they are unsafe," writes Peter Dorman,
citing a 1990 poll of blue-collar workers, 30 percent of whom
felt that their jobs were unsafe, with three-fifths of that 30 percent claiming to have been seriously injured on the job (12). Nor
are these injuries limited to people working around heavy equipment: repetitive motion disorders (RMDs) are now, due to increased production, "the occupational hazard of the new
economic environment" for both blue- and white-collar workers
(Dorman 19). The Japanese refer to deaths caused by work-re-
lated stress as *karoshi,* where a lifetime of overwork exacerbates
high blood pressure and leads to "fatal breakdown" (Rifkin, *End
of Work* 186). Given that Americans now work longer hours
than the Japanese, one wonders when a similar word will ma-
terialize in our vocabulary.

Nor does having a job eliminate the stress felt by unemployed
persons. While it's certainly better to have money coming in than
to have no income, writers like Jerald Wallulis (*The New Insecurity: The End of the Standard Job and Family*) document the
growing sense of anxiety in an age of "corporate restructuring,"
one of those polite euphemisms for massive layoffs. While family
income doubled between 1947 and 1973, Wallulis reminds us
that family income remained the same from 1973 to 1995 (xiv),
a cause for much of the anxiety fueling the contemporary need
for multiple-income families. In their book *Job Insecurity: Coping with Jobs at Risk*, Hartley et al. point out that the recession
and restructuring of the late 1970s and the 1980s turned the
workplace from a "rich" to a "poor" environment (9). As a result, "in the job market of the 1990s, loyalty has become a one-
way street": "It does not take much in corporate whim or change
in planning to put a long-time employee's job at risk" (Gamst
27). A *New York Times* survey showed that two-fifths of American workers were worried that they'd either be laid off or be
forced to take a cut in hours or pay, and the majority of these
respondents said that their communities were being affected by
joblessness (Rifkin, *End of Work* 13).

There are, of course, a great many kinds of work that are dangerous to the human spirit.

> For the many, there is a hardly concealed discontent. . . . "I'm a machine," says the spot-welder. "I'm caged," says the bank teller, and echoes the hotel clerk. "I'm a mule," says the steelworker. "A monkey can do what I do," says the receptionist. "I'm less than a farm implement," says the migrant worker. "I'm an object," says the high-fashion model. Blue collar and white call upon the identical phrase: "I'm a robot." "*There is nothing to talk about*," the young accountant despairingly enunciates. (Terkel, *Working* xiv, author's italics)

When I happened to mention in one of my undergraduate classes that I loved my job, several of the students were visibly taken aback. It took some time to convince one of them that I wasn't lying: "I've never known anyone in my life who loved their job," one student said. One of my former graduate students worked for a company that makes hospital software. For two years he held a job which, along with just one other employee, required him to read literally two billion lines of code as part of a Y2K project. He worked six, sometimes seven day weeks, logging in ten- and twelve-hour days. When he dragged himself to class at night, inevitably late, assignment unfinished, the toll that his job took on his body was immediately visible.

Certainly, teaching in academia remains by far one of the best jobs available—at least for full-time, tenure-track faculty. We have flexible schedules and spend time conversing with students and colleagues. Those of us with smaller teaching loads and those who are eligible for course reductions have the opportunity to write and conduct research. But fear, insecurity, and ugly political battles are as common in academe as they are anywhere else, if not worse (a story comes to mind about President Harding, who, when asked why he left the ivory tower for the presidency, replied that he wanted to get away from all of the politics). Hallway conversations at academic conferences are rife with accounts of colleagues driven to seek therapy as a result of departmental political battles, anecdotes about adjunct faculty being bullied or ignored by full-time faculty, and junior faculty being intimidated by senior faculty. The conversations on the theme "you think you've got it bad, well just listen to what my administration [or chair or personnel or budget committee] did" would merely be cliché were it not for the fatigue and frustration behind the stories.

Work Doesn't Pay Like It Used To

> We are a bunch of fools, aren't we? Today, we're actually earning less than we earned, in real dollars, in 1979! Millions of people officially are out of work—7,266,000. But the Bureau of Labor Statistics and the Census Bureau estimate another 5,378,000 are also unemployed but uncounted. Another 4,500,000 more are working part-time but looking for a full-time job. And then there are the 2,520,000 Americans who are working full-time and earning a wage that is below the poverty line. . . . That's nearly **20 million** people who cannot make the bare minimum they need to survive! [author's emphasis]
>
> MICHAEL MOORE, *Downsize This!*

In the last twenty years, wages for many workers have gone down 20 percent: "As big corporations paid their executives an average 8 percent to 12 percent increase each year, most workers received raises of only 2.5 percent on average, a figure which has not even kept up with inflation" (Aronowitz et al. 37). There is more: "In 1979 the average weekly wage in the United States was $387. By 1989 it had dropped to $335" (Rifkin, *End of Work* 168). Between 1973 and 1993, roughly 80 percent of workers saw their wages decrease by fifteen percent (Madrick 16). Between 1989 and 1993, the number of poor people increased by almost seven million, or 15 percent of the population, whereas in 1973 just 11 percent of the population was classified as poor (Madrick 152). Nor are these figures confined to the first few years of the 1990s. In my state, the gap between the rich and the poor is greater than in any other state, and throughout the 1990s most New Yorkers' incomes declined relative to the cost of living ("New York Incomes Decline").

It is not surprising, then, that "American and Canadian living standards have eroded since 1980: real wages have fallen, increasing the necessity of working mothers; the number of homeowners continues to decline; higher education becomes ever more unaffordable; and (for America only) the privilege of medical care is denied to growing millions of citizens" (Gamst 27). More than half of the millions of jobs created during the Clinton presidency paid less than the national average, and many of these were part-time and temporary positions without vacation or benefits (Aronowitz et al. 36). Almost 60 percent of the more than 1.2 million new jobs created in America in the first half of 1993 were part-time, low-wage, service positions (Rifkin, *End of Work* 167).

An appalling 12.8 percent of Americans were below poverty level in 1989, and that figure climbed to 13.7 percent in 1996. And while less than one in a thousand Americans claimed bankruptcy in the early 1970s, that number had risen to five in a thousand by 1997, a year in which personal bankruptcies increased by 20 percent, or about 1.4 million (Kurson 66). Comparatively, Europeans fare much better than we do when it comes to the poor working class: "The bottom tenth of our workers earns about half the salary that the bottom tenth of workers in Europe earns" (Madrick 154–55).

As if this were not bad enough, those who do make a comfortable living are often so brainwashed by our consumer culture that no salary seems high enough for peace of mind. In *The Overspent American*, Juliet Schor notes that "twenty-seven percent of all households making more than $100,000 a year say they cannot afford to buy everything they really need" and that, "overall, half the population of the richest country in the world say they cannot afford everything they really need" (6). In 1991 more people said vacation homes, swimming pools, second color TVs, and second cars were necessary items for "the good life" than said so in a 1975 poll—and yet, fewer people in 1991 said a happy marriage or an interesting job was necessary for that life than said so in the 1975 poll (Schor, *Overspent American* 16). As income has decreased, consumer addiction has increased due to increased cultural pressure to spend.

All of this has played some role in the decline in the average American's savings. American families now save less than 4 percent of their disposable income—50 percent less than the percentage saved in the 1960s and 1970s (Madrick 105)—and "in

1995 only 55 percent of all American households indicated they had done any saving at all in the previous year" (Schor, *Overspent American* 20). A 1999 article reported that Americans' savings dropped from 9 percent of their yearly salaries in 1982 to a mere 0.5 percent in 1998 (Feigenbaum F8). On the other hand, middle-class Americans are committing more time and money to acquiring not just the usual middle-class conveniences but also toys typically associated with rich lifestyles (Uchitelle, "Keeping Up With the Gateses?").

Most Work Is Unsustainable

> The consumer society fails to deliver on its promise of fulfillment through material comforts because human wants are insatiable, human needs are socially defined, and the real sources of personal happiness are elsewhere. Indeed, the strength of social relations and the quality of leisure—both crucial psychological determinants in life—appear as much diminished as enhanced in the consumer class. The consumer society, it seems, has impoverished us by raising our income.
>
> ALAN DURNING, *How Much Is Enough?*

Tragically, even if we could wave a Fourierian magic wand and change the landscape of work so that people everywhere were assured of just and continual compensation for pursuing their innate interests for twenty-five hours a week, it still would not be good enough, because business that is not sustainable is business that is no longer defensible. As long as work exists to promote a consumptive economy—an economy that thrives on consuming severely limited resources so that millions might buy billions of unnecessary things—it makes little difference how much one might enjoy one's job, how safe it can be, or how much time one has off from work. This is because work, as we know it, is inseparable from the idea of consumption. As Jeremy Rifkin reminds us, prior to this century "consumption" had only negative connotations, associated with destruction, pillaging, and tuberculosis: "The metamorphosis of consumption from vice to virtue is one of the most important yet least examined phenomena of the twentieth century" (*End of Work* 19). In fact, the United States created the first "consumption economy" at the turn of the century. Prior to the twentieth century, many Americans still believed in the value of sacrifice and saving for one's families: "For most Americans, the virtue of self-sacrifice continued to hold sway over the lure of immediate gratification in the marketplace. The American business community set out to radically change the psychology that had built a nation—to turn American workers from investors in the future to spenders in the present" (Rifkin, *End of Work* 19–20). So successful was this campaign that now, whenever I ask students to make lists of "what they want most of all," it's not uncommon for many of them to include a wardrobe of brand-name clothes within their top five wishes.

Until our jobs contribute to what Paul Hawken calls a "restorative economy," any pride one takes in one's work cannot help but be severely compromised. In *The Ecology of Commerce* Hawken eloquently calls for the radical reinvention not just of business practices but of the very concept of business itself.

> The ultimate purpose of business is not, or should not be, simply to make money. Nor is it merely a system of making and selling things. The promise of business is to increase the general well-being of humankind through service, a creative invention and ethical philosophy. Making money is, on its own terms, totally meaningless, an insufficient pursuit for the complex and decaying world we live in. (1)

What business must do, Hawken insists, is

> create an enduring society . . . a system of commerce and production where each and every act is inherently sustainable and restorative. Business will need to integrate economic, biologic, and human systems to create a sustainable method of commerce. . . . The institutions surrounding commerce [must be] redesigned. Just as every act in an industrial society leads to environmental degradation, regardless of intention, we must design a system where the opposite is true, where doing good is like falling off a log, where the natural, everyday acts of work and life accumulate into a better world as a matter of course, not a matter of conscious altruism. (xiv)

Whether we are talking about work, business, or education, we are ultimately talking about interconnected economic phenomena. All work is a form of business, and educational institutions, regardless of the rhetoric of their mission statements, are businesses in the business of selling a product (degrees) so that their customers (students) might (in theory) more "successfully" make a living. More importantly, those with college degrees are the ones who "inherit" and perpetuate business. If business is the main agent for creating a sustainable culture (John Davis 17), educational institutions play no small role in thwarting or assisting this pursuit, given their part in training not only business majors and MBAs but also virtually all students who eventually play significant roles in perpetuating the business world.

We should take Hawken's language and apply it to a new theory of curriculum. Where he writes "we need to imagine a prosperous commercial culture that is so intelligently designed and constructed that it mimics nature at every step, a symbiosis of company and customer and ecology" (15), the terms can be modified to fit the responsibility of the educator: we need to imagine a prosperous academic culture that is so intelligently designed and constructed that it mimics the local bioregion at every step, a symbiosis of institution and student and ecology. Similarly, when Liz Crosbie and Ken Knight write in *Strategy for Sustainable Business* that "the task of business leaders is to ensure that the organizations under their control can play their part in the move towards a sustainable-yield, global economy" (15), we can adapt this sentiment as well: educational leaders should help the students under their influence understand our collective responsibility to move toward a sustainable-yield economy.

Until this happens, our institutions of higher learning will continue to feed and, to a large extent, provide the foundation for a consumptive economy, promoting a world of work that privileges short-term gain at long-term expense and creating considerable violence along the way. Others have been quick to call attention to education's indirect role in promoting violence and consumerism throughout the world. Sulak Sivaraksa notes that where sustainably-minded Buddhist monks once served as government advisors in his native Thailand, the new "spiritual" advisors now come from the Harvard Business School, the Fletcher

School of Law and Diplomacy, and the London School of Economics, spreading the three poisons (greed, hatred, delusion) that drive Western consumerism (4). Jack D. Forbes, for whom consumerism is nothing less than cannibalism directed at poor and indigenous peoples, calls attention to the role that members of the educational elite have played in the failures of the twentieth century.[1] Birgit Brock-Utne reminds us of Virginia Woolf's claim that universities educate for war, a claim echoed in Paulo Freire's statement "all education is education for war" (124). And in his argument to deschool society, as if schooling were akin to a virus infecting the populace, Ivan Illich argues that "the escalation of the schools is as destructive as the escalation of weapons but less visibly so" and that, "in a schooled society, warmaking and civil repression find an educational rationale" (14, 72). Many have insisted that the military and higher education feed each other within a symbiotic circuit: "The few dozen big universities which set the pattern for higher education in the United States have ceased to be universities and have become research institutes for government, business, industry, the military" (Sledd 83). Mary Rose O'Reilley's idea of the "peaceable classroom" is predicated on her attempt to answer the question she once heard raised at a conference—"Is it possible to teach English so that people stop killing each other?" (9)—implying that our pedagogics fall far short of protecting our children from a violent society.

Meanwhile, my students are working more than ever before—coming to class, before and after their part- and full-time jobs, weary and distracted. Increasingly I feel that I have an obligation to listen to their stories about the work they do, and about their longing for a different kind of work. Just as investigating the nature of place is an important part of a curriculum of sustainability, so too is an extended inquiry into the reality of work.

What My Students Know about Work

Because the majority of them work at least twenty hours a week—it is not uncommon for my students to have full-time jobs while also taking eighteen credits of coursework—many of my students have considerable work experience to reflect upon. Many of my undergraduates have more insight into this phenomenon called work than I have. While practically all of my students are in college primarily or solely to get a certain kind of job (sometimes I ask the students in my classes whether they would bypass college if they could simply buy a degree, and most reply in the affirmative), the majority are all current employees in work environments that the majority of them find depressing, demeaning, or unfulfilling.

They write about family members who have spent long years working at difficult jobs.

> My father . . . really hates his job. When he came to the United States from Ecuador . . . one of his wishes was to open his own restaurant. [But] when he arrived here . . . my old man had no choice but to go out there and hustle in a cab because he had a wife and a baby boy. I asked him if his dream is still there and he told me no. He told me that all the years off having to fix cars and spending his money on them killed his dream a long time ago.
>
> My cousin works as a pay roll clerk at Jewish Home and Hospital. She told me that she had made big mistakes in her life that led her to work at a job that she does not enjoy doing. She told me that it hurts to go to work every day. She feels that she has no true control of her life. . . .
>
> FREDDIE

> After she and my father separated, my mother started making a career out of her hobby [sewing]. I think this was one of the most difficult things she ever had to do because sewing no longer was something she enjoyed doing but became something she was obligated to do. All of a sudden she had deadlines to meet. She became occupied with setting up meetings and purchasing materials. Before we knew it my mother's attitude started changing and we started feeling the effects. She became very short tempered and was running out of patience. She spent most of the day in front of a sewing machine or a table designing or cutting up patterns. Working consumed most of her time. . . . The whole experience didn't just change her but also changed the way I felt about her and our family structure.
>
> JEANETTE

> My father . . . used to work at a sticker factory, then he worked at a steel factory and his hands turned black from that job, and

his last job was working as a janitor in Bloomingdale's. My mother sewed clothes for Richelene, a corporation that sells their clothes to stores like Sax Fifth Ave. . . . . After my mother comes home from work, she immediately starts to cook and then helps us with our homework. [Once] when she was working long hours . . . she came home from work . . . started cooking and . . . left the rice and peas cooking in the kitchen to go use the bathroom. My mother never made it to the bathroom, she fainted on her way there. . . . The doctor later told us that she fainted because she had a nervous breakdown. That is when I realized why my mother was working and what for. It was for us kids.

MARTINE

My uncle's profession is dentistry, but he is not too fond of his work. He leaves early in the morning and returns late in the evening, and is dead tired by the time he returns. He confessed to me that he really hates his job. He stated that he was always around germs and diseases and that he was not working in a healthy environment. I asked him why he chose that profession and he responded by telling me that it was his parents' wish that he become a dentist. When I asked him who benefits from his work, he answered, "my patients do." He also stated that he benefited from his work too, but he said it slowly with disgust as if it were a horrible nightmare.

ANTHONY

Students also write about their own crummy job experiences.

The first job I had was working in McDonald's at Green Acres Mall in Valley Stream. It was when minimum wage was four dollars and twenty-five cents. . . . The boss was so intimidating that I got tense speaking to him. He would come too close to my face when talking to me which gave me no personal space. . . .

The uniforms that we had to wear were horribly tight. The pants were so tight that every time I ate I had to unbutton the zipper to eat and breathe. And there was also a cap included; the cap ruined the hairstyle that was provided by the measly thirty dollars a week check that I got from McDonald's in the first place. It was all I could afford with that amount of money I made every week.

I now work in the Lingerie department [at J.C. Penney] and I hate it. . . . I have to wear shoes and stand on my feet for long hours; my once beautiful feet are now a salad: with corns and bunions forming. The atmosphere is dull, I feel as if I am going to a funeral every time I go to work. . . . The manager is very rude every time I try and speak to her about a problem with my schedule she acts like what I have to say is unimportant; by not looking at me while talking to me and walking away as a way to say the conversation has ended.

Every day I have to go fishing for something to wear to work. And the clothes can never be jean materials, which is all I have. Therefore, I had to go and buy clothes and shoes just to work at J.C. Penny.

CHARISSE

St. Paul II in his encyclical "On Human Work" said, "Work is a good thing for man—a good thing for humanity—because through work man not only transforms nature, adapting it to his own needs, but he also achieves fulfillment as a human being and indeed in a sense becomes 'more a human being.'" [A]pparently he never worked in a sweatshop or any other type of factory where one does not see daylight until the end of the day.

I have worked ever since I was fourteen. Sorry to say I was misguided about the thrills of working. I started working at a pizza parlor. I worked from ten in the morning to about seven thirty in the evening for about four days a week. I only made about thirty dollars and some change a week. My boss told me by working off the books I wouldn't have to pay taxes. I continued to work there for about a year then I quit. I said to myself if this is what work is like I would rather become a bum living off the streets.

A year later I got picked up as a runner/clerk working for a law firm in lower Manhattan. I was making six fifty an hour working from nine to five for the whole week. As time went on my pay rose, but . . . I was still economically choked. I hated the work I did and despised my bosses who gave me the work. No matter what I did, whether I changed jobs or got more money, the work did not seem worth it.

Misery is what I go through every time I go to work. I just have my hands tied behind my back with only one of three options. Work to survive, not work and become homeless and poverty stricken, or work hard so that I might eventually work in a field I will enjoy. Either way you look at it I have to go through misery.

If I could, I would go back to live in my ancestral country Colombia on the farmland. The reason I won't go is the mere fact that my parents are all caught in the twisted American dream. And because I was taught as a child to honor my parents' wishes and become a doctor.

ERNESTO

Some of them articulate philosophies about work that are anything but uplifting.

I've been thinking about the concept of work a lot the past few weeks and I came up with one conclusion and that is that "work is imprisonment." From the day we are born, we are being groomed for a lifetime of prison. We all start out at the same point (school), then depending on what type of job we want, we choose if we want to continue with the grooming and training, or go straight to a cell (work). If you think about it long enough, you begin to picture the invisible chains that we have attached to us all.

Since I was small I've been working for my father in his bakery; I have two brothers who already followed in his footsteps and have become bakers, owning a bakery of their own. As for myself, I've always sworn I would get out, do something different; step off of one cross and nail myself on to another of my choice. So, I have chosen to continue the grooming process. Through the influences of my teachers I will be molded into a working class zombie, stand in line with other zombies with our legs chained together, while the wealthy take turns whipping us and slowly destroying our individualities day by day.

[I suppose I] could become a teacher and do some molding of my own. [But then] sucking the lives out of poor defenseless dreamers is not my cup of tea. Getting whipped by administrators and higher faculty doesn't do anything for me. . . .

I see myself sitting in a cubicle, with a desk full of paper work, thinking, "shit I should have picked something else." Do not get me wrong, I am not saying that all work is evil. It is possible to find a job with positive aspect to it, like shorter hours, higher pay and pleasant surroundings. . . . [But] there will always be something else you would rather do than work and somewhere else you would rather be. In the end I have come to the conclusion that we will be prisoners no matter what we choose to do. Freedom does not exist, there will always be someone around to whip you, and make sure you are doing what you are supposed to do. We begin to die from the day we are born.

KEN

They write of being overworked and having little time to themselves, and of the harmful side effects of work.

What happened to the days of working 9 to 5? I think I may have held two jobs that required me to show up for work at 9 AM and end my day at 5 PM. Are those good old days gone? Nowadays if you begin work at 8 or 8:30 AM, you should consider yourself lucky. Workforce etiquette dictates that one should always arrive early for work and always stay later; it leaves a good impression on the bosses and it shows that you take great pride in your work.

You find yourself bending over backwards to please your boss or those you work with. . . . Corporations try to get the most out of their money, when it comes to their employees. They hand you work that is impossible to complete within normal work hours, and then top it off with a deadline of yesterday. If you're lucky you might get rewarded with a thank you but in the long run, if you spend your lifetime catering to your employer, how rewarding is this really to you and your family?

LAURA

It starts from birth. From the minute we are born our parents start preparing us for the workforce. They teach us to read as early as possible so we can perform better in school. They teach us discipline and how to follow orders. Most of them start referring to us as a future "something." Whether it be a doctor or a lawyer or even the president of the United States, the expectations to succeed at a prominent career always linger in their minds—for every parent wants their child to turn out better than they did. . . .

We are killing ourselves trying to stay alive. Believe it or not, working is just like another form of drug. It can cure current problems, create new ones, become addictive or even kill you slowly. We spend so much time and money emphasizing the things that can hurt us physically or mentally or even kill us, yet we always seem to overlook the one thing that's killing us every day. We get repeated warnings about cigarettes and alcohol, how they can take over your life and hurt everyone that loves you or may even terminate your life, yet we get no warning about work. We never see advertisements telling us to stop working because it kills. Never do we get spokespersons telling us about how work is bad for us or informing us about the side effects of work.

GINA

For some, their work experiences help solidify and validate their views of our classist society, or emphasize the negative side of America's competitive work ethic.

I work at an expensive restaurant in Roslyn. There I am a valet parker. You might think, oh what an easy job, and at any other place I would agree 110%, the easiest job ever, piece of cake, parking someone's car. Although at this restaurant it is a different story. Three of us park between 80 and 150 cars every night. Every night is extremely busy. I have parked some of the nicest cars ever built: Mercedes-Benz, BMW, Bentley, Porsche, Aston Martin, Ferrari, Hummers, etc. You name it I've driven it. Anyway most of these people are the stingiest snobs in this city. These people are stockbrokers, doctors, accountants, have family money, own businesses, even the owner of the Knicks comes in from time to time. I'm not asking for a lot, the money's pretty good, just simply decent treatment. I expect not to be spoken down to, patronized, etc. [But] many of the people think that since they have money, that they're a better person or something. They are very superficial, pompous, arrogant. . . .

So many of the customers jump out of 100,000 dollar cars, spit on us on the way in, smoke a cigar and eat half a cow on the inside, then stumble out drunk and cranky and "hook us up" with a whole dollar bill on the way out. It's these kind of people that make me so pissed off. The richest people in America are some of the biggest assholes. Then when I see everyone else in school, out at bars, everywhere, they all want to be like these people. That's what gives me a sense of despair about the direction our country is moving in. Such arrogance by anyone turns my stomach. Just because you have money doesn't make you a better person.

Doug

They tell stories about friends who didn't get the kind of jobs they thought they would upon graduating.

I am in a fraternity here at school. Several of my brothers have graduated with business degrees, accounting degrees, numerous different degrees. For the most part though they are not working in their field of expertise. A friend of mine graduated a year and a half ago with a degree in marketing. Now this is my chosen major so this particularly worries me. Anyway, he worked for an insurance company for about two months, his closest shot at a "real" job, then he became a bartender/bouncer at a bar, and now he is driving a hearse for his uncle's business. I think that there just aren't enough jobs to go around. Another friend of mine graduated one year ago with a degree in accounting. He couldn't get a job either. He joined the police academy. He is now NYPD, which is not a bad job, but I don't think it's what he wanted to do when he decided to spend $40,000+ to get a degree.

Alonzo

They express concern over having their beliefs and values compromised by corporate culture.

> There is so much competition in the workplace that I sometimes feel like it is not even worth it to try. This may sound like I have no self-esteem and I do not believe that I am just as good as anyone else, but that is not the case. I feel that there is so much competition working in any job that I really do not look forward to getting mixed up in such rivalry among other people. So many people are "out for blood" and will do anything to get what they want that I do not even think people worry about the consequences. This is why competition bothers me so much because although everyone is out in the work force trying to make a living, I feel that too much competition to get a job done just makes the workplace a place where people go to hurt others at any cost. . . . If I have to work, I would want to work in an environment where my beliefs and morals are not subjected to change by any company. It is bad enough that I have to work to survive, I really do not need any corporation telling me what to believe in.
>
> JULIE

Such tales of workpain are directly related to the mission of higher education. These are not just stories about bad jobs told by students who, upon completing their degrees, will magically enter a world of "good jobs." These stories remind us—especially those of us who are full-time faculty with flexible schedules, some degree of pedagogical autonomy, and the opportunity to pursue our research interests—what work is like for a significant portion of the population.

Grooming for Workpain and Active Participation in Consumer Culture

> Our present educational institutions are predominantly geared to the reproduction of industrial, affluent, consumer society.
>
> TED TRAINER, *The Conserver Society*

It is not the academy's job to simply help its students "get jobs." For one thing, the majority of our students have already entered a world of work without our help: more than half of the nation's undergraduates spend at least twenty hours a week working while taking a full course load (Jones 299). Many students know more about work than do some of their professors who managed to get teaching positions right out of graduate school. Surely to some extent it is the responsibility of the academy to help its students find their way not just into jobs but into good careers. However, if writers like Rifkin, Aronowitz, DiFazio, Gamst, Frank, and Cook are correct in their forecasts for variations of jobless and workless futures, it will become increasingly difficult for colleges to prepare students for a workforce where so many positions are being eliminated, or at least where so many jobs have limited opportunity for advancement due to winner-take-all market forces. It is now necessary to provide students with the tools with which to critique existing work opportunities through the lens of sustainability, to explore sustainable work options, and to critically imagine the various work landscapes that might exist for them in the near future.

But the academy is less concerned with helping students imagine and explore the possibilities of sustainable, pain-free work environments than it is with demonstrating its success in "placing" students in jobs, regardless of the ethical philosophies motivating the companies and corporations that hire these students. Nor does the academy seem overly concerned with making students aware of forecasts predicting a decline in jobs, due to advanced technology. For example, describing the effects of desktop computer technology on the publishing industry, one reporter quotes a partner in a graphic communications consulting and analysis firm: "In 1990, there were 6,200 typographers, service bureaus, separators and platemakers, employing 83,000 people in the United States. . . . By 1997 this segment had lost almost 1,800 businesses and more than 13,500 employees. The value of these jobs is somewhere in the neighborhood of $700 million annually" (Joss 1). If our undergraduates knew that a rising number of their college professors are adjuncts with advanced degrees who get paid, on average, between $2,000 and $2,500 per course before taxes, don't receive benefits, and spend their weeks commuting between two or three job sites, it might dawn on them that a graduate degree, let alone a bachelor's, is hardly a guarantee of economic success. If the academy refuses to take care of its own employees and graduate assistants, what investment does it have in the futures of undergraduates once they leave the institution?

If educational institutions really prepared students for work as it now exists in the late twentieth century, they might offer required courses that teach strategies for coping with workpain in the ensuing decades—the ever longer work weeks, the increasing physical and psychological tolls, the wages that fail to meet costs of living, and the ongoing disappearance of challenging and creative jobs. Students could take "corporate health" classes that teach ways of reducing stress in an increasingly stressful work environment; "economic simplicity" courses that help them break consumer addictions and adopt simpler lifestyles in preparation for likely lay-offs, downsizing, and future job scarcity; and seminars in community work and third sector employment where students research ways of directing their talents and interests toward local agencies and organizations.

Because the academy often fails to critically examine work for what it is—an often degrading and exhausting commitment to environmentally and socially irresponsible enterprises—it plays a role in perpetuating workpain and the unsustainable economy. In fact, higher education has permitted business to shape the curriculum without first critically challenging the nature of business. Business tells the academy what it wants in its graduates— essentially, how the university should do its job—but the flow of critique is rarely two-way. Business leaders visit institutions of higher learning, letting administrators, faculty, and students know the kinds of skills they want to see cultivated in our students. But administrators and faculty generally do not initiate dialogues with corporations to tell them how to conduct their affairs more ethically and responsibly. Almost all colleges have a career services program where staff help students assemble their résumés, conduct mock interviews, and invite corporate representatives on campus to discuss job preparedness. Faculty are encouraged to alert their students to job fairs—but not to critique the ethics practiced by the participating companies. In the land of career services, any job, it would seem, is a good job. These are not sites where high priority is given to helping students assess the level of workpain at a particular company or investigate a business's commitment to its local community. Internships play an important role in many departments and programs, but here the goal is for the student to assimilate into that particular work arena, not to help make the agency more sustainable or more responsive to workers' needs.

Certainly education should be work-relevant and professionally oriented. Those who advocate pedagogies that pretend to be above the mundane realities of work simply perpetuate the world of work they disdain by ignoring it. Colleges should have career centers, and internships can obviously play a vital role in the learning process. Teachers should want their students to find meaningful work just as much as they themselves want to hold onto their own jobs. But the academy also has a responsibility to initiate a two-way dialogue with the companies and organizations that need our graduates if they are to continue operating. Business leaders want to see better communication and writing skills in graduates? Fair enough, but, in return for teaching students certain "basics" deemed important for professional communication, the academy ought to use whatever leverage it has to insist that businesses demonstrate a commitment to sustainable "basics" and the elimination of workpain. Of course, academies that are themselves unsustainable, that perpetuate brown instead of green campuses, and that promote their own versions of workpain throughout the university corporation, are in no position to make such demands.

And so higher education continues to roll over and let business directly and indirectly dictate curricula. Consider the language in a recent collection of essays intended to convince English faculty to make the classroom workplace-relevant. The contributors to *Expanding Literacies: English Teaching and the New Workplace* (Garay and Bernhardt) want English teachers—writing and literature faculty alike—to abolish the school-versus-work mentality that is common in academia, replacing it with pedagogies that foster a synthesis between school and work. To this extent, such an idea could be useful. Departments, particularly those in the humanities, don't do enough to help their majors realize the potential relevance of their coursework and disciplinary skills for existing and evolving careers. Again, this is nowhere more acute than in graduate programs that, on the one hand, require students to take advanced courses, pass comprehensive exams, and write theses and dissertations, but, on the other hand, fail to help them find work with their advanced degrees. Garay and Bernhardt's emphasis on making the discipline work-relevant, while written for an audience of undergraduate faculty, would be even more appropriate if written for an audience of graduate faculty in English, who for the most part have yet to effectively reconceptualize the goals of their English curricula in response to the job crisis confronting today's graduate students.

The problem with such a collection of essays is that it assumes that teachers must unquestioningly serve the workplace as it now exists, and that those who manage the workplace and all it symbolizes are above critique. The contributors want English instruction to change "in response to a changing workplace" (ix), to "fit instruction with the needs of particular industries" (ix), to "upgrade . . . courses to include skills that will make . . . students work ready" (115), to help students "find a niche in the changing job market" (149), and "to produce the skillful workers that business wants" (151). "It is critical," concludes one contributor, "that new entrants to the workplace have the background and education needed to meet or exceed the higher skill level requirements of the current manufacturing world" (116–17). But the assumption that "manufacturing" is inherently good and right demonstrates a distressing lack of critical thinking and ethical interrogation. One of the editors goes so far as to urge faculty to "suspend negative stereotypes of the workplace" (44), revealing a romanticization of work that is at odds with the millions of readers who made Scott Adams, creator of the *Dilbert* cartoon strip, the number one author for months on the *New York Times* nonfiction bestseller list.[2]

The contributors to this volume also refer repeatedly to a 1991 report issued by the Labor Department's SCANS Commission (the Secretary's Commission on Achieving Necessary Skills), titled *What Work Requires of Schools*, which they present as a blueprint for pedagogical reform. Unfortunately none of the contributors explores the functionalist biases and assumptions running throughout such a document, as did writers like Knoblauch and Brannon five years earlier (*Critical Teaching* 75–90). And in another collection of research on professional and nonacademic writing, *Writing in the Workplace: New Research Perspectives* (Spilka), although there is one essay arguing for pedagogies that influence workplace communication practices and apply "strategies for effecting social change in the workplace" (Spilka, "Influencing Workplace Practice" 213), social change is defined there in only the most limited of contexts, as in promoting collaboration and invention within professional writing communities. Whether or not organizations are engaged in sustainable and socially responsible activities is, we are to assume, an unrelated matter. Ultimately volumes like this—along with much that gets published under the rubrics of technical communication and business writing—are not interested in using a lens of sustainability to cross-examine the social and environmental implications of the workplaces they take for granted; rather, they regard organizations and corporations as generally neutral entities.

When I was a senior undergraduate in 1985, a number of my friends worried about leaving the safety of the campus behind and launching into the "real world." While one still hears these concerns spoken by undergraduates positioned to leave college behind, it seems increasingly that more of the students I advise are impatient to get out as quickly as possible. Far from being strangers to the "real" world of work—again, the overwhelming majority of my students work at least twenty hours a week, and have done so throughout the bulk of their undergraduate years—they are eager to work more hours, in order to make more money and begin paying off their school loans and living lifestyles expected by their parents and their peers. In many ways, that "real world" has been there with them all along. I see it in the student who, having come to class after a twelve-hour shift, dozes off in the front row of the classroom. I see it in the students who are chronically late after fighting traffic to get to campus. I see it in the tired expressions of students who regularly get no more than five hours of sleep a night, due to working full-time in a factory somewhere. Workpain walks into the classroom the moment our students do: we see it in their tardiness, their weary faces, their disorganized appearance, their forgetfulness, their apathy. Some come to our classes right from work; others race out of our classes to get to work. And as online courses and distance learning continue to infiltrate the curriculum, I suspect that an increasing number of our students will "attend" our classes while sitting in front of a computer at their "real" jobs.

Work is always there, with us in the classroom, and where there is work there is workpain. As for the students we pass, who in turn use those passing grades to eventually complete their degrees, and who use those certificates to help them get jobs, we have played some small but undeniable role in helping them reach these positions. If our students find work as marketing executives for Nike or some other corporation built on the backs of Third World indentured servants, or as accountants doing the books for distributors selling chemicals to companies that make environmentally harmful pesticides, or as telemarketers who invade the lives of other people at home while they are recuperating from their own forms of workpain,[3] or as architects whose plans are used by developers encroaching on open space, or as writers producing advertising copy for junk mail catalogs, we have played some part in helping them get there. I agree that this can be a cynical way to envision the end results of our teaching; what, after all, of those students who go on to become teachers, third sector employees, counselors, activists, health advocates, ecologists, caretakers, artists, and caring, attentive parents? But it is even more cynical to turn a blind eye toward the many kinds of business environments that perpetuate workpain and that work against sustainability—businesses and workplaces that higher education continues to feed.

In Chapter 3, I argued that throughout the curriculum we need to create opportunities for students to examine their immediate communities, since without heightened local awareness one cannot develop an understanding of sustainability. The same is true of creating contexts in which students can write about the jobs they and their families hold and the careers they intend to pursue. Again, in the composition classroom, one can go only so far in making connections between students' work experiences and the need for more sustainable employment. But a necessary first step is to at least listen to what our students have to say about their often crummy jobs, and then gradually introduce the idea of more enriching and sustainable employment opportunities. Certainly the bulk of such conversations will have to take place throughout the curricula, particularly within students' junior and senior years and during advanced courses in their chosen majors, and especially throughout graduate curricula. But in some small way, the entry-level composition classroom can initiate conversations about the differences between good and bad work—conversations rooted in the experiences of our students and their families, conversations that move eventually toward exploring possibilities for fulfilling students' needs and desires in more sustainable career paths.

CHAPTER FIVE

Future

In short, if I am compelled to guess the future, I would estimate that the global system will, indeed, probably experience a series of terrible events—wrenching calamities that are economic or social or environmental in nature—before common sense can prevail. It would be pleasing to believe otherwise, but the global system so dominates and intimidates present thinking that I expect societies will be taught still more painful lessons before they find the will to act.

WILLIAM GREIDER, *One World, Ready or Not: The Manic Logic of Global Capitalism*

For the last twelve years this thing called "the future" has been a preoccupation with me. For the most part my concerns have revolved around attaining economic stability: the worries of a grad student in the late 1980s seeking interviews, an adjunct in the early 1990s searching for full-time work, and then a junior faculty member preoccupied with getting tenure. But this admittedly selfish focus began to broaden sometime around 1993 with two events: becoming a father with the birth of my son, and reading a paragraph in a book by Paul Ryan. The first event speaks for itself. Having a kid will bring about the most radical of paradigm shifts in one's consciousness. As other parents know, you find yourself contemplating futures you never noticed before, regarding them with a mixture of awe, excitement, and terror. As the arrival of my son was rearranging my psychic furniture in profound ways, I was also reading Paul Ryan's exceptional book, *Video Mind, Earth Mind: Art, Communications, and Ecology*, which begins:

No one can say for sure how long we humans can go on abusing the ecosystems that support our life. Some think the time is short. In 1990, the respected Worldwatch Institute predicted the earth could only endure another forty years of overpopulation, ozone depletion, rain forest destruction and global warming. And then? Then we pass a threshold of irreversible environmental destruction. The door to a healthy life on earth deadbolts behind us. We watch our grandchildren garbage-pick their way through life in ecosystems that are terminally ill. (1)

At that time, such deadlines were new to me; I had no idea that experts in so many fields had begun to formulate such horrific predictions. Since then I have tried to assess how many others agree that our species has a forty-year window of opportunity. What I discovered, as mentioned in Chapter 1, is that, to many, four decades now seems very wishful thinking; indeed, a growing number of observers seem to believe that time has already run out.

Much of the impetus for this book lies in those two experiences: the quiet joy of watching my son grow up, and the growing frustration and fear that comes with paying attention to never ending forecasts about a world in a state of overwhelming crisis and decline. Not surprisingly, I started bringing "the future" into my writing courses, asking my students to contemplate various future scenarios while writing their own versions of what they thought life would be like in twenty-five years. I did this partly out of need for company: I wanted to be around people who, even if they were only half my age, were also contemplating our common future several decades from now. I did it also because there are few if any opportunities in my students' other courses for them to compose future forecasts on the basis of available information—a curious absence given the surge in writings by futurists in recent years. Finally, as with most of my writing assignments, there was at bottom a need to create opportunities for students to testify about something they considered important: the articulation of their hopes and fears for the next twenty-five years. This chapter looks at excerpts from a number of those testimonies, and attempts to provide a rationale for creating classroom contexts where students can pursue this kind of exercise. As with the investigations into one's local community and one's current and future jobs, looking into the near future is something I consider an essential component of sustainability-based thinking.

The Art of Forecasting

Whether they call themselves futurists, futurologists, or scenario builders, nonfiction writers who tell stories about the future are nothing new. Back in 1968 an introduction to Donald Michael's *The Unprepared Society: Planning for a Precarious Future* described the author as a new breed of futurist, not to be confused with the old-school futurist thinking associated with social planners of the 1930s (ix). Several years later, Alvin Toffler's *Future Shock* captured the imaginations of readers around the world with what probably remains the most widely read work of futurist thinking. In the 1980s John Naisbitt's *Megatrends: Ten New Directions Transforming Our Lives* appeared, along with the widely translated State of the World reports from the Worldwatch Institute (Brown et al.). As we approached the new millennium, it came as no surprise that the 1990s saw an acceleration of titles in "future studies."

Contemporary speculative nonfiction now takes a number of forms. Many, such as Peter Schwartz's *The Art of the Long View: Planning for the Future in an Uncertain World* and Taylor, Wacker, and Means's *The 500-Year Delta: What Happens After What Comes Next,* are positioned in the realm of strategic management, intended for an audience of entrepreneurs. And many examples of futurist thinking, such as Bill Gates's *The Road Ahead* and Yorick Blumenfeld's *2099: A Eutopia,* offer unabashedly optimistic views of life in the first century of the new millennium. On the other end of the spectrum are those works that describe dark times ahead: Eugene Linden's *The Future in Plain Sight: Nine Clues to the Coming Instability,* Smith et al.'s *Global Anarchy in the Third Millennium? Race, Place, and Power at the End of the Modern Age,* Robert Kaplan's *The Coming Anarchy: Shattering the Dreams of the Post Cold War,* William Greider's *One World, Ready or Not: The Manic Logic of Global Capitalism,* and, most disturbing of all, Jay Hanson's archive of articles and editorials at his www.dieoff.org Web site. Somewhere in the middle are the fork-in-the-road hypotheses by writers who see our society poised at a critical juncture where we have no choice but to choose either the path of sustainability or, in the words of planning organizations like New York's Regional Plan Association, "irreversible decline" (Yaro and Hiss). Examples include Hartmut Bossel's *Earth at a Crossroads: Paths to a Sustainable Future*, Hazel Henderson's *Creating Alternative Futures: The End of Economics*, Ed Ayres's *God's Last Offer: Negotiating for a Sustainable Future*, and Alan AtKisson's *Believing Cassandra: An Optimist Looks at a Pessimist's World*.

According to Peter Schwartz, who has called himself one since 1975, a futurist is someone who posits scenarios about likely (not to be confused with merely possible) futures in hopes of "changing mind-sets" and "reperceiving the world" (10). By gathering information from a variety of sources—and having a feel for what to examine and what to disregard—the futurist makes stories about the coming future, usually in hopes of influencing the decisions of policymakers. In his *Foundations of Future Studies: Human Science for a New Era*, Wendell Bell lists nine "major tasks of futures studies" and starts the list with "the study of possible futures" and "the study of probable futures" (75–97). Of course, what all of these futurists are doing is telling stories, and in this regard a work of speculative fiction like Octavia Butler's *Parable of the Sower* and Eugene Linden's nonfiction work *The Future in Plain Sight* have much in common (in one course that I teach, "Writing the Future," I treat both works as belonging to the same genre of futurist literature). It is this desire to tell stories about the near future, regardless of whether one concludes with happy or sad endings, that many of my students seem to share.

My Students' Futures

In the last four weeks of my composition courses, I have my students read a handful of futurist forecasts, samplings from all four categories listed above: business-minded, optimistic, bleak, and fork-in-the-road scenarios. As students familiarize themselves with some of these texts, they write their own statements about what the next twenty-five years will bring. I don't ask them to write about what they hope to see, or what they think should come to pass, although in the classroom many of our conversations revolve around such longings. Rather, I ask that they articulate their gut feelings about what will happen, for better or worse, or both.

While I know that my own biases cannot fail to enter the classroom, I think I do a fairly good job of creating an environment where students feel comfortable expressing a range of views about the future but aren't ever really sure what my own thoughts are (afraid of influencing them too much, I wait until the end of the semester, after they have turned in their work, to briefly mention my own chameleon vision, as expressed in Chapter 1). Throughout the last four weeks of the semester, we spend most of the time discussing each other's drafts in workshop situations where the students make each other aware of their views and explain where they agree and disagree with one another. I often end up playing the role of devil's advocate, questioning everyone's positions so that they might anticipate various counterarguments in the course of revising their own narratives. Some discussions are given over to clarifying and questioning points made in the readings. Most of the classroom time, though, is spent in small groups where students discuss and argue with one another their reasons for viewing the future as they do.

Many of my students, of course, can't wait for the future to get here. They predict continued economic growth, increasing tolerance among different cultures, and a heightened sense of respect for and awareness of community and environment. Alexis ends an essay by claiming that "we will realize what is truly important in life: family, love, happiness, being kind, values, giving and receiving respect, and preserving the earth." Maria writes that, even though the future might not be so rosy, she is buoyed by her faith in the ability to change the world: "I have always believed that the actions of a few could affect the world, both in their actions and what they preach. I am thankful that I know a lot of people who agree with me. So as long as I do not lose my faith, I have already made things better." Lots of my students, enamored of technology, anticipate future technological breakthroughs that will make life better than ever: George is excited about the recent availability of DVDs and the futuristic "concept cars" he sees at auto shows; Chuck writes of how MP3 and flat television screens have improved his life, and how he looks forward to "floating cars." Pamela looks ahead with approval to a future where crime decreases as a result of harsher penalties, more prisons, and an increase in gated communities, which she thinks will be equipped with hi-tech motion detectors, retinal scans, and electric fences. Many of my students are confident that electric cars will be the norm in ten years or so. Some, like Carmine, a student planning on becoming a doctor, see life expectancy rising to 130 years or more, the elimination of most diseases, and a global rise in intelligence—all due to "increased technology." In all of my classes there are some who, like Zhu, exhibit confidence that technology will "solve all our problems" in the years ahead; another student writes that "technology will prevent any disasters . . . and make for a perfect society."

Others predict that things will get worse before they get better, but that inevitably things will get better.

> I envision the future as growing, flourishing, expanding, reaching new horizons in technology, and great advances in all areas of science and technology. I envision a world . . . that seems or appears similar to the cartoon show "The Jetsons" or the television show "Star Trek," maybe without all the gizmos and gadgets but one very close to it. A world where manual labor is replaced by machines, where man's next great exploration is space, where . . . the problems that concerned humanity ten years ago (i.e. overpopulation, over-consumption, shortages of energy and food resources, etc.) will no longer be a problem for humanity in approximately twenty-five years.
>
> ROGER

And still others, of course, find this whole business of imagining futures a waste of time:

> Personally, I have no fear of the future. I feel that what is going to happen will happen, no matter what. There is no such thing as "changing the course of history." If it is going to end, what are we supposed to do? Absolutely nothing! At that point, there is nothing that can be done anyway. Let the world end. . . . Whatever should happen will happen. (You can quote me on that.) The future can come and go as it pleases.
>
> LARRY

Yet many of my students do not see things this way. While I have been teaching this assignment for only the last four years, in that time at least half, and sometimes as many as two-thirds, of my students in each course think that the future is going to be considerably worse—not in every way, of course, but enough so that they describe their overall outlook as pessimistic. I find this to be noteworthy for a number of reasons, not the least of which is the degree to which their sense of what the future holds seems to stand in stark contrast to the rosier futures arguably implied in University mission statements and the curriculum at large.

Some focus on overpopulation as the main problem on the horizon and argue for various forms of birth control—a rather gutsy position considering that those who argue this are not only Catholic themselves, but aware that, in our Catholic institution, many of their peers and professors will be made uncomfortable by such views:

> Overpopulation will be the major problem that we will have to contend with in the future. It is the kind of problem that leads to other problems. These include an increase in vulnerability to diseases, an increase in pollution, depletion of the ozone layer and global warming. . . . That's why population decline must become a priority. If we act now and take initiative while our current population is still controllable we may have a chance at avoiding a catastrophe.
>
> AMANDA

> There is no way, unfortunately, to save the future, unless our generation finds a way to educate the world about overpopulation and the secondary problems that stem from overcrowding.
>
> ERICA

> Today we live in a society that is slowly deteriorating into nothing. Our environmental atmosphere is also decaying, only faster. The only solutions I can think of can only be achieved through a single totalitarian government that rules the entire planet. . . .
>
> What we need to do about this situation is what's being done in China. We need to control the amount of children that a family can have. Those who exceed the amount, have to pay fines for doing so. . . . Unfortunately, as long as we live the way we are now, in 25 years human existence will be no more.
>
> WEI-YI

Others write about increased crime and violence, which some of them correlate with phenomena such as increasing technological advancements and a widening gap between the poor and the affluent.

> It is more than likely that there will be a continuous increase in computer technology, but that may not all be for the better. . . . [A]s computer technology increases so will the gap between the haves and the have nots. As computer technology increases only those who are computer literate will succeed and those who are not will be left behind. This means an increase in crime and poverty.
>
> MARTY

> The rich get richer and the poor get poorer. Which leads to an increase in crime. The crime will increase to the point that the world seems out of control. Jails will be overcrowded (more than they are now). Violent crimes such as murder, rape, robbery, and abuse will be at a disgustingly high level.
>
> MELISSA

Some, of course, write future scenarios influenced by apocalyptic imagery circulating in the media:

> The future seems bleak. Everyone [in the media] is talking about theories of how the world is going to end [and it] frightens me. Such theories are of how we are getting closer to the sun, or that we might get hit by a meteor, or a 3rd world war occurs. A fear of guerilla warfare flashes in my head, as I watch the world news. What is stopping that from happening here in the United States? Automatic weapons can easily be accessible, if the right person has the wrong idea. Thoughts of people carrying guns on the streets, stealing and random killings is what I see occurring. Countries that were once allies now bombing each other because one of them interfered with their ways. This is my fear, when world leaders snap and go crazy. Action movies come to reality. The phrase survival of the fittest comes into play. Words from the book of revelation start becoming true.
>
> ANTHONY

Others expect *more* crime—a view conflicting with news reports in recent years of declining rates of crime in New York City.

Unfortunately, I am worried about the future. The crime rate seems to rise as the years pass. There are so many cruel people in the world that like to harm others. This bothers me because I do not want my kids to grow up in this society. There are numerous children who are afraid of going to school every day for fear of their safety.

AMY

Other students describe a future shaped by ensuing environmental catastrophes:

I expect by the year 2050 and I am seventy-one years old, that I probably will be wearing gas masks on my face because the air we breathe will be unclean and can cause death. . . . We would no longer have a winter season. It will always be hot and the humidity will be high. But that's not the worst part, there is scarcity in water because we have been taking it for granted, rain would no longer fall as much as it used to and the water that we use for our baths we would use to flush the toilets. The earth would be covered in garbage because we no longer have a place to throw out our trash. Because of the trash diseases are going to come about that will threaten our society. The antibiotics that some people are taking to prevent colds will be the very things that kill them. The viruses would take different forms and our body would not be strong enough to get rid of them. . . . The forecast I give for the future is disaster.

LORRAINE

I see some positive events emerging in the future but unfortunately more negative ones. As for the negative, I think the destruction of the ozone layer will continue. More and more people on a daily basis have to protect themselves from the sun's ultraviolet rays. There was once a time when my mother could go out on a hot sunny summer day without any type of sun block but those days are now over. My mother is extremely sensitive to the sun and has been urged by her dermatologist to take precaution. I never really thought it was a problem until it hit home. Now I realize that many people have to protect themselves from the sun's dangerous rays.

YOLANDA

I have a pessimistic view about our future. . . . There will be more natural disasters, such as flooding, mudslides, and droughts. We're going to have to change our energy: oil suppliers will be depleted, and we're going to have to substitute this with another energy source, namely coal. Unfortunately, coal will further enhance climate change, air pollution, and acid rain. To prevent this from happening, people are going to have to participate and get involved. By this I mean, volunteer your time in various programs, and try to make a difference in your community as well as in society. But, to be honest, I don't see this happening.

This is what's going to happen if we don't stop abusing and neglecting the environment and its resources: technology, rising population, and the people that live here today are going to cause a major catastrophe, like wiping out the entire population. How are we going to feed 8 billion people down the road from now? . . . I do believe that people will become more educated on what we need to do to take better care of our environment, but won't go that extra step to do so.

VINCENT

Some write about a future dominated by greed and excess:

All I see is a corrupt world that is filled with greed. Greed is one of the diseases that science could never cure. People are and always will be greedy. People will lie and cheat to get to the top; not all people, but most of them. The future will show the two extreme sides of humanity. The violent, selfish one and the flip side; the giving and caring side. Only time will bring about both sides. I believe that the world will reach rock bottom; filled with evil, murder, violence, crimes, disease, greed, hunger.

SAMANTHA

I predict in the next twenty-five years more and more people will buy more and more junk. We will just destroy the environment and we will still not provide ourselves with a fulfilling life. What will become of the planet in twenty-five years? My personal opinion is disaster and organized chaos.

OSCAR

At the rate we are going now, I see the future as a world full of people who dread their lives instead of loving them. Of course it is always possible to have a beautiful world, but to reach that goal there would have to be intense sacrifice, hard work and dedication. Unfortunately, the societies of the world today base themselves on personal gain and are hardly willing to sacrifice anything.

JEAN

One student anticipates more sexual predators, greater decline in race relations, and increased intolerance for immigrants:

> Twenty-five years from now I see a world where people will have no regard for their fellow person. Everyone will be very suspicious of everyone else, you won't know who to trust. Today we have students killing classmates, teachers, their parents. Next door neighbors molesting children on the block. Fathers and uncles abusing their daughters, nieces. Grown men sleeping with and manipulating the minds of little girls. And the Internet which is supposed to be an important part of our society today, you can't even allow your child to surf the web for information. Next thing you know some pervert has lured your son or daughter miles away from their home and you thought your child was just "chatting" on-line. I don't see these things getting better, so our kids will not be able to play or associate with anyone. Even the adults will have to be very careful about who they interact with. . . .
>
> In terms of race relations I don't see things getting any better, just worse. Twenty-five years from now I don't think this whole cultural diversity thing will make one bit of difference. Instead of people really understanding another culture people will just be hypocrites and smile in your face but behind your back still have the same prejudice feelings inside. The media is a big cause of the race relations in our country, because the regulating companies allow them to report biased and misleading information. . . .
>
> TANYA

Some of my students are confident that the only winners in the future will be the rich; the poor will either die off or go on living lives unchanged by advancements in technology.

> With the amount of technology available, there will be successful attempts to get around [problems associated with global warming and overpopulation]. The only problem will be that not everyone will have access to these new ways of survival. The only people who will survive this are the ones that helped create the problem. They are the rich and the powerful. They are the ones that supported all the changes that caused the disasters to begin with. They are the ones who will have enough money, know the right connections that will get the tools needed to survive in the "new world." . . . Unfortunately, for the rest of us, we will be the ones dying of cancer from ultraviolet rays.
>
> GISELLE

I have lived all my life on a one way street of the Bronx. In my block, there are two grocery stores, a laundromat, and, of course, buildings. These things have not changed since I've been here . . . . The same people might not still live here but the same kind of people are around. . . . Drug dealers have been here for a while and then they go. . . . Because before you know it someone else is in charge of the drugs. Those obese ladies that sit outside with all of their seven children gossiping about everybody in the block may leave, but others come. All I've seen these years has led me to believe that twenty-five years from now we won't be any different. We have generally been the same for so many years and will continue being the same.

What I predict will happen in my neighborhood in twenty-five years in the future is simple. My two grocery stores will go from the colors yellow and red to green and purple and still a little yellow. . . . The stores will be remodeled in the inside with a few more aisles added. . . . The laundromat will no longer be there. Since business was not going so well they will have had to sell the place. Instead we will have one of those cheap fast food places. . . . We won't have the same landlord because he is in his 50s now and I don't believe he'll be able to do the same work he does now. Our new landlord . . . won't have to work much because the machinery will be so advanced. Instead of using the broom and mop there will be other tools used to maintain the building. Most of the people will have left the neighborhood, be deceased, or are still there. . . .

Basically I am predicting the world will change for the better but will have little impact on this neighborhood. . . . Generally it will still be the same old Findlay Avenue.

JASMINE

In the year 2025 . . . a large number of people will be forced to live in unsafe neighborhoods. There will also be more prisons for the increasing number of criminals. Crimes will increase unbelievably . . . due to the lack of a steady family life and the lack of a fair and just education system for people of most classes. A lot of New York City will change for the worse, but of course the rich, high-class neighborhoods will still exist. It will be like two completely different worlds. On one side, you'll have the poor, the violence, and the fear, and on the other side, you'll have the beauty, the peace and the life everyone deserves to live. . . . For the middle class, it will get harder and harder to live a comfortable life. I could even see this happening to my family. Opportunities for my parents seem to be vanishing right before our eyes, and there isn't anything they can do to stop it.

GEORGIA

Some predict that education will suffer.

Education is decaying as we speak. As gaps widening between rich and the poor, educational factors can leave holes in the world's social mixes. If it is not taken care of, the gaps soon turn into pits. In turn we will need a "root canal" to fix the problem. Education is needed to attain an above minimum wage job. If education is decaying how will people be able to attain work, if the rich become richer would not the poor become envious and revolt in ways. [And yet] in the future I can honestly say the rich will prosper and flourish while the poor try to survive.

CARL

When I think about what life will be like twenty-five years from now it seems very bleak, I get very depressed and feel very sad to even think about the future, our future. Unfortunately, I don't have a very positive outlook based on the way things are headed now. If our direction now is any inclination of what life will be like in twenty-five years I feel sorry for whoever is around during that time, including myself.

Economically, I believe there will be an elimination of the middle class. The rich will be even richer, and the poor will get poorer. Presently, the middle class is already suffering. There are students who cannot get a college education because their parents make a supposedly decent living—but decent according to whose standards? Is $40,000–$70,000 really enough to pay for a car, house, food, clothes, and a college education? You have to be really rich to be able to afford college or really poor to be eligible for financial aid to go to college.

When you think about it why even get a college education, what are we going to use it for. The workforce seems to be less dependent on humans and shifting towards more reliance on computers and automated systems.

DIANA

Some anticipate that consumer culture will further weaken family structure:

I see the family unit disintegrating, along with all traces of traditional lifestyle. Consumers represent the largest portion of society. Wealth is equal to purchasing power, and shopping has superseded baseball as our nation's favorite pastime. . . . Years ago, a family was considered lucky to have a radio, and a television practically put you in a class by yourself. Today, people have satellite dishes that receive channels from all over the US, and they still are unhappy. . . . Life for many has become a quest for happiness; happiness being defined as constant accumulation of material possessions. Therefore, parents will be struggling to work in order to pay for the material desires of their children. Kids, for the most part, will never have a parent waiting for them after school. Instead, daycare will play an increasingly large part of our children's lives. TV and video games will replace family outings and the passing down of morals and values. Parents will be judged by their children based on how well their desires were fulfilled. The family structure will be redefined, the purpose of quality time forgotten. For many, life will become a matter of convenience. How to get places the fastest, what is the quickest meal to prepare, and what is the latest gadget I can buy that will "make my life easier?"

JANET

Although the student quoted below holds a generally positive outlook on the future—new technological advances will, in her eyes, put an end to most crime, pollution, and disease—she also foresees the construction of new myths and legends brought on by paranoia and isolated living habits:

People will be more fearful of the "outside." No more kids playing on the streets, or in backyards (like I used to). There will be so many myths and tales of "the world around us," and "things you don't know about." These would be called the "Hidden Tales." People will be paranoid so they wouldn't want to go into the "dirty" world.

ANDREA

Some are confident that a barrage of sociological and environmental factors add up to bad times ahead.

My view of the future can be viewed as one of a pessimist, because it is kind of bleak. I don't doubt that there will be some positive advances in the future but the bad things that will happen in the future will overshadow them. . . .

Television will become the most important part of people's lives. To children it will become like another parent, they will look to it for guidance and answers to all their questions in life. Gang violence will surge in the coming years. Today people are afraid to let their children go out alone, but in the future I think that the problem will get worse. . . .

With all the new technology coming about, people will soon lose their jobs because there will be no need for them anymore. There will also be another depression or recession, returning the U.S. to the way it was during the "Great Depression." I say that because business always has a cycle, and with all the prosperity we are having now we are bound for a downfall. . . .

Ecologically I see the worst developments for the future. With our extravagant "live now . . . pay later" lifestyles, all of our natural resources will be used up. The landscape will be totally different. We will see trees, but sparsely placed. Since everything will be so barren around us we will be living in a "concrete jungle." People will start to adopt the earth friendly lifestyle from using solar energy to cutting down on waste but it will do no good; the damage will already be done. The hole in the ozone layer will grow to double or maybe even triple the size it is now. Either it will melt all the icecaps causing mass flooding, killing us all or life will be so unbearable with all the UV rays shining down on us, life expectancies would drop. Coupled with all the air pollution caused by the green house effect people will have no chance.

JESSE

Some write about future decline in a disturbingly matter-of-fact manner, as with the student who imagines his life in 2025 as an online salesman for an anti-pollution gas mask company—or in the case of this next student, who equates the rise in technological dependence with decline, thereby presenting a point of view that clashes with academia's faith in the value of online curricula and wired campuses:

In 25 years, things will be worse than they are today. There will be a lot of technological advances and with these advances there will be a rise in more complicated problems. Natural resources will become non-existent because they are using more and more of it to produce new technologies. The population is increasing rapidly and eventually can lead to famine and more pollution and damage to the environment. The ozone layer is thinning out and probably will disappear in the years to come. The Internet . . . will lead to less socializing and [more] laziness. Technological advancements may seem great and helpful to us but underneath it all there are consequences that come with it. . . . We will only get lazier and unhealthy due to the Internet and all its capabilities. . . . Technology isn't going to make life easier and faster but it is going to destroy us slowly.

NATALIE

Some students use this exercise in scenario building as an opportunity to make claims about human nature. More of them, I have found, make arguments for our species' inherent selfishness than believe humans can set aside personal desires for the good of community:

> People today are lazy. We want what we want, when we want it and how we want it. We work hard to get into high paying jobs but we don't want to work to save the earth. . . . Today's society is a "me" society. We do things for the good of our families or ourselves, not for the good of the society, nation or world. The reason we have so much waste and our planet is slowly being destroyed is because years ago people just didn't know any better. No one knew that aerosol cans had something in them that was deteriorating the ozone. Today, people are well informed. Yet no one seems to care. We sit there and look at the horrible things that are happening around us and say how sad it is but most of us don't actually do anything about it. . . .
>
> Twenty-five years from now people will look back and begin to regret what they and their ancestors have done to this world. Some will want to try and repair it, while others will take no more than a mere five minutes to consider the damage they did. The ones who realize the destruction will find out that nothing can be done to reverse this rapidly increasing cycle of destruction. . . . As much as I hate to admit it, in my opinion our future isn't very bright.
>
> PAULA

Most unsettling of all, at least a few students in every class are convinced that the human race will extinguish itself within this or the next generation.

> This is a mess. We are definitely moving towards our end. Whatever you want to call it; the End, our extinction, Armageddon or whatever else we often refer to it as. Whatever we now know will soon no longer be. We will soon have an epidemic that will end all of our lives. Overpopulation will do what it does best . . . destroy. It will demolish not just everything around it, but life itself. It will obliterate the human race, as we know it. It will take the form of a cancer. It will start out very small and almost undetectable and soon grows too large that even chemotherapy won't help. The population rate is no different from that of a cancerous disease. Already, we're starting to see that the population rate is

moving too fast. It's as if we're on a train moving full speed ahead where no one person can be the operator.

. . . In a nutshell, in about fifty years from now, we will actually be closer to our extinction. It will feel as if we're in a room where all the walls are closing in on us, each wall representing a factor aimed at our destruction. Fifty years from now when we find ourselves in this room, life will be dramatically different. The population will double from what it is today. Technology will turn the table around, instead of us controlling it, it will be controlling us. The environment will be exhausted and worst of all, hatred will consume most of our hearts. In this room will stand two types of people, the ones who've accomplished all they've dreamt about and those who won't dare to dream—only these walls won't be able to make the distinction.

LYNETTE

I think that in twenty-five years it will be a more technologically advanced time, which at first will make life a bit easier. [But] with this technological advancement will come chaos and ultimately our destruction. Someday machines will run the world . . . . If a computer can think and if it's smarter than any human then it will not be long before it starts thinking that it shouldn't be under the ownership of a human. It will start thinking of gaining its supremacy. In twenty-five years I think humans will be slaves to their own creations.

VICTORIA

Because of overpopulation the environment will be destroyed. We will have to cut down trees to build apartments and houses for people. There will be more cars than ever before. And because we had to cut down trees there will not be enough oxygen around. Overpopulation will cause an increase in the spread of diseases. If a person on a crowded subway car has tuberculosis and coughs, chances are more than half the people on the subway car will catch the disease, because everybody is breathing the same air.

There will be a struggle for food. Homes will be built in substitution of farms and because there is less land there [will be less] space to grow vegetables and fruits. As the population increases so does crime. While building more homes, more prison systems will also be built. By the year 2024 there will be very few people who are not diagnosed with skin cancer, and cataracts because of the sun's ultraviolet rays. Because we have used chemicals in the past to make our fruits and vegetables bigger and more attractive, we will lose most of the rich soil that we had to grow these plants.

Also in the year 2000 everybody is going to know someone who either has AIDS or died from it. Even if cures for diseases are found by the year 2024 new diseases will begin to form and old viruses will begin to mutate.

Everything outside our homes will pose a threat to us. There will be nothing we can do, we will soon be extinct just like the dinosaurs, moving on for some other species to take over the earth possibly aliens, you never know.

MARCELLA

If the environment isn't cleaned up, population isn't controlled, and values aren't restored, the earth may be in for an ugly, dark future, even with the next 20 to 25 years. I probably won't be alive to see the Armageddon or the second coming of Christ, but God may not have to inflict these punishments on the human race if we don't set ourselves on the correct path very soon.

ROBERTO

Such narratives are made all the more compelling when we realize that these students are not simply writing about the near future, but forecasting the deaths of themselves and their families.

I see a place of useless junk and a disease-filled, all-night day, a Dark City if you will. . . . We always assume there will be something to save our behinds in this world, so we think we can do all the bad we want. The motto of the world is, "We will figure it out later." I asked my friend today, what do you think is going to happen in the next twenty-five years? She responded with the notion that we would all be extinct.

MANNY

In twenty-five years, the world will be in utter chaos both physically and morally. This society will care only about consuming products, making life more comfortable, and attaining more wealth. This world can only get worse and worse. . . .

Countries will team up on the US to bring its downfall. Since so many countries have nuclear arms, they will eventually use it. They won't just show off their weapons anymore. A nuclear holocaust will take place. The US will come out on top, but the destruction of the US will last a long time. . . .

This society will also become a society without values. As of now, people step all over each other for personal gain. The future will be even worse. Everyone will be fighting amongst each other to consume products and gain wealth. . . .

As I look into the future, I can only see more evil and despair in this world. This society will become valueless and lazy. Personally, I hope god's day of judgment does come soon, because I wouldn't want to live in a world like this.

LOUIS

For some the threat of nuclear war is as real as it was for people of my generation who grew up in the 1960s and 1970s, and, combined with other global calamities, it fuels apocalyptic scenarios. When asked his opinion on the future of New York City in twenty-five years, this next student told the rest of the class that he was confident that New York City would by then have been obliterated in a nuclear attack—and himself along with it, since he didn't foresee moving away.

Sometimes I believe that Nostradamus and the bible were right about Armageddon or a nuclear holocaust. People laugh about it and say it's not going to happen. But we are approaching the next millennium with the U.S. fighting wars in Yugoslavia and Iraq. North Korea has nuclear capacity and so does India and Pakistan. Many third world nations are at war or fighting huge famine and poverty. Throughout the earth there are great disasters like earthquakes in Colombia and floods in the Midwest. Islamic fundamentalism is on the rise. Racial tensions are hot and getting hotter. For example the Louima case and Rodney King riots. If we don't see to these problems, we will be the first species to make ourselves extinct and destroy the planet. We will put the gun to our own heads. Only our actions can determine if the trigger will be pulled.

RICARDO

To help further explain the logic behind his scenarios, this student attached an appendix to this particular essay, a collage of headlines taken from the *Daily News* on the day he was writing this paper (April 10, 1999): "Killer Storms Hit Midwest," "Safir: Diallo Furor's About Race,"[1] "Tales of Horrors in Serb Army Camp," "Russia's Warning Against Invasion," "U.S. Hits Iraqi Missile Sites."

And even students who exhibit a stoic determination can paint rather dismal pictures in their narratives of self-reliance:

Where will I be in the next couple of decades? What will become of me in the future? Will I be a piece of shit on the sidewalk that people laugh at as they walk by, or will I be a successful million-aire with mad loot to spare? It is depressing to think about what will happen in the future. You always think of the great things that could happen in the future, but no one ever thinks of the bad stuff in your future. No one grows up thinking that they will become a homeless alcoholic, but it does happen to some unfortunate people, that could be you in twenty years. . . . Thinking like this gets me scared of the future and makes me want to stay 18 forever. I am happy or at least content with this world and I do not want it to change because of the fear of the bad stuff that could happen to myself.

I am scared of what is to come in my future. This fear is due to the uncertainty of the future. Whatever does come to my plate will be hit and hit hard. I will not crawl up and die.

RONNIE

Did I influence my students? Of course I did; simply by having them read excerpts from bleak futurist scenarios, I introduced ideas that many of them had never considered before. On the other hand, the same is true for more positive information—the synopses in the Worldwatch Institute's annual publication of *Vital Signs: The Environmental Trends That Are Shaping Our Future* (Brown et al.) contain both disturbing and promising trends. In the information I make accessible to students during this sequence, I try to keep an even balance between hopeful and pessimistic forecasts. Besides, while it is obvious that I personally put more stock in many of the negative scenarios than the positive ones—mainly because those who present the gloomier scenarios seem to me to have conducted more exhaustive research—the last thing I wish to do is promote cynicism and despair among my students, let alone within myself. Part of me cannot take seriously the kinds of grim futures that Eugene Linden paints, where memories of plagues and continued risk of viral contamination have turned Manhattan in 2050 into a sanitized mall-like infrastructure where sterilization procedures and containment protocols have eliminated much of human contact. Such renderings smack too much of what David Matlin calls the "sensuality" of apocalyptic thinking, the seductiveness of which must never be fully trusted. But neither can I begin to accept the optimistic forecast that Peter Schwartz gives of a world in 2005, which, despite his status as "one of the world's leading futurists," reveals (at least in his book *The Art of the Long View*) a glaring ignorance of ecological economics. The truth is, I'm not exactly sure what to do with these scenarios, other than continue reflecting upon the lot of them, observing the degree to which they continue to influence my own pedagogical and curricular decisions.

Are these views the norm among first-year students in colleges across the country? Or is this just a New York City or Long Island thing? I'm not sure. In many respects I'm sure my students are no different from so many others living in urban and densely suburban areas: they work long hours outside of class, spend a lot of their nights going out to clubs, and are preoccupied with fashion. Sometimes they're enthusiastic in class, and sometimes they doze off. Sometimes they talk with considerable animation during class and in one-on-one conferences, and sometimes they appear bored out of their minds. They seem pretty much like the students one would expect at any large, metropolitan university with a diverse student body coming from urban and suburban homes. Certainly the prevalence of pessimistic scenarios is not surprising, given how many of them live in undesirable or boring neighborhoods, or whose first- and secondhand experiences with work are largely negative. I would not be surprised if, were this same assignment sequence given to students of other economic means and living in different kinds of neighborhoods, the number of hopeful scenarios would increase; I wouldn't be surprised if there was a correlation between financial independence and rosy forecasts. But somehow I have a hunch that even among more affluent students we might find signs of similar worries and reservations. If my students' views of the future are in any way representative of what other college students think, then this fear, this cynicism, this frustration, runs like an invisible current beneath whatever curricula we impose on our students. How irrelevant and disconnected our professional preoccupations with literacy, outcomes assessment, and core requirements must seem to a student body that harbors, consciously and unconsciously, so many reservations about the next several decades.

In the 1974 publication *Creating the Future: A Guide to Living and Working for Social Change*, the authors Charles R. Beitz and Michael Washburn write that "we all have an obligation, in our personal lives and in our social-political lives, to invent a little bit of what we want to see exist in the future" (406). Theirs was a primer for the "social visionary," a breed of thinker they found lacking in the culture at large.

> The social critic, philosopher, and visionary activist is the most potent social change force we can imagine. Yet few, if any, people in a generation combine in themselves all these capacities. . . . Our visions of world community are by and large pitifully juvenile, generally coming down to a single slender principle, "All right, brothers and sisters, love one another."
>
> This, then, is a plea. If you are somehow inclined to be a planner, a philosopher, a visionary, a poet, see if the idea of global society is not worthy of your prolonged creative energy. (408)

One finds a similar plea in Timothy Beatley and Kristy Manning's more recent *The Ecology of Place: Planning for Environment, Economy, and Community*. The authors argue that making sustainable places

> is about carrying on a sustained dialogue about how the community wants to grow and evolve, what it wants to look like in the future, what will likely be the results if no changes in practice and policy are made, how it will address its moral obligations (for example, to future residents and generations), and so on. One of the early steps in getting started, then, is to begin to structure a community dialogue about the future and to identify mechanisms, procedures, processes, tools, and techniques for carrying out such a dialogue. (205)

Beatley and Manning write of communities in Portland, Chattanooga, and Pasadena where citizens collaborated on vision statements and growth resolutions that reflected their desires and concerns for the future of the community, sometimes engaging in planning charrettes, "one- or two-day, intensive participation exercises often focused on the design and development of a particular site or area" (206–7).

Future scenarios are inevitably vision statements. Having students read narratives and arguments that point to various future scenarios might make them more aware of the complex forces at work in shaping their lives, and of their involvement in the perpetuation and resistance of such forces. A roomful of students playing the game of futurist, arguing with one another about where they see things headed, becomes a conversation fueled by idealism and cynicism, hope and fear, optimism and pessimism. It can be the beginnings of a sustained dialogue the likes of which I doubt exists in many homes or classrooms—and certainly not in the popular media. Unfortunately there is currently little context for such discussions in our curricula. Academic committees spend a great deal of time debating the objectives and rationales implicit in their mission statements, fine-tuning and revising the language therein, and then discussing the degree to which their institutions' curricula reflect that mission. But in the process we overlook our students' own vision statements about the confusing futures they expect for themselves. We cannot foster sustainability-based thinking within our classes, our research, and our curricula unless we begin actively imagining likely future scenarios that are informed by available facts, and then collectively assessing, and ultimately acting upon, the implications of such scenarios.

CHAPTER SIX

Reconstructive Design

The future is not easy to contemplate, but it is, obviously, where we are going to spend the rest of our lives, and if those lives are to be anything more than the nasty, brutish, and short passages we are experiencing at the close of the twentieth century, it has to be an ecological future.

KIRKPATRICK SALE, "The Columbian
Legacy and the Ecosterian Response"

That Hollow, Falling Feeling

In *The Rise and Fall of English: Reconstructing English as a Discipline* Robert Scholes asks,

> If the culture itself is sick, how should we prepare students to live in it and maintain a state of ethical health? How, that is, can English studies help students become fit for life in a world like ours? (19–20)

Scholes continues this line of questioning by quoting Jacques Derrida:

> "We might perhaps ask ourselves: where are we? And who are we in the university where apparently we are? *What* do we represent? *Whom* do we represent? Are we responsible? For what and to whom?" (44)

And in the opening pages of Michael Blitz and C. Mark Hurlbert's *Letters for the Living: Teaching Writing in a Violent Age*, similar questions nearly assault us with their urgency and frustration:

If educators everywhere are teaching and conducting research toward the understanding and remaking of culture and society, why are our culture and society so chronically unhealthy? Why are our children inheriting a desperately polluted planet, an outrageously unbalanced global economy, dramatically intensified racism, sexism, homophobia, urban squalor, a booming prison industry, mass media aimed at dulling preadolescent intellects, elected officials who have decided that it is more cost effective to allow a rise in poverty and homelessness than to make a commitment to schools and training and long-range socioeconomic justice? What are the crucial differences between what we think we are doing in higher education and what we really are and are not doing? Are we creating anything of value? Value to whom? Do we make things? For whom? Do we make things happen? Do we prevent things from happening? Do we know what we're doing? (3)

Scholes's resuscitative response to what he calls our "hollow, falling" field of English (18) is to "reconstruct English" as a bona fide discipline grounded in textuality and methodology, where the English teacher's responsibility is to get students to "read, interpret, and criticize texts in a wide range of modes, genres, and media" (84). What intrigues me more than Scholes's idea of dividing English studies curricula into three methodological zones (grammar, dialectic, rhetoric) is the way he interprets the seriousness of our historical moment, and the English educator's obligation to respond. Scholes calls for teachers to help students "develop better intellectual equipment for the lives they are actually living and will continue to live" (142), and he concludes that

> Now, more than ever, the graduates of our schools and colleges will live in worlds different from those in which they were born and went to school. A discipline called English must help them prepare for unknown conditions. The best preparation we can give our students will be the highest level of competence as readers and writers, producers and consumers of the various texts they will encounter. (154)

Yet if our graduates continue to be producers and consumers at current levels of production and consumption, those future worlds will not be so unknown or mysterious after all. So long as we continue on our current paths of accelerated unsustainable growth, those futures can only get worse. Thus, concurrent with meeting Scholes's call for "a canon of concepts, precepts, and practices rather than a canon of texts" (120), we need also to lay the foundation for a pedagogical ethic that promotes an awareness of and striving for sustainability.

Annette Kolodny nods in this direction in *Failing the Future: A Dean Looks at Higher Education in the Twenty-First Century*, when she urges reform in higher education with the aim of having academics redefine themselves "as responsible partners in a healthy and sustainable habitat" (44). Kolodny writes that her purpose "is to suggest ways of surviving the presently bumpy road in such a manner as to prepare ourselves for what lies ahead" (44), though her project never actually gets around to exploring sustainability. Still, what remains striking about these writers' statements is the degree to which terms like "survival," "health," and "uncertain futures" are now directly related to the mission of higher education, and specifically to the mission of English studies.[1]

I agree with Scholes's and Kolodny's claims that, as educators, whether in English studies or elsewhere, we have an obligation to help our students develop the ability to maintain ethical health in a sick culture while anticipating and surviving an uncertain future. My own response is not to call for a radical transformation of English departments into, say, the triad that Scholes envisions, or to call for any other imposed methodological restructuring. While one can imagine a department successfully orchestrated around the rubrics of grammar, dialectic, and rhetoric, one can just as easily imagine lively departments alternatively designed in response to different criteria growing out of the local needs and concerns of their specific institutions and student bodies. My own initial attempts at imagining a pedagogical ethic of sustainability have been fairly simple, even anticlimactic. Until new opportunities arise that allow more radical restructuring of departmental and core curricula around themes relating to sustainability, my efforts have focused on course design and on contemplating alternative approaches to imagining curricula. One of my courses is presented in Appendix B. In this concluding chapter, I will focus on two design strategies I consider necessary for advancing a sustainability-focused theory of education. The first strategy—seeking a more symbiotic balance between the concepts of specialization and generalization—has been widely discussed but is worth revisiting in the context of sustainability. The second strategy involves mining the work of scholars in a range of fields (I have tended to focus on artists, architects, planners, and environmental educators) for theories and design solutions that might lead us to frame new approaches to course and curriculum design with sustainability in mind. Though ultimately it matters less what we call our methodologies than what they actually accomplish, I have chosen, for what it's worth, to assemble these gestures under the label "reconstructivist design," certainly less a distinct theory than a pastiche of related impulses.

Beyond the Specialist/Generalist Polarity

By far the biggest cliché to have come out of environmentalism is the credo "think globally, act locally," and the main problem with this dictum is not that it should be "think locally, act locally," as Wendell Berry argues—the World Wide Web, the Global Positioning System, instantaneous international news reportage, and other global technologies have all irreversibly brought the idea of the global, no matter how idiosyncratically engineered, into our psychic landscapes. Rather, the flaw rests in the fact that the injunction to "think globally, act locally" proposes a false gap between cognition and behavior. Instead of pretending that thought and action occur in separate realms, we need to explore the relationship *between* the "local" and the "global"—or perhaps, as New Urbanist planners Andres Duany, Elizabeth Plater-Zyberk, and Jeff Speck (whose work will be touched on below) write, to "think globally, act locally, but plan regionally" (225). In other words, to bridge the ends of this spectrum not by exaggerating the individual, nor by remaining preoccupied with "universal" concerns, but by emphasizing collaboration and cooperation between adjoining communities.

The pitfalls of the global/local split are also exhibited in the ongoing academic debate between specialization and generalization. Academics, if they are to approach sustainability seriously, must think on some level as holists, since sustainability is inherently a cross-disciplinary idea. (This has been one of the central

quarrels that ecological economists have with "regular" economists: that to fully grasp economic theory one must move beyond the realm of classical economics and develop an
understanding of such concerns as watersheds, carrying capacity, environmental ethics, steady-state economies, entropy, and
thermodynamics.) On the other hand, one can hardly expect academic culture, which from its inception has partitioned intellectual inquiry into autonomous departments and fields, to simply
reject the intrinsic culture of specialization that serves as its very
institutional code. Ultimately the only response is to value the
fruits of both the expert and the generalist, emphasizing the
strengths of each without belittling or demonizing the other.
Having said that, the first step toward a more synthetic balance
between these two perspectives is to acknowledge the academy's
failure to take holism seriously, as well as its continued reinforce-
ment of the cult of specialization. The academy suffers from an
overemphasis on specialization while stigmatizing generalists,
which is obvious in the degree to which specialists teaching up-
per-level and graduate courses are granted more prestige, money,
time, and power than are generalists hired to teach introductory-
level core courses. In what follows, I juxtapose critiques of specialization by environmentally oriented writers with arguments
by educators who are critical of the academy's privileging of specialization at the expense of more panoramic inquiry.

Gene Youngblood's claim that "one can no longer specialize
in a single discipline and hope truthfully to express a clear picture of its relationships in the environment" (41) embodies the
distrust that ecologically grounded writers have felt toward specialization. R. Buckminster Fuller, who wrote the introduction
to Youngblood's 1970 publication of *Expanded Cinema*, wrote
elsewhere in that same year:

> I find it surprising that society thinks of specialization as logi-
> cal, necessary, desirable, if not inevitable. I observe that when
> nature wants to make a specialist she's very good at it, whereas
> she seems to have designed man to be a very generally adapt-
> able creature—by far the most adaptable creature we know
> of. If nature had wanted man to be a specialist, I am sure she
> would have grown him with one eye and a microscope on it.
> She has designed no such creatures. I observe that every child

demonstrates a comprehensive curiosity. Children are interested in everything and are forever embarrassing their specialized parents by the wholeness of their interests. Children demonstrate right from the beginning that their genes are organized to help them apprehend, comprehend, coordinate, and employ—in all directions. . . .

. . . [But] we got all specialized, with everybody minding his own business—and now nobody can mind everybody else's business in order to put things together. That's where we are right now. We're all dressed up with enormous capability and absolutely no ability to coordinate the affairs of the earth. (15–16, 52)

Seven years later Wendell Berry presented this condemnation of specialization:

The disease of modern culture is specialization. . . .

The first, and best known, hazard of the specialist system is that it produces specialists—people who are elaborately and expensively trained to do one thing. We get into absurdity very quickly here. There are, for instance, educators who have nothing to teach, communicators who have nothing to say, medical doctors skilled at expensive cures for diseases that they have no skill, and no interest, in preventing. More common, and more damaging, are the inventors, manufacturers, and salesmen of devices who have no concern for the possible effects of those devices. Specialization is thus seen to be a way of institutionalizing, justifying, and paying highly for a calamitous disintegration and scattering-out of the various functions of character: workmanship, care, conscience, responsibility.

Even worse, a system of specialization requires the abdication to specialists of various competencies and responsibilities that were once personal and universal. Thus, the average—one is tempted to say, the ideal—American citizen now consigns the problem of food production to agriculturalists and "agribusinessmen," the problems of health to doctors and sanitation experts, the problems of education to school teachers and educators, the problems of conservation to conservationists, and so on. This supposedly fortunate citizen is therefore left with only two concerns: making money and entertaining himself. He earns money, typically, as a specialist, working an eight-hour day at a job for the quality or consequences of which somebody else—or, perhaps more typically, nobody else—will be responsible. And not surprisingly, since he can do so little else for himself, he is even unable to entertain himself, for there exists an enormous industry of exorbitantly expensive specialists whose purpose is to entertain him. . . .

It is rarely considered that this average citizen is anxious because he ought to be—because he still has some gumption that he has not yet given up in deference to the experts. He ought to be anxious, because he is helpless. That he is dependent upon so many specialists, the beneficiary of so much expert help, can only mean that he is a captive, a potential victim. If he lives by the competence of so many other people, then he lives also by their indulgence; his own will and his own reasons to live are made subordinate to the mere tolerance of everybody else. He has one chance to live what he conceives to be his life: his own small specialty within a delicate, tense, everywhere-strained system of specialties.

. . . The specialist system fails from a personal point of view because a person who can do only one thing can do virtually nothing for himself. In living in the world by his own will and skill, the stupidest peasant or tribesman is more competent than the most intelligent worker or technician or intellectual in a society of specialists. (19–21)

Berry's attack—leveled as much at those who would permit themselves to be victims of specialization as at the specialists themselves—anticipates James Goldsmith's argument two decades later against a socially and environmentally destructive global economy:

We must . . . reject the concept of specialization. We need the contrary, a diversified economy, for only such an economy will allow our populations to participate fully in our society. Specialization inevitably leads to chronic unemployment and to lower wages. . . . In addition to the large corporations, we need a society based on a multitude of small and medium-sized businesses and crafts workers covering a wide range of activities, and we need a decentralized economy. Everything must be done to return life and vigor to the small towns and villages throughout our nations. (179)

Shifting to critiques of academic specialization, we find John Dewey faulting what he perceived to be the failure of elementary schools to bridge their curricula with the student's local experience: "From the standpoint of the child, the great waste in the school comes from his inability to utilize the experiences he gets outside the school in any complete and free way within the school itself; while, on the other hand, he is unable to apply in daily life what he is learning at school. That is the isolation of the school— its isolation from life. When the child gets into the schoolroom he has to put out of his mind a large part of the ideas, interests, and activities that predominate in his home and neighborhood" (75). More recently, New York City public school teacher John Taylor Gatto has attacked the curricula of compulsory public education for being arbitrarily designed by educators in isolation, resulting in chaos and confusion:

> Even in the best schools a close examination of curriculum and its sequences turns up a lack of coherence, full of internal contradictions. Fortunately the children have no words to define the panic and anger they feel at constant violations of natural order and sequence fobbed off on them as quality in education. . . . Confusion is thrust upon kids by too many strange adults, each working alone with only the thinnest relationship with each other, pretending, for the most part, to an expertise they do not possess. (2–3)

And echoing Berry's definition of specialization as a sickness, Mary C. Savage characterizes "academentia" as an academic "disease" brought on in part by a

> long period of training [that] produces the delusion that the disciplines are intellectually powerful as a result of their specialization. Actually, the reverse is true. Separation produces a naive and nonreflective cleric[al]ism that may be irreversible. . . . Unfortunately, advancement in the academy depends more on the discipline than on service to the institution where one works, and certainly much more than it does on service to the wider civic community of which one is part. (14, 15)

Savage argues that those at the top of academic hierarchies tend to work in "pure" disciplinary realms like "'hard' science and literary theory," perpetuating a patriarchal system where teachers concerned with "nourishing the young and preparing them for their places in society" occupy the lower rungs of the hierarchical ladder (15). Pushing her metaphor further, Savage celebrates writing teachers who unabashedly "carry their impurity like a badge" (15), and whose "vision of human dignity and . . . hope that people, including professionals and intellectuals, can act in solidarity with the marginalized to transform society"—practicing what she calls "neighborliness"—offers an antidote to academentia (17).

Continuing in this direction, Michael S. Gazzaniga, in "How to Change the University," offers a radical plan for redesigning faculty neighborhoods:

> The modern university is partitioned along academic lines that no longer truly reflect today's intellectual life. These academic groupings are now just categories that accountants and business managers use to build a budget. . . . It is time to reorganize the whole university, and not by doing it piecemeal. My suggestion is that the university administration announce to its faculty that while continuing to function as they are for 1 year, they are free to reorganize themselves in any way they see fit, planning new curricula, graduate programs, special emphasis groups, and all the rest. For instance, faculty from different departments could combine to teach about an area, such as the mind. They would request space for their new venture and spell out the teaching load they would share. At the end of the year, the new organization of the university should reflect the new configurations of the academic world. After regrouping, people would be better prepared for the intellectual work of the next century. (237)

These critiques of specialization are not without their flaws. Some of them exaggerate or inflate the problem of specialization in their demonization of the specialist as a self-absorbed, naïve, and even amoral villain. Specialization is a degree of intensity, less an indication of any measurable quality than a gauge of time spent in specific pursuits. R. Buckminster Fuller's "Dymaxion" principles and geodesic domes owe much to his time spent as a specialist in architecture and engineering; Wendell Berry's essays reveal him to be something of an expert on agriculture; and even Mary Savage, in her romanticization of the noble practitioner devoting more of his or her time to assisting undergraduates than to writing literary theory, is herself a publishing academic, and one, we might speculate, who is not beyond characterizing herself as a specialist when such labeling helps one advance to tenure (and, certainly, those academics best suited to make arguments against specialization are those who enjoy the job security that comes from fully participating in the academic culture that privileges the role of the specialist).

But such caveats are obvious and, ultimately, less important than the impetus beneath any hyperbole. The problem lies not with specialization per se; it is, rather, a problem of context and relevance: What is the purpose of "specialized" information? What is its relationship to other forms of information residing "outside" the boundaries of that particular specialty? Don Byrd helps here, as he recasts the dichotomy in terms of common and disciplined knowledge:

> The common knowledge might be properly contrasted to disciplined knowledge. The domain of the common knowledge has no preexistence. It comes into being only when contingent beings come into relationship. The common knowledge leads not to certainty of mind but to confidence of action. It consists not of propositions to be communicated from A to B but of orientations in fields of meaning, measures by the scales in which humans share not a perspective or a belief but a world that opens to this or that particular vantage and practice. (23)

In the end the problem with academic specialization is the implicit xenophobia found in sites of disciplined knowledge making. The problem lies not in the making of specialized or disciplined knowledge, but in the academic culture that privileges disciplined knowledge at the cost of the common. Our concern now is one of synthesis and bridging: how to create intellectual and social environments where information spillage and exchange might lead toward enlightenment and amelioration of existing problems. To quote Duany, Plater-Zyberk, and Speck, the challenge now is to build community by "creat[ing] expert generalists" (243).

The Suburbanization of Curricula

Disciplined knowledge as characterized by Byrd leads to what environmental educator David Orr calls the creation of boxed thinkers:

The great ecological issues of our time have to do in one way or another with our failure to see things in their entirety. That failure occurs when minds are taught to think in boxes and not taught to transcend those boxes or to question overly much how they fit with other boxes. We educate lots of in-the-box thinkers who perform within their various specialties rather like a dog kept in the yard by an electronic barrier. And there is a connection between knowledge organized in boxes, minds that stay in those boxes, and degraded ecologies and global imbalances. (*Earth in Mind* 94–95)

Such scholar-in-the-box thinking has led to the suburbanization of curricula. Suburban sprawl fails to satisfy largely because it is designed by market experts, traffic engineers, homebuilders, fire chiefs, and modernist architects—all specialists within their realms who not only work independently of one another but who also fail to design in accordance with the local needs of the residents or in conjunction with the unique characteristics of the local environment: "The term *homebuilder* describes the house as a product that exists independent of its context. This approach would be appropriate if houses floated freely in space, or in some other environment where actual interaction between neighbors was neither possible nor desired. But houses are not meant to exist in isolation, so to think of the individual house as the ultimate outcome of the builder's craft robs that craft of its broader significance" (Duany, Plater-Zyberk, and Speck 110–11). Something similar happens when faculty are expected to design courses but not curricula. I don't want to push this analogy too far; certainly the diversity of college courses today is fundamentally more enticing than the interiors of suburban dwellings. But there are still relatively few opportunities for faculty to collaborate with colleagues in other disciplines to design new courses.

Even where a steady rise in "interdisciplinary" courses and programs has helped make the gated enclaves of traditional departments less balkanized, such efforts at collaboration and hybridization are overshadowed by that final academic rite of passage, the dissertation ritual. In what is still too often an exercise in fetishization, graduate students are expected to demonstrate a specialist's expertise by preparing a document written for what usually amounts to an audience of fewer than five. The frustration that graduate students typically experience while manufacturing this document is commonly attributed to the perils of negotiating the usual committee politics, but the angst must also have something to do with a system that rewards mandatory connoisseurship which too often has little or no local social relevance. One of the themes in Richard Powers's novel *The Gold Bug Variations* is an implicit comparison between the complex simplicity of the genetic code that unites all living beings and the specialist's pursuit of information detached from contemporary relevance, represented in a doctoral candidate's moral quandary that prevents him from completing a dissertation he considers too removed from the sociopolitical concerns of his time: "the whole, colossal impertinence of studying Art History—the delicate, gessoed, tempera conflagration—in a world setting *itself* on fire" (68).

There are plenty of reasons to specialize in art history of course, even if the world around one is going down in flames. Again, the problem has nothing to do with specialization per se or with the pursuit of disciplinary knowledge. Like anyone else, teachers and scholars have a right, an obligation even, to go wherever their intellectual itches take them, and to pursue them to whatever obsessive degree. Specialization happens for legitimate reasons. It feels good to know quite a bit within a particular realm; the collector, the fetishist, the medical specialist, the craftsperson, and the academic all understand the erotics of concentration. The problem arises when sustained concentration eclipses wide-angle vision. A kind of multiple, simultaneous focusing is in order: to train the eye toward one's chosen realms of study while not losing sight of the degree to which one is embedded within other informational flows.

What is needed is something like mosaic theory applied to our construction of courses and curricula. If I understand it correctly, mosaic theory attempts to describe how arthropods with compound eyes see. Bees see more than one way. The bee eye discriminates differently depending upon its online (in-flight) location and in accordance with its aim: "The visual processing itself depends on the activity at the time, i.e., *walking, flying, fixating,* or *landing*" (Horridge 877). In some cases, a two-dimensional-pattern vision is used as the bee hones in on a target, distinguishing it by edge patterns. At other times the bee measures the range of landmarks in three dimensions. Researchers are now studying the mechanisms by which insects actively see in flight by altering their head movements in response to their environments (reconfiguring their vision depending upon their position) so that they can be written into software for robot vision.

Conceptualizing courses and curricula should be an exercise in cross-pollination. It has become necessary to think like bees see, missing neither the forest nor the trees. As educators, we need to strive, as Robert Costanza argues, for synthesis between specialization and "transdisciplinary problem solving" (95). But if, "in the future, problem solving will become the primary function of academics, occurring through multiple activities, not just research publications," as Costanza anticipates (100), current academic culture, with its "social traps" that insist on faculty, especially junior faculty, remaining rooted in specialized discourse communities measured by one's publications in peer-reviewed journals, will not be the place for such a "new transdisciplinary, intellectual Renaissance" (105). Because "young faculty cannot afford to stray from narrow disciplinary boundaries" (100), Costanza calls for the creation of transdisciplinary studies and colleges coexisting with and yet also outside traditional university programs. But as much as I would enjoy teaching in such an environment, the proposal can seem as pointless as Gazzaniga's call above for radical academic reorganization, especially in an era where faculty positions are increasingly being outsourced to adjuncts and TAs.

And so while I argue that much of what educators and their institutions need to be doing is collaboratively examining ways in which their curricula might not only honor the disciplinary needs of their departments but also work toward improving the daily environments in which our students live and work, I also know that opportunities for such horizontal, transdisciplinary dialogue and brainstorming are rare in academic environments where faculty are already overburdened by teaching loads and a paucity of full-time colleagues. However, as difficult as it might be to actively invent and implement a curriculum of sustainability that transcends disciplinary lines, each of us can at least construct our own working pedagogical stances that seek to promote sustainability within our courses and our research. Toward this end I have found myself prospecting among writings by artists, architects, planners, and environmental educators for metaphors and strategies that might inform my own sense of course design; the next two sections invoke some of these influences.

From Site-Seers to Landing Sites

In her edited collection *Architecture as a Translation of Music*, Elizabeth Martin refers to a liminal zone between disciplines, a zone that is the site of what she calls the "*y*-condition."

> Let's say . . . that there exists a definable membrane through which meaning can move when translating from one discipline to another. What I mean by membrane is a thin, pliable layer that connects two things and is, in this case, the middle position of music + architecture. The membrane is similar perhaps to the role of a semi-tone or semi-vowel in the study of phonetics. A semi-tone is a transitional sound heard during articulation link- ing two phonemically contiguous sounds, like the *y* sound often heard between the *i* and the *e* of quiet. I am suggesting that some- thing similar occurs, a *y*-condition, in the middle position of music + architecture when translating one to the other. (16)

This *y*-condition might be better understood not as translation but as transformation. The issue is not so much to move mean- ing from one site to another, converting it in the process, but to explore how such migration forces us to rethink those sites and our relationship to them. The essays in Martin's collection are less about how music and architecture announce themselves within each other than they are about how both categories change as a result of such boundary spillage. Thus *y*-condition thinking urges us to leave behind what once appeared to be autonomous disciplines and direct our attention toward evolving hybrids. Be- cause I consider curriculum to be the educator's artspace, and since sustainability is in many ways a design problem, my own version of a *y*-realm heuristic draws me to the theories and prac- tices of artist and writer Robert Smithson, architects Paulo Soleri and Lucien Kroll, New Urbanist designers Duany, Plater-Zyberk, and Speck, and the poet/artist/architect team of Arakawa and Madeline Gins—all constructivist thinkers whose work presents useful metaphors for educators interested in sustainability.

The work of the artist Robert Smithson lies within Martin's *y*-spectrum, and not just because his work involves such a coexistence of writing, drawings, sculptures, rocks, and earthworks, although this would be enough to mark him as an intermediary thinker. Much of Smithson's work forces us to become more conscious of our situatedness between, within, and outside art and place. Fascinated by both the sterile nonspaces of museum galleries as well as the fringe spaces of ignored and forgotten landscapes throughout suburban and rural wastelands, Smithson chose to use these two spatial arenas as bookends between which a viewer contemplates his or her own relationship to the artwork and its referent. One of Smithson's projects was the "non-site." He would pick a site—something antipicturesque, like a mineral dump—from which he would collect rocks and other debris, cart them back to the museum space, and exhibit the materials in bins, which then become the "non-sites." In the title of one of his essays, Smithson coins the term "site-seer" (340), and although he doesn't define this term anywhere in his writings, we might read it as referring not only to "earth artists" like himself but also to the contemplator of such works. Smithson's dialectic between site and non-site forces the viewer to locate him- or herself in a *y*-realm as a reflective agent at the nexus between the abstract, three-dimensional "map" of the non-site, and the remote site itself, an inaccessible place somewhere out there on the "unfocused fringe" (249).

Something similar is happening when I read my students' narratives about their own sites—their neighborhoods, workplaces, and imagined future landscapes. The sites they write about are real, even though I have access to them only via the non-sites of their writings and photographs. And while they are writing in response to assignments emanating from a composition course, and thus working "within" a disciplinary realm, to some extent their testimonies bring themselves, and me, closer to some interdisciplinary membrane. We become site-seers, contemplating our relationship to the sites we live in (homes and neighborhoods), the non-sites we also work in (classrooms and workplaces, which can be like non-sites in that students' conversations and photographs refer to homes unseen by others), and the imaginal sites we envision for our future selves, families, and communities. Part of the reason that I have chosen to make this book more testimony than pedagogy, spending more time quoting students than reflecting upon my own classroom dynamic, is to emphasize that our students' stories are as pedagogical as anything we can construct. Their testimonials about neighborhoods bring the status of their homes into the classroom, their accounts of workpain remind us of the workaday world surrounding the classroom, and their narratives about possible futures speak volumes about their own states of mind, and, implicitly, the role of the academy in fostering or challenging those states of mind.

Paoli Soleri's ongoing project is a fusion of architecture and ecology into what he calls "arcology." Soleri envisions a sustainable architecture that is three-dimensional: not sprawling outward horizontally, or rising upward vertically, but evolving in both directions organically, simultaneously. As Soleri writes:

> The problem is the present design of cities only a few stories high, stretching outward in unwieldy sprawl for miles. As a result of their sprawl they literally transform the earth, turn farms into parking lots and waste enormous amounts of time and energy transporting people, goods and services over their expanses. The alternative is urban implosion rather than explosion. In nature, as an organism evolves it increases in complexity and it also becomes a more compact or miniaturized system. Similarly a city should function as a living system. It must follow the same process of complexification and miniaturization to become a more lively container for the social, cultural and spiritual evolution of humankind. The central concept around which these developments revolve is that of arcology—architecture and ecology as one integral process. Arcology is capable, at least theoretically, of demonstrating positive response to the many problems of urban civilization, those of population, pollution, energy and natural resource depletion, food scarcity and quality of life. Arcology is the methodology that recognizes the necessity of the radical reorganization of the sprawling urban landscape into dense, integrated, three-dimensional cities. *(Arcosanti 1997 Construction Workshops)*

Soleri's work is a logical extension of twentieth-century modernist artists' attempts to imagine and refer to fourth- and n-dimensional geometries within their work (Linda Dalrymple Henderson). Soleri, along with a constantly changing group of volunteers and students, has been building a prototype of the arcological city (Arcosanti) on a mesa in central Arizona since 1970.

A year before construction began on Arcosanti, the Catholic University of Louvain, Belgium, began plans to build the University's medical school in Brussels. Students insisted on a campus architecture woven into the landscape of the local neighborhood. Although the University rejected the students' proposal that community residents play a role in designing the campus, the students were allowed to choose the architect to build the University. They chose Lucien Kroll, known for his organic, collaborative, antihierarchical approach to design. Kroll created a campus where students, faculty, and administrators were consulted throughout the design process, and where engineers are encouraged to approach the project as artists (interpreting ducts and brick walls, for example, as functional sculptures). From the beginning, Kroll's intention was to provide a forum for a collective of voices as a means of resisting the authority of the institution.

Kroll was faced with the task of designing "forty thousand square meters for studios, twenty apartments, two hundred rooms for single students, two hundred rooms for grouped apartment living, a theater, a restaurant, a nursery school and kindergarten, places for worship, a post office, a metro station, and offices for student services and administration" (Dutton 180). His response was "to express the diversity of individuals and not the authority of institutions" (Kroll, qtd. in Dutton 182): masons, carpenters, landscape architects, and engineers were strongly encouraged to work as imaginative artisans, and dormitory spaces were made to be readjustable to suit a variety of student needs. As a means of integrating the campus Kroll put the medical school director's office right across the hall from the nursery school and near the graduate student apartments, so that whenever his window was open he would hear the daily sounds of the community's children and families (Dutton 182). When one obtains "the space and the means to allow the inhabitants to organize their own buildings," Kroll wrote, "a process of accretion starts, which grows like a biological organism" (Kroll 29–30).

Both Kroll and Soleri present, in different fashion, shared desires: to conceptualize architecture as an organic, collaborative, procedural event within a nonhierarchical framework. Soleri's fusion of architecture and ecology, and Kroll's interest in bringing together the needs and desires of all individuals involved with the campus (local residents, blue-collar workers, students, and administrators), both generate questions and opportunities for those involved with designing the "architecture" of curriculum: To what extent are students' needs and desires reflected in projected courses? How might curricula be designed so that links and bridges might be made between courses and disciplines—what are the opportunities for incorporating cross-disciplinary cohesiveness and relevance within the larger curricular design? What role does ecology play within the greater curricular landscape?

Interestingly, we find further links between both the exotic desert arcology of Arcosanti and the motley structure of Kroll's medical campus with the increasingly influential New Urbanist vision of designers like Duany, Plater-Zyberk, and Speck—architects and town planners who have successfully designed hundreds of community revitalization plans that reintroduce elements of the traditional town into suburbia. Duany, Plater-Zyberk, and Speck's *Suburban Nation: The Rise of Sprawl and the Decline of the American Dream* gives a lucid argument against the proliferation of suburban sprawl, arguing convincingly for community planning that privileges the cooperation and collaboration of all community members in the shared goal of creating cross-cultural, mixed-income neighborhoods designed for pedestrians as opposed to cars. The New Urbanists are not antisuburbia—the majority of Americans now live in suburbs, and to resist that tide would be as elitist as it would be futile—as much as they are in favor of a more civic-minded approach to suburban design. Their answer is disarmingly simple, even conservative: to incorporate features of the traditional town as much as possible within the construction of new suburban centers, replacing the housing subdivisions, shopping centers, industrial parks, isolated civic institutions, and excessive roadways that characterize suburban sprawl with neighborhood centers, mixed-use communities, street networks, narrow streets, and civic institutions woven throughout the community landscape. One of their overarching goals is to encourage readers to think more critically about their environments, and about how "form can dramatically affect the quality of our lives" (242), a concern we need to attend to more intensively throughout our curricula.

In response to what they perceive to be the tendency of contemporary architectural schools to retreat into solipsism—seduced by fashionable French theory while rejecting the needs of local communities—Duany, Plater-Zyberk, and Speck insist that design does indeed affect behavior and that "the design of new places should be modeled on old places that work": "Invention must be laid upon the solid foundation of precedent, as it is in medicine and jurisprudence" (240).

While Arakawa and Madeline Gins would agree that design affects behavior—or rather, they might revise this to say that design is behavior—it is hard to imagine two architects more opposed to the traditionalism of New Urbanism than this pair of artists/poets/philosophers/architects. And yet, albeit in a decidedly more avant-garde manner, Arakawa and Gins are equally concerned with the relationship between form and consciousness. I know of no other architects or artists working today who provide us with such a range of new lenses, maps, and exercises through which we might reconceptualize the interweaving of mind, body, and site. The ongoing Arakawa/Gins project leads toward what they call a "postutopian future" characterized by constant self-invention, where the self is no longer an entity separate from one's surroundings but an architectural body-person continually remade anew via its constantly shifting perceptions.

Arakawa and Gins belong in the company of thinkers like Gregory Bateson, Humberto R. Maturana, and Francisco J. Varela, who make us aware that selves are not isolatable phenomena but are ever in relationship with other circuits of living. It is less appropriate to say that we are selves moving through a world than it is to think of us as minds/environments bringing our worlds into being by virtue of our existence: "nothing of the body is strictly its own" (Arakawa and Gins, *Architecture* 106). What

Arakawa and Gins have done is apply this orientation to architecture. Instead of being bodies that move around in architectural domains, "human beings are born into architecture and are from then on conditioned by it" ("Architectural Body" 169). The problem is that the homes and cities and landscapes that we are born into and that wrap around us have the effect not only of deadening our senses but also of conditioning our actions so that much of one's daily movements occur as if one were on autopilot. Believing that "one is one's own artwork" (*Architecture* 121), and that one's "one" is never confined to one's body or mind but is a condition of perpetually changing interaction with immediate environments always in states of flux, Arakawa and Gins seek to decompartmentalize living:

> The living of a life will no longer be put into separate compartments. For example, one will not have to pick oneself up to go [to] a museum to find art. Instead, where one lives will be a plentiful-enough source of artworks. Dwellings will turn dwellers into self-knowing artworks, ones that will even be capable of freeing themselves from having to be artworks. Simply going to visit a neighbour will be as if one had become a member of a great dance troupe. (*Architecture* 121)

One of their heuristics is their concept of the "landing site." To recognize something is, for Arakawa and Gins, to have landed on it—the landing site is an "outpost of sentience" of any volume or dimension, and it is either perceptual, imaginal, or dimensionalizing (*Architectural Body*). To partially illustrate this—for the concept is more elaborate than I can summarize here—imagine sitting in a living room for one minute. Everything that your eyes take in, as well as everything you perceive through your senses as you sit in this room, can be considered a perceptual landing site. So too do all of the things that you know to be "there" but with which you are not perceptually in contact—a section of floor beneath your chair, for instance, or the adjoining room, or the "neighborhood" outside, and so on; these are all imaginal landing sites. And finally, consider your awareness of the formal limits of the architectural surroundings—say, the distance between your eyes and the ceiling, or the location of one's body in relation to all of those other sites. This mapping and contextualizing of sites constitutes, for Arakawa and Gins, yet another type of landing site, the "dimensionalizing" kind. Now imagine that, for the duration of that minute, conceptual threads connect your body to each of these illimitable landing sites (which are embedded within each other), accruing as time passes. Very quickly, a web of crisscrossing lines will have extended throughout (and beyond) the room, mapping your "architectural body" for the duration of that minute. What Arakawa and Gins want is for us to be conscious of the perpetually fluctuating webwork of landing sites that we construct all the time, whether we are walking through a room, sitting in our cars, or taking walks in a city. The implications hark back to Gregory Bateson's concept of the mind/environment, where mind and environment are two sides of the same coin, or to Maturana and Varela's notion of autopoiesis: To think of the self, or the body, as an autonomous entity separate from its "outside" environs is a bad habit that we need to break. Instead, we are mind/environments and architectural bodies, profoundly and dynamically woven into and conjoining world(s) that are ever in the process of becoming.

We tend to function as if we were independent entities moving arbitrarily through or remaining at rest within whatever environments happen to surround us. We take our surroundings so for granted that when we drive our cars we are not conscious of driving, and, in fact, we forget, for lengthy periods of time, that we are hurtling (or creeping) along in two-ton steel boxes. In walking down a hallway on campus or from the bedroom to the bathroom in our homes, we are so preoccupied with whatever is on our minds that we tend to be oblivious of our surroundings. Arakawa and Gins wish to jam the cognitive mechanisms by which we put ourselves on autopilot. It is precisely our surroundings, which were never separate from us in the first place, that they want to see registered as components of that mindfulness. To help facilitate this kind of awareness, they have designed structures such as the "modular labyrinth house," the "morphed twist house," the "rotation house," the "indeterminacy house," the "knotted passage house," and the "ubiquitous site house," all of which are homes intended to continually throw their inhabitants off balance (there are no level surfaces), constantly disrupting their expectations about how bodies are supposed to interact with their architectural surroundings. Consequently these architectural environments possess multiple horizons, are built on undulating, tilting surfaces, and have barriers and walls running through spaces (kitchen tables, bathtubs) where one wouldn't expect to find them.

From this brief description it might seem at first that Arakawa and Gins, with their desire to make us more aware of how conventional architecture conditions us by hypnotizing us into unawareness of our more expansive "architectural bodies," have simply imposed their own vision onto others. If the goal is to engage in a process of sustained self-invention, then ultimately even Arakawa and Gins's architectural visions would have to give way to other manifestations constructed by the dwellers. But they anticipate this as well, making it clear that their architectural experiments must always contain a built-in tentativeness. They refer to their designs as "tentative constructed plans":

> In some sense, the most vital part of any architectural work is the plan, after which comes only one form or another of entombment. Like it or not, whatever is constructed without a built-in— an insisted-upon—tentativeness entombs, sooner or later, now and forever. . . . Not wanting to entomb but rather to augment, we turn to the plan and hold onto it (fluidly-tentatively) for dear life. We wish to make every element at every stage in an architectural work behave not as a fixed and finished thing, but as if it were still only in plan form. Any construction can be made to act as a plan by building tentativeness into it. Built-in tentativeness sits at the opposite end of the spectrum from built-in obsolescence. . . . (*Architecture* 85)

It is in the spirit of this built-in tentativeness that I present my own thoughts on sustainability and its import for our work in composition, English studies, and beyond. Whether it comes in the form of designing new courses, building new sustainability-focused service-learning projects, or imagining a Sustainability Across the Curriculum movement, thinking sustainably is for me a combination of reeducation and invention: educating ourselves about the complex interrelationships between site and self, while experimenting with new approaches to teaching, to theorizing, and to conceptualizing our responsibilities as educators working with a threatened generation.

Few of us will visit Cordes Junction, Arizona, where Arcosanti sits at the end of three miles of dirt road on a mesa in the desert— a grand, if unrealized, idea in sustainable design [despite claims of being an "urban laboratory," fewer than two dozen people were living and working at the site when I visited). Nor should we hold our breath waiting to see our campuses redesigned in sync with something akin to Kroll's vision of a self-organizing, dehierarchized university where high-level administrative offices are located across the hall from day-care facilities—boards of trustees do not open their proceedings to their own students and faculty, let alone conduct them within earshot of infants. To experience Arakawa and Gins's structures, one has to travel to places like Yoro, Japan, or East Hampton on Long Island. Nevertheless these constructive architects bring us metaphors that can be used to help us fashion new theoretical frameworks for curricula of sustainability. Soleri and Kroll create a context for buildings and complexes that are innovatively designed by the community members who will live in them. Duany, Plater-Zyberk, and Speck, whose influence is certainly more pervasive than that of these other thinkers—their architectural firm has designed hundreds of new neighborhood plans—seek to make everyone an expert generalist committed to the art of community making. Arakawa and Gins, like Robert Smithson, make unconventional maps that invite us to reimagine the profoundly complex interrelatedness of mind, body, and place. All of these projects are examples of inventive mapmaking, of arcological cartographies that move us toward an understanding of art, architecture, and ecology as shared dimensions of the same project. Imagining curricula is an architectural endeavor. Thinking through the implications of a curriculum of sustainability requires designing connections between disciplines, the campus, student neighborhoods, local businesses, and the watershed. These visionary artists and architects provide us with tentative scaffolding from which to contemplate such construction.

A Reconstructivist Ethic

In closing, a tentative sketching of a "reconstructivist" ethic or theory is offered—certainly not as a definitive model for any readers to follow, but more as both map and testimony of the kinds of influences that have played a role in my own thinking. My use of the term *reconstructivism* is grounded in work by an amalgamation of Russian constructivist artists, collage and outsider artists, and Theodore Brameld's reconstructionist educational philosophy, all of which are briefly explained below, followed by a listing of the characteristics I associate with a reconstructivist ethic.

Constructivism

Early in the twentieth century, Russian artists discovered that sculpture could involve more than adding to or subtracting from mass. Instead of the carving of blocks of stone, wood, or casting metal, sculpture could be a method of drawing in space via the fastening, welding, and gluing of materials, thereby causing space to play a more integral role in the work. Constructivist art conjured space, inviting viewers to do the same. To walk around constructivist sculpture is to participate with that work, as one's movement through space alters the spatial relationships within and surrounding the piece. Imagine standing in front of Vladimir Tatlin's 1919 revolving tilted spiral tower of metal and glass (his intention, never realized, was for the sculpture to rise to 1300 feet)—or beneath Alexander Calder's sweeping mobile, suspended in the National Gallery, which, although propelled by a motor that turns the mobile continually in slow circles, reminds one of Francisco Varela's thought experiment of a delicate "mobile mobile" drifting along autonomously throughout a room, "an autonomous cognitive system: an active, self-updating collection of structures capable of informing (or shaping) its surrounding medium into a world through a history of structural coupling with it" (52). Or, from a different tack, imagine running a hand along Richard Serra's monolithic steel plates—so immense that there are only two ship-building foundries on the planet able to manufacture them—which bend and twist the space that flows around them, distorting your sense of balance as you walk next to them. As Frank Stella writes in *Working Space*, a series of essays decrying much of contemporary abstract art for being too flat and never breaking out of its "spatial cocoon"(43), "the aim of art is to create space—space that is not compromised by decoration or illustration, space in which the subjects of painting can live" (5). Constructivism was aware that space is less a field through which we move than a condition of our being. Space is us, making it happen.

Recycling

One of the more fecund outgrowths of constructivism has been the development of collage and found-object assemblages. War-ravaged Berlin turned Kurt Schwitters into a hunter-gatherer collecting textile scraps and cigarette wrappers as he developed a rhetoric of garbage picking.

> I felt myself freed and had to shout my jubilation out to the world. Out of parsimony I took whatever I found to do this, because we were now a poor country. One can even shout out through refuse, and this is what I did, nailing and gluing it together. I called it 'Merz,' it was a prayer about the victorious end of the war. . . . [E]verything had broken down in any case and new things had to be made out of fragments: and this is Merz. I painted, nailed, glued, composed poems, and experienced the world in Berlin. (Schmalenbach 96)[2]

For Schwitters, consciousness was liberation: the reuse of refuse, salvation through salvaging.

In an extension of this approach, Jess, a contemporary master of collage, explains that his chosen form is "all about rescuing or resurrecting image. . . . [P]asting up is a marvelous way to rescue so much and see the dialogue that takes place" (Auping 25). Jess's work gives us a new vocabulary for the rescue of images. There are his "paste-ups," which include constructivist-inspired ransom notes, reconstituted Sunday funnies, and the explosive collage murals that are probably his best-known work; his "translations," which are copies of found images repainted in densely textured and idiosyncratically colorized pigment; his "salvages," or reworkings of amateur paintings found in rummage sales and thrift stores; and finally his "assemblies," which are carefully balanced "impromptu sculptures—strange, homemade lamps, statues, or groups of found objects balanced on top of or inside each other" found throughout his home (Auping 52). These last constructions are sometimes unattached, with the components carefully balanced in an unfixed, temporary composition.

Recently, attention has fallen upon visionary and intuitive artists generally lumped together as "outsider artists," and within this constellation are a curious subset of outsider environmental artists—individuals who constructed, often over decades, ever-growing, mutating installations in their backyards. Where Schwitters made merzbaus—interior spaces cubistically recomposed—outsider environmental artists have fashioned their own merzbaus turned inside out, thus making private lots and hillsides into sacred labyrinths and shrines (Beardsley).

This fusion of constructivist and collectivist impulses—collectivist not in the sense of a hobbyist or aesthete but in the way that a child gathers rocks and rubber bands and seashell fragments—reinvigorate the banal concept of recycling. As Jess has described it: "Everything has to fit, not only in terms of form but also in its mythic, spiritual, or psychological presence. And just as importantly, it must all remain in flux so that no single story dominates" (qtd. in Auping 26).

Reconstructionism

For Theodore Brameld, writing in the 1950s, there were four categories of educational philosophies, and only the fourth made sense (74–79).

Much of what Brameld saw as constituting the traditional curriculum at the time was informed by what he called essentialism, which conservatively held that education existed to preserve the existing (mainstream, dominant) culture. Essentialism emphasized the teaching of the so-called basics—that is, the essentials, hence the name—as "the tried and tested heritage of skills, facts, and laws of knowledge that have come down to us through modern civilization" (74). Here the teacher's job was to serve as a conduit, passing along the world's knowledge to the waiting student, whose job was to absorb what he or she received. A recent manifestation of essentialist themes is found in E. D. Hirsch's campaign for cultural literacy, with his emphasis on the teacher's role in passing along the kind of information "every American needs to know."

Progressivism, the second educational philosophy in Brameld's quartet, pointed to a more liberal critique of essentialism, one that privileged problem solving through rational, scientific inquiry. In order for society to progress, schools had to be democratic institutions where "student-citizens," thinking "critically and responsibly" (75), refined existing knowledge. Unlike the essentialists, the progressivists viewed skills, facts, and laws not as static but as elements that required constant fine-tuning.

Perennialism, Brameld's third category, referred to a retrograde position that was impatient with both Enlightenment essentialism and pragmatic progressivism. Perennialists advocated an Aristotelian conviction in self-evident truths and irreducible axioms, leading to a fundamentalist, even medieval approach to education as a quasi-religious training for elites: "to train intellectual leaders so brilliantly endowed with the intuitive capacity to recognize first principles that we may, for the first time in centuries, be led out of the darkness that threatens to engulf mankind and into the light of a rationally determined order" (75).

Brameld's proposal was a reconstructionist philosophy of education that not so much rejected these three schools as it reconstituted elements from each into an argument for a more forward-looking, future-oriented curriculum. Like the essentialists, Brameld believed in such things as facts and appreciated the need for a functionalist perspective. Like the progressivists, he appreciated that "critical and responsible thinking" in a democratic society would mean different things to the different cultures within that society. And like the perennialists, he shared a sense that current society was inappropriate and in need of radical change. But because the essentialists sought to preserve an existing order, and the progressivists sought a more "gradual, evolutionary change," and the perennialists wanted to return to a (fictionalized) former age, what was called for was an emerging reconstructionist philosophy, one that "would solve our problems not by conserving, or modifying, or retreating, but by future-looking" (77). The reconstructionist "would build a new order of civilization, under genuinely *public* control, dedicated to the fulfillment of the natural values for which humanity has been struggling, consciously or unconsciously, for many centuries" (77).[3]

Reconstructivism

A reconstructive consciousness is an arachnid consciousness. It involves the art of cross-disciplinary, cross-temporal thinking—*reaching*—from a vantage point grounded in one's local conditions. Consider a spider, equipped with multiple eyes, engineered to spin different gauges of webbing, adept at extending itself into and thereby altering, and maintaining, its limited, local universe.

Reconstructivism extends the constructivist tradition in art where disparate materials are connected in ways that make us differently aware of our relationships to space and place. It learns from the hunter-gatherer aesthetic of assemblers, collagists, visionary recyclers.

Reconstructivism reaches backward and forward temporally, simultaneously, aware that to look behind is also to look ahead. Our present historical condition needs to be considered through the rise and fall of past indigenous cultures. At the same time we must become artists in scenario creation and (future) story building, imagining likely narratives of our own rising—and falling—contemporary culture as it spins its way onward.

Reconstructivism modifies Brameld's notion of reconstruction, concerning itself with choreographing immediate future conditions but through an ecologically informed awareness of sustainability and ecological economics.

Reconstructivism recognizes the fallacy of seeing ourselves as isolated individuals and finds it more sensible to think of us as fields of self (Livingston 138–39). We are cyborgs, "offspring of . . . technoscientific wombs" (Haraway 14), at once organic and technical. People don't exist in place but *are* place, intricately interwoven within local bioregional and technological terrain. Winifred Gallagher makes this clear in her reflections on pre-emies in a neonatal intensive care unit (101–15). Wendell Berry reiterates the interconnectedness of self and land in observing that "we and our country create one another, depend on one another, are literally part of one another; that our land passes in and out of our bodies just as our bodies pass in and out of our land; that as we and our land are part of one another, so all who are living as neighbors here, human and plant and animal, are part of one another, and so cannot possibly flourish alone" (22).

Reconstructivism works against pedagogies that promote irresponsible consumption, recognizing instead that being able to distinguish between needs and desires must be at the center of a contemporary curriculum.

> I can help them to learn standard English, telling them all along "upward mobility" is a crock. I'm not going to help them in the struggle for upward mobility. I will do all I can to help them get food, clothing, shelter, medical care, a job that won't destroy their soul, some leisure. But upward mobility simply means putting your neighbor's nose out of joint by wasting more than your neighbor can, and . . . no, . . . never. (Sledd 32, author's ellipses)

Reconstructivism recalls Eugene Youngblood's observation in 1970 that

> for some years now the activity of the artist in our society has been trending more toward the function of the ecologist: one who deals with environmental relationships. Ecology is defined as the totality or pattern of relations between organisms and their environment. Thus the act of creation for the new artist is not so much the invention of new objects as the revelation of previously unrecognized relationships between existing phenomena, both physical and metaphysical. So we find that ecology is art in the most fundamental and pragmatic sense, expanding our apprehension of reality. (346)

A reconstructivist seeks to revive Youngblood's hopefulness within the design of courses and curricula. As part of this project, a reconstructivist looks to the findings and designs of other educators engaged with sustainability. Marvin E. Rosenman, director of Project EASE (Educating Architects for a Sustainable Environment), organized several meetings in the mid-1990s for educators to determine how sustainability-based thinking might influence architectural schools. Among the suggestions they came up with were tying studies to more "real life problems"; developing "a fabric of many voices in studio instruction"; replacing the "architect as hero" model with "architect as team player"; "acknowledging the curriculum as one phase in life-long learning"; "promoting an interdisciplinary/collaborative approach among designers, sociologists, ecologists, etc."; and "developing a solid theoretical and research base" (Boyer and Mitgang 45).

Ted Trainer, after cataloging the many ways in which schools perpetuate an unsustainable culture (166–69), envisions an alternative educational philosophy designed and organized by the learners, where skills useful in one's neighborhood and home are emphasized, and where much of the learning would be voluntary, self-directed, hands-on, cooperative, and "informal or spontaneous, occurring during the process of growing up in the community or working with other members of it" (170).

C. A. Bowers's important yet largely ignored books—*Education, Cultural Myths, and the Ecological Crisis: Toward Deep Changes* and *Educating for an Ecologically Sustainable Culture: Rethinking Moral Education, Creativity, Intelligence, and Other Modern Orthodoxies*—remind those arguing for curricular reform that one cannot understand culture without also considering the natural systems within which culture happens: "Individuals [are nested] in the symbolic systems of culture, and cultures in the natural systems that are the source of the many forms of energy humans rely upon" (*Educating* 126). As a result, "we need to adopt a view of the individual as an interactive member of the larger and more complex mental ecology that characterizes the culture/environment relationship" (*Educating* 15). (As obvious as this is, it is remarkable how much of the work done in "cultural studies" fails to keep this culture-environment relationship in mind.)

David Orr presents us with a series of foundations for a new pedagogy of sustainability: teachers would have to understand that "all education is environmental education" (*Ecological Literacy* 90). Environmental education could no longer be considered a single discipline but would be taught across all disciplines. Learning would occur through mutual discourse rooted in each person's sense of local space. The success of the curriculum could be measured not just in how people talk and write but also in how they act. Education would involve ample firsthand experience in the natural world. And ultimately education would be the cultivation of "good thinking," which Orr defines as the offspring of "friction between reflective thought and real problems" (*Ecological Literacy* 92).

Paul Ryan has designed a "curriculum for sustainability" called the "Earthscore Method," which consists of five components: (1) understanding three comprehensive categories of knowledge (firstness, secondness, and thirdness, taken from the work of American philosopher Charles Peirce), (2) pedagogical organization according to an awareness of cybernetics and relational circuits, (3) cooperative learning, (4) the ability to picture a sustainable future, and (5) interpretation of ecological systems. Ryan's goal is to "raise education about sustainability to the level of an art form" ("Earthscore").

There is no shortage of blueprints, heuristics, or design proposals for imagining sustainable environments. We have only to apply and revise them for our own local, curricular needs. But there is nothing easy about this: "In some institutions, a university-wide culture of environmental stewardship and leadership from top-level university administrators will be strong and visible; in many others, it will appear to be limited, ineffective, [or] nonexistent, or [the campus culture will] even seem detrimental to campus environmental stewardship" (Creighton 274). Such difficulties can only be exacerbated by the increasing number of universities which are investing less and less in tenured faculty—those best able to initiate pedagogical, disciplinary, and curricular reform—and which are replacing them with part-timers and teaching assistants who, overworked and treated like intellectual migrant workers, have little leverage or time to work actively toward long-term changes within their institutions.

But we haven't reached a dead end yet. How might those of us with a fair amount of autonomy over the courses we design, and some influence over the surrounding curriculum, reconstruct these sites of learning more sustainably? How might those of us who work with graduate students encourage them to conduct more cross-disciplinary research in these areas? How might those of us who have the administrative support to collaborate with other colleagues, especially those in other disciplines, go about inventing new courses, programs, and curricular initiatives that imaginatively foster awareness of sustainability? How might those of us who have to publish to keep our jobs use this as an incentive for designing and implementing the kind of higher educational reform only hinted at in this book? How might we construct environments where we listen more closely to our students' survival stories and use their experiences and insights to help us reform our curricular goals? As distance learning, online education, and service-learning place new demands on faculty, how might we approach these growing arenas with new sets of sustainability-informed objectives? How might those of us expected to write grants focus our energies on those that support cross-disciplinary, environmentally based initiatives? How might we overlay against the backdrop of the institution a map of student and local residential lives, neighborhoods, communities, and families, or a grid highlighting student and residential fears, hopes, and concerns? How might we replace the image of the university as a self-contained universe with that of the university as *locality*, as a distinctly regional entity inseparable from the psychotopological flows and contours ever implicit within its students, faculty, administration, and neighboring residents? How might we design mechanisms for realizing such maps and networks? How might those mechanisms be integrated into the machinery of the curriculum?

One of Charles Fourier's proposed methods of educational instruction was the butterfly approach, which he suggested for those who suffered from short attention spans. For such individuals the appropriate learning environment was one where students would be permitted to flit from subject to subject, and, over time, so he thought, they would develop the necessary depth of knowledge as a result of approaching it on their own terms (Zeldin 135). The metaphor is still useful if considered from the other side; that is, even as contemporary life and culture often encourage a short-attention-span mode of being, our ability to dance from informational realm to informational realm in a constructive, connecting way has atrophied. Appreciating the demands inherent in a sustainability-based philosophy of education—of living and surviving—requires simultaneous comprehension in multiple dimensions. A butterfly approach to curricular design and research becomes necessary: a delicate choreography of intellectual cross-pollination. And, if we learn—quickly—to think like butterflies, then perhaps it will be our wings that create those seemingly insignificant ripples destined to have far-reaching effects.

Laughing Cages

On the cover of John Cage's collection *A Year from Monday* there are three photographs of him. In the first he is straight-faced and serious. In the second his mouth has broken into an open smile and he is laughing. And in the third his eyes are scrunched tightly shut and his head thrown back as he lets out a hearty belly laugh. All three images are partially superimposed; the first overlaps the second, which overlaps the third.

The book's opening, its center, and its conclusion are made up of the collection's three main texts, all with the title "Diary: How to Improve the World (You Will Only Make Matters Worse)" followed by the year in which they were composed (1965, 1966, 1976). These "diaries" are dangling mobiles of quotations and insights assembled around a paradox of the kind Cage loved: his keen awareness of the need to make the world inherently better, coupled with an understanding that humans keep on screwing things up. In an anecdote prefacing these texts, Cage shows how well his mother understood this paradox:

> I told [my mother] I'd written three texts on world improvement. She said, "John! How dare you? You should be ashamed!" Then she added, "I'm surprised at you." I asked her, in view of world conditions, whether she didn't think there was room for improvement. She said, "There certainly is. It makes good sense." (145)

Survival now means both crying and laughing at the same time. The crying part is easy: we have only to listen to what our students say about where they live, how they work, where they think they're going to end up. (For that matter, the same goes for so many of our part-time colleagues, our neighbors, our family members, even ourselves.) I realize that the only appropriate response to much of the information and many of the testimonies I have brought into this book might be tears (see Appendix A). And yet oddly—or perhaps not so oddly, when we think of Cage's laughter—in the course of my research I have also grown strangely happier, more exhilarated. Apparently fear can engender joy. I am as worried as ever about what my son is going to have to live through. But the walks I take with him now have become, if that is possible, even more—acute? necessary?—than they were before. Being able to work at a job that not only gives me the support to pursue such distractions as book writing but also enables me to spend more time with my wife and son makes me realize how unspeakably lucky I am to have landed this kind of job, something academics like me too often take for granted. And now that I understand a little more the circumstances that have led to the absurd design of my ridiculously planned suburban neighborhood, I no longer even react to the view outside my window with contempt as much as with a curious sense of familiarity: if nothing else, the flawed places we live in are reminders that they are human constructs. Which means that they are not permanent, and that they can change.

In an interview not long before his death Cage said,

> What we're basically in, it seems to me, is a greater population than the earth has ever experienced before and we just don't know what's happening or how to deal with it yet. We're inexperienced, we're uneducated, and so forth, about the reality of the present circumstance. . . . [W]e don't know much about what we're doing. But I do believe that we're on one earth and I think more and more people realize this. And if we could give up this silliness of the difference of nations and concern ourselves with problems that affect all of us we would make a great step forward. . . . ("Conversation" 99)

In moving forward we find that teaching can mean constructing zones of active inquiry where states of felicity are more valuable than the consumption of things. Teaching can mean subverting our pursuit of distractions (self-imposed hibernation) so as to distinguish the difference between desperate desire and informed need. It can mean rethinking the role of the classroom as a field where our accelerated ecological crises become not more "issues" tacked on to the educator's already overburdened social agenda, but the hub out of which spiral future pedagogies of sustainability.

In *A Year from Monday* Cage writes, "once one gets interested in world improvement, there is no stopping" (52). Here's to not stopping.

Bad News: A Compilation of Observations and Forecasts

Climate Change

A study released in June 2000—*Climate Change and a Global City: An Assessment of the Metropolitan East Coast Region*—concluded that in the ensuing decades New York City residents can expect flooding, debilitating heat, drought, violent downpours, heavier smog, power outages, and increased mosquito infestation due to climate change: "Many of these scenarios don't even sound like predictions; they're already happening," said one of the report's authors ("City Living Looks Gloomy"). At no other time in the last six hundred years have temperatures risen as dramatically as they have in the last ten years (Flavin 58); January 2000 through April 2000 were the hottest months in 106 years of U.S. record keeping ("More U.S. Drought"). In the Northern Hemisphere Spring arrives a week earlier than it used to (McKibben). For decades the world's oceans have been absorbing much of global warming, and concern is growing over the impact of this heat's eventual release: "Some experts believe that about half the greenhouse warming is still in the oceanic pipeline and will inevitably percolate to the air in the decades just ahead" (Stevens). Over the next century, average U.S. temperatures are expected to increase between five and ten degrees Fahrenheit, resulting in hotter cities, extreme precipitation and drought, systematic ecosystem damage, more heat waves, and shrinking coastal wetlands due to rising sea levels ("Federal Report on Global Warming"). Both the Arctic and the Antarctic ice covers are melting at a higher rate than at any time since record-keeping began (Mastny), and flora that once could not survive above the arctic tree line are now thriving there ("Polar Regions");

in a decade, ozone depletion in the arctic stratosphere might become just as bad as current ozone losses over Antarctica ("Arctic Ozone in Jeopardy"). Because of climate change, 70 percent of the world's great coral reefs will be destroyed as early as 2030, and, at this rate, they will all be gone by 2100 (Hoegh-Guldberg). Despite problems brought on by climate change, policymakers (that is, those who have tried) have been largely unable to make the consumer class aware of how its lifestyles contribute to a proliferation of heat-trapping gases (Revkin, "Struggling"). Because of the rising rate of domestic electricity usage, for instance, which causes the release of more carbon dioxide, thereby accelerating climate change, one study concludes that television watching now plays a large role in global warming (Kirby, "Climate Change Risk from TV"). And even if the public could be alerted in time, "many experts are convinced that whatever action [about global warming] is taken, the world's political and economic systems are probably not capable of responding fast enough to keep carbon dioxide concentrations in the atmosphere from rising" (Sterngold). For reasons like this, a recent international conference on global warming ended in "atmospheres tinged with gloom" (Crossette).

Vanishing Resources

Despite examples like Easter Island, whose inhabitants, we now know, caused their own extinction due to overuse of limited resources (Diamond), we continue to consume limited resources with abandon. We lose twenty-three to twenty-five billion tons of topsoil each year (conventional farming methods and eradication of forests result in fallow ground, thus accelerating erosion, in which topsoil and organic nutrients are carried away by wind and precipitation). In 1924 the Agricultural Research and Education Center sunk a concrete post nine feet into protected Everglades soil until hitting bedrock. Fifty-five years later, a five-foot-long portion of the pole was exposed (Ehrenfeld 172). The fertile topsoil lost each year is the equivalent of all of Australia's wheat fields (Hawken 3). Half of the people on the planet will not have enough water by the year 2050 (Simon). If every human suddenly became a vegetarian and we were able to repeat record harvest levels of 1985–1986, we still couldn't feed 1.5 billion of our present humans at the 1993 U.S. level of consumption (Ehrlich and Ehrlich, "Why Isn't Everyone" 61). Brazil's Amazon rain forest is disappearing twice as fast as previously suspected ("Study: Brazilian Rain Forest"). Asia's environment in the next century might "completely collapse" due to looming catastrophes brought on by soil degradation, wide-scale deforestation, rampant industrial and municipal wastes, toxic air, and elimination of biodiversity. Asia's carbon dioxide emissions are expected to increase 25 percent over the next century, which leads one expert to state that "clearly, then, the resolution of the global warming problem hinges on what happens in the Asia-Pacific region" ("Asia Faces Looming Environmental Disasters"). Less than 0.08 percent of all the world's water can be used by humans. However, over the next twenty years our use of water is expected to increase 40 percent: "If we go on as we are, millions more will go to bed hungry and thirsty each night than do so already" (Kirby, "Dawn of a Thirsty Century"). The forecast is no better concerning fossil fuel: "Within the next decade, the supply of conventional oil will be unable to keep up with demand. . . . Using several different techniques to estimate the current reserves of conventional oil and the amount still left to be discovered, we conclude that the decline will begin before 2010" (Campbell and Laherrère). More than twenty-two billion barrels of oil are consumed globally per year, but only six billion gallons are discovered globally each year. Massive disruptions of transportation and of the global economy are expected around 2010, when the final peak of production of all petroleum liquids is followed by irreversible decline (Thomson).

Population Growth

It is projected that by 2050 India will have another 519 million people, China another 211 million, and Pakistan another 200 million. The populations of Egypt, Iran, and Mexico are expected to increase by more than half, and "in these and other water-short countries, population growth is sentencing millions of people to hydrological poverty" ("Population Growth Sentencing Millions"). Nor is the overall picture hopeful: "World population is projected to increase . . . to somewhere between 10 and 14 billion within the next century. Suppose population growth halted at 14 billion and everyone were satisfied with a per-capita energy use of 7.5 kilowatts (kW), the average in rich nations and about two-thirds of that in the United States in the early 1990s. A human enterprise that large would create a total impact of 105 TW [i.e., 105 terawatts, or 105 billion kilowatts], eight times that of today and a clear recipe for ecological collapse" (Daily, Ehrlich, and Ehrlich). The current level of production would have to be increased five to thirty times over simply to provide basic amenities to this increased population. This is clearly ecologically unsustainable, given current technologies and resource-use strategies (Shrivastava 10).

Ecosystem Decline and Mass Extinctions

A World Resources Institute Study released in 2000 concluded that most of the world's ecosystems are in decline. Some of the report's statistics:

Half of the world's wetlands were lost during the last century.

Logging and conversion have shrunk the world's forests by as much as half.

Some 9 percent of the world's tree species are at risk of extinction; tropical deforestation probably exceeds 130,000 square kilometers per year.

Fishing fleets are 40 percent larger than the ocean can sustain.

Nearly 70 percent of the world's major marine fish stocks are overfished or are being fished at their biological limit.

Soil degradation has affected two-thirds of the world's agricultural lands in the last fifty years.

Some 30 percent of the world's original forests have been converted to agriculture.

Since 1980, the global economy has tripled in size and population has grown by 30 percent to six billion people.

Dams, diversions or canals fragment almost 60 percent of the world's largest rivers.

Twenty percent of the world's freshwater species are extinct, threatened, or endangered. At least 10,000 freshwater fish species are threatened globally. ("New Analysis of World's Ecosystems")

At current rates of extinction more than half of our existing species will disappear in the next five decades (Leakey and Lewin 221). Fifty-five percent of the world's most species-rich habitats (rain forests, where nearly half of all plant species are found) are gone. Conservative estimates say 5,000 species become extinct each year. Other estimates say we lose 150,000 species a year (Goodland). Still others put the figure at "27,000 species a year, seventy-four per day, one every twenty minutes, due in no small part to the 500,000 trees that are cut every hour in tropical forests" (Hawken 29). Twelve hundred bird species "could become extinct in the next 100 years, with 600 to 900 more on the verge of joining the list" ("One in 8 Birds"). Because of pollution, overfishing, and coastal development, a "dead zone" the size of New Jersey now extends into the Gulf of Mexico (Yoon "'Dead Zone'"), and "humans may already or will soon have destroyed enough species that it will require a full 10 million years for the planet to recover—20 times as long as humans have already existed" (Yoon "Study").

Pollution

The Commission for Environmental Cooperation, created by Canada, Mexico, and the United States in relation to the North American Free Trade Agreement (NAFTA), concluded that industrial pollution increased in 1997 for the first time since NAFTA officials began monitoring pollution in 1994. Industrial pollution was up 27 percent over 1995 levels—certainly an understated figure considering the data focused mostly on metal companies but did not include electrical plants, coal mines, agricultural operations, dry cleaners, service stations, cars, or trucks ("Study: North American Pollution"). Children living in Mexico City, Beijing, Shanghai, Tehran, and Calcutta, because of the air they breathe, "inhale the equivalent of two packs of cigarettes each day" (O'Meara 129). Residents of Mexico City breathe a daily mix of poisons (which includes airborne fecal matter) so strong that on one occasion "fully half of the metropolis's 18 million residents became sick with some respiratory ailment" (Preston). In 1998, fires in Jakarta, Indonesia, caused a toxic haze to cover much of southeast Asia: for weeks people wore masks, suffered from respiratory illnesses, and drove with lights on during the day (Kristof A1; Mydans). California beaches were closed in 1998 for a total of 3,273 days, compared with 745 days in 1991; most of the closures were due to sewage spills and urban runoff ("Where Bacteria Meet the Beach").

Globalism and Growth

"[There is] a developing worldwide crisis driven mainly by a phenomenon called overcapacity: the tendency of the unfettered global economy to produce more cars, toys, shoes, airplanes, steel, paper, appliances, film, clothing and electronic devices than people will buy at high enough prices. . . . The danger is that at some point this house of cards must tumble down. . . . The global economy appears, in effect, to be capable of self-destruction" (Uchitelle, "Global Good Times"). There are more than twenty-three thousand McDonald's restaurants in 113 countries, and, in 1997, McDonald's opened five new restaurants a day (Gardner 150). In 1950, Scottsdale, Arizona, was no bigger than a single square mile, and only two thousand people lived there. In 1996, the population hit 165,000, and the size had grown to more than three times that of San Francisco. Scottsdale currently covers some 185 square miles. In nearby Phoenix, "the air is so bad at times that people who came to the desert seeking good health are warned to stay indoors" (Egan, "Urban Sprawl" A1). Recent economic euphoria has overshadowed what the Worldwatch Institute considers the two main crises facing humankind: stabilizing the

climate and the population: "If we cannot stabilize both, there is
not an ecosystem on Earth that we can save. . . . As the Dow
Jones goes up, the Earth's health goes down" ("Information
Economy Boom"). Two articles side by side on the front page of
the February 27, 1999, edition of the *New York Times* illustrate
the kind of selfishness that William Greider associates with the
rise of globalism: next to a new story on surging growth in late
1998 is another documenting the drop in food donations to soup
kitchens and private charities (Nasar; Revkin, "As Need"). Meanwhile, waste increases: "Every American consumes about 136
pounds of resources a week, while 2,000 pounds of waste are
discarded to support that consumption" (Hawken 37). "The
Western world's desire for beef has doubled the cattle population
in the past 40 years. There is now one cow for every four humans
on the planet. Bacteria that break down the cellulose in the guts
of cattle convert between 3 and 10 percent of the food the cattle
eat into methane, which comes out the other end. It is estimated
that the *flatulence factor* adds almost 100 million tons of methane to the atmosphere each year" (Gordon and Suzuki 12).

Environmental Injustice and Rising Incarcerations

Christian Aid issued a report in 2000 claiming that the increase
in climate-related catastrophes in less developed countries is the
fault of rich nations such as the United States and Britain ("West's
Pollution Blamed"). Even though "most Americans breathe polluted air, only 57 percent of whites reside in counties with feder-
ally substandard air quality, while 65 percent of blacks and 80
percent of Hispanics live in counties with similar or worse conditions" (Dowie 144). Similarly, "in parts of the United Kingdom
where average household income is below £15,000 a year, there
are 662 polluting factories," but "in parts where average income
is above £30,000, there are five" (Kirby). Despite drops in crime
rates throughout the 1990s, prison building is one of the United
States' leading growth industries: "Since 1985 the nation's jail
and prison population has grown 130 percent, and it will soon
pass two million, even as crime rates continue a six-year decline.

No country has more people behind bars" (Egan, "War" A22). In fact, "for an American born [in 1999], the chance of living some part of life in a correction facility is 1 in 20; for black Americans, it is 1 in 4" (Egan, "Less Crime"). Seven million children in this country have at least one parent who is incarcerated or on parole (Butterfield). In fact, "the scale of imprisonment in America is now unmatched in any democracy, and is greater than even most totalitarian governments have ever attempted": in 1998, "one in every 150 American residents (children included) was behind bars" ("More than Any Other Democracy" 30).

Sustainability in a Composition Course

Variety and relevance are important factors when I put together an introductory composition course. Students are given an opportunity to write in a range of styles and genres, since composing in various forms can elicit various kinds of thinking and approaches to problem solving. Students write informal responses, letters, essays, results of interviews they have conducted, journals, and, if they want to, poetry, fiction, and experimental hybrids. (For more on my interest in promoting a variety of so-called "experimental" and "alternative" compositional forms, see my book *Resisting Writings [and the Boundaries of Composition].*) Informational variety is just as important, and the readings I bring into the classroom explore a range of subjects: anthropology, art, Buddhism, business, ecology, economics, environmental studies, education, future studies, philosophy, planning, sociology, and urban studies. The cross-disciplinary nature of the readings has little to do with any desire to help "prepare" students for their selected majors and colleges—something I consider well beyond the reach of any composition course. My university comprises many different colleges, including the College of Liberal Arts and Sciences, the School of Education and Human Services, the College of Business Administration, the College of Pharmacy and Allied Health Professions, the College of Professional Studies, and several others; students from all of these widely differing colleges wind up in my composition courses. Since the students come from departments throughout the university system, my objective is to create a context where students, regardless of their academic interests, explore concerns shared by most of them, and where they do so in a manner that connects their thinking to a variety of cross-disciplinary texts. By creating assignment sequences aimed at getting students to think about the places, people, cultures, workplaces, educational settings, and futures that matter to them, and by linking these different sites of reflection to texts culled from a range of sources, I try to help students see links between their personal interests or obsessions and those of ecologists, educators, philosophers, planners, sociologists, and so on. The goal is to create an atmosphere where students simultaneously reflect upon local matters of personal concern and synthesize a steady flow of important information.

Obviously, the kinds of information I pull into the classroom are determined by my need to foster the beginnings of an awareness of sustainability in a semester-long conversation where students might become more aware of the need to think about sustainability within the context of their own local conditions. My philosophy here has been influenced by writers like Carolyn Merchant, who at the beginning of her book *Radical Ecology: The Search for a Livable World*, shows that in order to articulate an environmental ethic one must first explore the cultural and familial values of one's ancestors, the historical and economic forces that have socialized us, and the goals and worries we have for our futures (1–8). It is also an approach that has benefited from Edward Goldsmith's insistence that education be taken out of "specialized institutions" and resituated within our students' families and communities:

> Modern education is concerned with training people for a career in the predominantly urban industrial world. It is said in India that when a young person gets a high school diploma, he leaves his ancestral village for the nearest town; when he gets a university degree he moves to the city; and when he gets a Ph.D., he leaves the country for Europe or America. Instead of providing the village with a means of renewing itself, education thereby provides instead a means of assuring its inevitable demise.
>
> Education is one of the many key social functions that the state has usurped and that, in an ecological society, must once again be fulfilled at the level of the family and the community, so that young people should learn once again to fulfill their social, ecological and cosmic roles within the context of their specific culture. (335)

To fault Goldsmith's faith in maintaining some notion of cultural purity when culture is constantly in flux and undergoing hybridization is to miss the larger argument that the higher one ascends within academic culture, the easier it is to feel that one has left one's "home" behind. And so ultimately in my writing courses I seek to "bring things home" by helping students situate their needs and desires within a cross-disciplinary range of conversations grounded in many of their local concerns.

In my department I teach what are called "developmental," "intermediate," and "honors" composition courses. Using student SAT scores as the primary and usually only criteria for placement, my institution's administration, not my department, separates each first-year or transfer students into one of these three categories. Because I consider such a placement process flawed—I feel all courses ought to be constructed as if they were "honors" courses, with smaller class sizes, challenging assignments, intense conversations, and high expectations, since students who are told that they do not belong in "honors" or "advanced" classes might well come to believe such lies—I disregard these categories and teach the same writing course regardless of how the university has labeled these students. I make no attempt to dumb down the course for those classes where students are assumed to have had less reading and writing experience; indeed, my "developmental" students sometimes confide in me that they don't feel challenged enough in their other courses. I try to work individually with students as best I can to customize when the need arises: If a student has very limited experience in reading and writing in English, I will cut back on certain readings. For students who don't have easy access to a computer at home, who haven't learned how to type, or who have never written anything longer than two pages in their lives, I let them write assignments early in the semester that are shorter than the minimum page-length requirement, and then take it from there. For those students who have an easier time with the readings or who have more extensive writing experience, I'll often give them optional supplementary readings. As for their assigned readings, I rarely order books, choosing instead to keep an extensive file of articles and chapters on reserve in the library.

Designing for a fourteen-week semester, I divide the course into four phases lasting three weeks each; the remaining time is used for an introductory week and, in the middle of the semester, a "catch-up" week for students who have fallen behind. During each phase, students work on an assignment sequence. For the first and last phases, everyone in the course works on the same assignments; for the second and third phases students get to choose the sequences of their choice. If none of the assignments is to their liking then students can design a sequence for themselves.

The theme of the first phase is the concept of place. The themes for the second phase are tribe, oral history, and eutopia, or students can undertake a service-learning project or design a sequence of their own; students pick the approach that interests them. Themes in phase three are work, education, and consciousness, or, again, students can conduct a service-learning project or design a sequence of their own, and, once again, students select their sequence. In phase four everyone writes on the theme of future. In each phase, the three weeks of assignments are interrelated, with the second week's assignment often picking up where the first week's left off. Most of my students say they like the approach, since it gives them enough time to immerse themselves in a particular topic or theme but doesn't go on for so long as to become tiresome. (For a while, I tried dividing my courses into three phases instead of four, but overwhelmingly my students said they wanted the greater variety that came with four assignment sequences.)

Because students are working on different projects during the second and third phases of the semester, I treat the class during this period as if it were two, three, or sometimes four different miniclasses, all held simultaneously. Sometimes the groups work separately on their own themes—the oral history people take over one corner of the room while the tribe people commandeer another corner, with students in each group reading and commenting on each other's work. At other times I mix the groups up so that people from different groups can discuss with each other their projects and the readings they've been looking at. Consequently students are sometimes talking to peers working on the same project, and sometimes with classmates completely unfamiliar with their topics. Not surprisingly, things can get chaotic during the middle two phases, but the payoff is that students have more choice in selecting their assignments, which I think makes them more involved in their writing.

During most weeks, two kinds of writing assignments are due: a primary assignment, which develops, over the course of the three-week phase, into a longer piece of writing (e.g., an essay, interview results, or a memoir), and, often, a reading response, where students reflect upon one or more assigned readings. Informal peer critiques, where groups of students offer each other feedback via e-mail, are also required at the end of each phase. With the exception of two or three weeks during the semester when other commitments keep me from doing so, I respond to student writing every week, spending most of my time on their primary assignments, which I consider their most important pieces of writing. When I have extra time I write comments on their "reading responses," but some weeks all I have time to do is read them and make mental notes of recurring questions and insights that ought to be brought up in class. Either way, the reading responses serve to promote conversation in class (as well as ensure that students do the readings).

The grade I give after each of the four phases is based on the student's writing portfolio, which includes everything written for that phase, including e-mailed peer responses. Student participation is also taken into consideration when formulating a grade; for those students who have considerable difficulty speaking up in class, whether for cultural or other reasons, I encourage them to participate in other ways, either by holding conferences with me or by communicating online. If a student is unhappy with the grade for a particular phase, he or she can submit a significantly revised version of the final text within two weeks, in hopes of getting a better grade—something I encourage students to do repeatedly, all semester long if they wish, except for the fourth and last phase, when there is no time left to revise since grades are due. There are no tests and no midterms or finals, although I suppose the reading responses serve as quizzes of a sort, as an incentive to make sure students do the weekly readings.

My approach to grading students' writing portfolios has obviously been influenced by my former teachers, Cy Knoblauch and Lil Brannon, who urge composition instructors to evaluate according to growth rather than performance: "Symptoms of growth—the willingness to take risks, to profit from advice, to revise, to make recommendations to others—may appear quickly, even if improved *performance* takes longer" (*Rhetorical Traditions* 169). In other words, if students are doing all of the assignments in a timely fashion, taking the initiative to meet with me, paying considerable attention to the work of their peers, demonstrating a willingness to continually revise their work, preferably in conjunction with our university's writing center (which I also direct, a fact which makes it a little easier for me to encourage my students to use this facility), chances are good they'll end up with an A, whereas a more experienced writer taking a less active interest in the class might not do as well. In every class I teach, undergraduate or graduate, I remind students that if they ever receive a grade that is not to their liking, all they need to do is meet with me to discuss how they might revise their work for a new grade. While I will never lower a grade, I do raise students' grades if they indicate a willingness to seriously revise their assignments. My stance here is very much in opposition to those who insist upon entrance and exit exams as a means of assessing student writing. For those who still cling to the need to offer end-of-semester writing exams, I would invoke not only the work of writers like Knoblauch and Brannon—particularly their chapter "The Development of Writing Ability: Some Myths about Evaluation and Improvement" in *Rhetorical Traditions* (151–71)—but also Bill Readings's chapter "The Idea of Excellence" in *The University in Ruins*, where he dissects this omnipresent academic trope and finds it not only meaningless but also indicative of the university's transformation into little more than "another corporation in a world of transnationally exchanged capital" (43).

All writing and reading assignments are due at the beginning of each week, with the rest of that week's classes spent discussing both the students' writings (in small and large groups) and the weekly readings—usually in that order. Because this is a writing course, I try to make sure that at least three-fourths of class time is spent discussing students' writing, with whatever time is left devoted to discussing assigned readings. Because of the at-times overwhelming number of articles and chapters I assign throughout the semester, a considerable portion of this reading never gets thoroughly discussed in class, and some readings never get discussed at all. While this is inevitably frustrating in that there are always details and meanings within the readings that many students don't catch or fully comprehend, I will always spend more time in the classroom talking about their own writings; it is enough for me to know that they are encountering a variety of "text for thought," even if they aren't reading the material as closely as they might for other classes. Anyway the goal is not for them to study these readings as if they were to be tested on them, but rather for them to get used to encountering and processing a cross-disciplinary flow of information. I know of colleagues who balk at this, arguing that the presence of so much assigned reading in a composition course risks taking attention away from the students' writing. My response, while perhaps a selfish one, is this: because I am continually hungry for information, and am intrigued by the ways in which new sources of information continually force my own thinking to evolve, I try and create an atmosphere of information overload that is stimulating but not threatening. Students are never "tested" on this information— even the responses to the readings are generally not supposed to be summaries but simply students' own reactions to and opinions about the readings. Of course, students complain about all the work I make them do, often telling me that I require more work than their other professors. Again, since they know I'm not grading them on the degree to which they've fully understood everything in the readings, but am concerned mostly that they work hard at managing their time so that they can wrestle with a variety of texts, and in the end extract several ideas worth contemplating, the majority of the students manage to get all of the work done.

Some complain, of course, that a few of the assigned readings are "boring" or not as entertaining as they would like. My response to this is that as a culture we already have more entertainment than we know what to do with, and besides, the classroom is a place not for entertainment but for discovery and enlightenment. Consequently it matters not whether the information one encounters is or isn't entertaining; what counts is what one manages to construct from the interaction with that information—a concept that, admittedly, some students have trouble with, conditioned as they are by previous classroom encounters with teachers for whom pedagogy is largely a matter of performance. Ultimately, though, complaints about the number of assignments or the nature of the readings never predominate, since, as I mentioned, the bulk of the classroom time revolves not around the reading responses but around discussions of students' primary writings.

The remainder of this appendix is the entirety of the assignment packet that I give to students in my composition courses. Although the assignments included here have resulted from years of tinkering, none of this is written in stone. Every semester, after thinking back to students' in-class comments and their end-of-semester evaluations, I rewrite parts of this packet, drop some readings and add others, and modify the themes. The course has evolved in response to the local conditions in which I teach, and it is influenced by who my students are, where they live, the kinds of work schedules they have, and the feedback they give me. Readings, especially in the first and final parts of the course, have been chosen in part because they refer to places and subjects familiar to students living in the New York City–Long Island region. Now that our university has built residence halls, and more students from farther away have started enrolling in the university, this regional emphasis will expand, and readings will include communities within other states. Consequently, the materials presented here represent merely the latest manifestation of this course.

It should also be noted that my objective in presenting this information is not to imply that this is how a writing course *ought* to be taught. The sequence approach seems to work for me—for now, any way—but it is hardly the only way to go. Some composition teachers require more readings than I do. Others assign no readings aside from student texts. Some courses require a different "essay" each week, where others have students work on just one or two extended projects or books. I don't consider any of these alternative approaches inherently good or bad, their success depending, obviously, on how effectively the teacher and students work together to create a writing environment that they find intellectually and culturally related to their local conditions.

The text of the following assignment packet is presented here exactly as it is handed out to students, with a few comments added in brackets. Also, in the original assignment packet all bibliographical information is included, whereas here this information can be found in the Works Cited list at the end of this book.

Assignment Packet

Objectives

My objectives in this class are that by the end of the semester you will feel like a more confident and creative writer; demonstrate attentiveness and interest when discussing ideas with other people; have made revision and proofreading automatic parts of your writing process; be better at catching and correcting errors or inconsistencies within your prose; feel more adept at critically reading a large amount of material in a short amount of time; and gain experience in drawing connections between your own lives and concerns, and the information found in a variety of cross-disciplinary texts. In addition to these objectives, I have designed these assignments with a general theme in mind, one that runs throughout the entire course. That theme might be summed up in two questions: "What do you value, and how will you live?" I'm hoping that this course will give you a chance to investigate some of the things that matter most to you, consider how those things might be affected by changes in the near future, and reflect upon the implications of those potential changes.

Course Overview

Our course is divided into four phases. In the first phase you will write about where you're living right now, or some other place that matters to you. In the second phase you will have a choice: you will either write an oral history, investigate a particular culture (I tend to use the term "tribe") you belong to or are familiar with, imagine ways of designing "eutopia" (a word I use to mean the "good place," not to be confused with "utopia," which means "no-place" or a perfect place), or conduct a service-learning research project. In the third phase you will write about either your own or someone else's work experience, about your own philosophy of education, or about consciousness, or you will pursue a service-learning project. In the fourth and final phase of the course you'll write about the future twenty-five years from now (this will be your chance to tell others what you think the future has in store for you and the rest of us). Also, if during the second and third phases you don't like any of the assignment sequences, you can always create your own writing assignments— just meet with me at least one week in advance so we can work something out.

Please take the time now to look ahead at all the different options for phase 2 and phase 3. If at this time you think you're going to want to select either the service-learning project or the "your choice" option, see me in the next week so we can talk about these options in more detail.

Unless what you're writing about happens to be very personal and you can't bring yourself to share it with others in the class, expect to have your writing discussed in small and large groups throughout the semester. (If at any time you're handing in work that is too personal to share with others, just write "For Your Eyes Only" in big letters on top, and I'll make sure not to distribute it for workshops.) Ultimately, if you want to, you can also publish some of your assignments on a Web site I've put together expressly for this purpose. There are also two student journals that you might wish to contribute to, since a number of our assignments lend themselves to the kind of work those journals publish.

Assignment Schedule
[Were this were an actual assignment packet, I would insert the dates for each assignment.]

Week 1: Introductions & individual conferences

Phase 1
Week 2:   Assignment 1.1 due
Week 3:   Assignment 1.2 due
Week 4:   Assignment 1.3 due

Phase 2
Week 5:   Assignment 2.1 due
Week 6:   Assignment 2.2 due
Week 7:   Assignment 2.3 due

Week 8:   "Catch-up week"

Phase 3
Week 9:   Assignment 3.1 due
Week 10:   Assignment 3.2 due
Week 11:   Assignment 3.3 due

Phase 4
Week 12:   Assignment 4.1 due
Week 13:   Assignment 4.2 due
Week 14:   Assignment 4.3 due

Assignment Sequences

An assignment is due at the beginning of every week of the semester, with the exception of the first week and the "catch-up week." With a few exceptions, each week's assignment is actually two assignments: a "primary assignment" and a "reading response." Also, a third type of assignment—peer critiques sent over e-mail—will be expected at the end of each phase.

The "primary assignments" for the first two weeks of each phase will directly or indirectly lead up to the third and final primary assignment due at the end of each phase. The "reading responses," although still written assignments, are intended to help you familiarize yourself with the readings and give you something to refer to when we discuss them in class. When you write your reading responses, keep in mind that, unless otherwise indicated, these aren't supposed to be summaries of what you've read, but your own personal reactions to what you've read. (We'll talk about the difference more in class.) All writing assignments should be double-spaced and written on a word processor (see me if you're going to have trouble getting access to a computer).

PLEASE NOTE: In phase 4 there are a lot of reading assignments, so you should plan on reading some of this material before phase 4 begins. I suggest you use the "catch-up week" to get a head start on some of this material.

Phase 1

For this phase everyone in the class will be writing on the theme of place.

Introduction

It's easy to think of ourselves as somehow detached from the places we move through and live in. But self and place influence each other in profound ways. The scientist Gregory Bateson referred to the concept of "mind/environment," where one's mind and one's environment are not separate phenomena but a shared, coexistent process. As Jack D. Forbes writes,

> I can lose my hands, and still live. I can lose my legs and still live. I can lose my eyes and still live. I can lose my hair, eyebrows, nose, arms, and many other things and still live. But if I lose the air I die. If I lose the sun I die. If I lose the earth I die. If I lose the water I die. If I lose the plants and animals I die. All of these things are more a part of me, more essential to my every breath, than is my so-called body. What is my real body?
>
> We are not autonomous, self-sufficient beings as European mythology teaches. Such ideas are based upon deductive logic derived from false assumptions. We are rooted, just like the trees. But our roots come out of our nose and mouth, like an umbilical cord, forever connected with the rest of the world. Our roots also extend out from our skin and from our other body cavities.
>
> Nothing that we do, do we do by ourselves. We do not see by ourselves. We do not hear by ourselves. We do not breathe, eat, drink, defecate, piss, or fart by ourselves. We do not think, dream, invent or procreate by ourselves. We do not die by ourselves. (145–46)

One way of getting a little closer to understanding what Bateson might have had in mind when he wrote of "mind/environment" is to study places that matter to us.

Assignment 1.1
<u>Primary Assignment</u>

Write a detailed description of where you're living right now. (If you are living in one of the residence halls, then write about your permanent address, the place you go back to when the residence halls are closed.) Or, if you are uninterested in where you're living right now, write about some other place you have lived in the past. Your goal is to describe this place so that your readers can form a detailed and relatively accurate picture in their heads of what it is (or was) like, and of its influence on you. Bear in mind that it doesn't matter whether you like or dislike this place; many students have written very engaging essays about places that they dislike or that frustrate them for various reasons, just as others have written engagingly about places that they have enjoyed. **Length: at least 3 pages.**

If you're going to write about where you're living right now, spend some time describing the house or apartment building you live in, and even more time describing the surrounding area. What is the street like outside your front door? The adjacent buildings? Is it a residential or commercial area, or both? Are there stores nearby? What are they, what do they look like, and what kind of an impact do they have on you—that is, how do they make you feel? Is there traffic, and if so, how would you describe it? Are there parks or fields or lots nearby? Open spaces? Are there lots of people around, and if so, what kinds of people—age, culture, appearance? What do the people do in your neighborhood? If there aren't many people around, describe what that's like. Think about your neighbors: What kinds of jobs do you think they have? How do you think they spend their days? What is the name of the street you live on? The town or village? What are the names of the nearby neighborhoods, and are they similar to yours or different? If there are things that strike you as positive and good about your neighborhood, tell us about them. If there are things that are negative, let us know what they are. If you feel your place is "boring," try to explain why, exactly. If you feel indifferent about your neighborhood, and find it neither "good" nor "bad," try hard to explain why you feel that indifference. Do you think your neighborhood is similar to many others, or unique? In general, how does this place make you feel, and why?

By the time one of your classmates has finished reading this assignment, he or she should have a very vivid picture of what your place looks and feels like. That picture won't be exactly the same one in your head, of course, but it should at least complement the image you're trying to depict. Your reader should also be able to look on a map of the borough or county you live in and point to the general area where you live. In other words, be as specific as possible in mentioning where exactly you live, without actually divulging your address.

One last thing: if you're writing about a place that you can visit now, get hold of a camera and a roll of film this week and take some pictures of your neighborhood. (If this is impossible, or if you don't know anyone who owns a camera, see me.) Take pictures of the places that come to mind when you think of this place. Don't worry if the pictures you take aren't "scenic" or "picturesque;" in the past students have taken pictures of dumpsters behind bodegas, strip malls, abandoned swing sets, street corners, parking lots. Just make sure the photographs you take are of the actual places that appear in your mind when you think about the place you're writing about. Take these pictures, and get them developed so that you can bring them into class within the next few weeks.

If you're writing about a home that is not nearby, you can take pictures of this place if you go back to visit over a break in the semester. And if the place no longer exists, or is too far away to visit, perhaps there are old family or childhood photographs you could locate and use for this assignment. In either case, see me.

Reading Response

Read "Place: A Fragment" by Sven Birkerts. As you read pick out four sentences. Let two of them be sentences that convey specific visual images. Let the other two be sentences that are more concerned with conveying some kind of idea. In class we'll discuss what some people mean when they talk about the difference between "showing" and "telling," as well as how writing detailed description can sometimes lead to the raising of questions and conclusions.

Assignment 1.2
Reading Response

Read and write a response to the following two excerpts: "Working Landscapes" (Chapter 5 from Tony Hiss's *The Experience of Place*) and "Scary Places" (Chapter 1 from James Howard Kunstler's *The Geography of Nowhere: The Rise and Decline of America's Man-Made Landscape*). As you read these texts, feel free to agree or disagree with the authors, or perhaps both. **Length: at least two pages.**

Primary Assignment

Both Hiss and Kunstler describe how specific places have changed within their lifetimes. Both refer to places not too far from St. John's: a farm in Queens, and a suburban development on Long Island. Hiss is interested in how, during the twentieth century, this farm managed to retain much of its original character while the surrounding area became increasingly developed. Kunstler views his boyhood home on Long Island as an example of what he considers to be many "no places" all across America— a housing development where all the houses look more or less alike, a place designed for cars rather than humans, where there is no common square or village center—in sum, a place marked by sameness, monotony, boredom (whether or not you agree with Kunstler is up to you).

Both of these writers are making arguments for what makes "good" places good. As you read these two passages think about where you live: Would you describe it as a good place, or not? What exactly is good about it? What is bad or problematic? Do you plan on living here for years to come? If so, why? If not, why not? If this isn't the kind of place you want to live in for much longer, what *is* the kind of place you want to live in? What would it have that this place lacks? If you don't have any desire to move far from this place, what does it have that is keeping you here? Your goal in this assignment is to describe in further detail the desirable and/or undesirable qualities associated with your place. (This assignment will help you get ready for next week's assignment, in which you provide a more complete portrait of this place and indicate, directly or indirectly, whether or not you consider it to be a "good place.") **Length: at least 3 pages.**

Also: bring in the photographs from last week's assignment, so that the rest of the class might see them and hear you talk about them for a few minutes.

Assignment 1.3
Primary Assignment

In this assignment I want you to present a detailed portrait of the place or community you've been writing about. As you do this, be sure to let your readers know what exactly it is about this place that makes it good, or bad, or both. As you write this piece, reflect upon what your definition of a "good place" would be. What must it have? What shouldn't it have? What constitutes a "good neighborhood" as opposed to a bad or undesirable one? Feel free to use anything you wrote in the previous two assignments. But remember that I want you to significantly revise your work; don't simply cut and paste together paragraphs from those two assignments. By revising I mean rewriting.

Also, if you were able to take some photographs two weeks ago, incorporate these into your essay. (You can insert them into the actual text or attach them at the end as an appendix.) As you do this, think about how the photographs and words can complement each other within your final piece. **Length: at least five pages.**

Reading Response

All members of our class, and indeed all students, professors, and staff members at St. John's University, have at least one thing in common: our lives have all been shaped by Robert Moses. Read the short article "The Father of Parks, and Traffic" (Lambert), then the longer article "The City-Shaper" by Robert A. Caro. The first article looks at how Robert Moses, more than any other person, designed Long Island and much of New York City. The article gives a quick introduction to Robert Caro's biography on Robert Moses and the controversy it has caused. In the second, longer article, by Caro himself, he talks about the making of his famous and very lengthy (about twelve hundred pages) book about Robert Moses. Caro considers Moses to be something of an evil genius—a man who preserved a lot of land (many of Long Island's beaches, for example), but who, Caro argues, was "antidemocratic, corrupted by power, ruthless, vindictive, underhanded and racist [and who] sabotaged mass transit, enforced de facto segregation by race and class, bulldozed neighborhoods and callously displaced half a million New Yorkers under the banner of slum clearance, urban renewal, road construction and assorted other civic improvements" (Lambert 14:6). As you read these two articles, think about the various ways in which Moses shaped this entire region. Write a response in which you express your opinion of Robert Moses. If you were a historian, would you mostly praise Moses, or find fault with him? **Length: at least two pages.**

Phase 2

For Phase 2 you can choose one of the following assignment sequences: oral history preservation, tribe, eutopia, service-learning, or a project of your own design. All of these options are described below. Read through them all before you decide which one you want to pick.

Oral History Preservation Project
Introduction

By the middle of the twenty-first century approximately 50 percent of today's languages will be extinct (Kane). With them will disappear cultures, stories, histories, knowledge, and memories. This writing sequence gives you an opportunity to play the role of preservationist: you will record and write an oral history, thereby preserving portions of one person's life, memory, and history.

Assignment 2.1
Reading Response

Read the following first: Cynthia Stokes Brown, *Like It Was: A Complete Guide to Writing Oral History* (34–47). You needn't write anything for this; just read the text.

Primary Assignment

Find someone who matters to you, ideally someone much older. This person could be an older relative, a friend of the family, a neighbor, or an acquaintance. The person need not be living nearby, so long as you can talk to this person on the phone at least three times in the next three weeks for at least thirty minutes per call. If you don't have any family or friends or neighbors you'd like to interview, but still want to do this assignment, see me and we'll come up with someone else to work with, possibly a St. John's staff member, or somebody in a local nursing home.

After you've selected your person do the following:

a. Write down a list of questions you'd like to ask this person. Let this list be at least several pages long. Be sure the questions can't be answered with "yes" or "no" but are worded to get the interviewee talking as much as possible.

b. Interview the person for *at least* half an hour.

c. Write down the results of that interview. It's up to you whether to print this up in an interview format or to compile the results in a narrative. In the former case the text will read something like a play, with each paragraph preceded by your name or the interviewee's name, followed by what was said. In the latter case your text will look more like a narrative, in which you've compiled and probably rearranged the results of the interview, "gluing" it together with your own comments. Either way, be sure to accurately and truthfully record what the person says—don't "clean up" his or her English, or alter what he or she said because it "sounds better." The more accurate you are in getting down the person's voice, and his or her responses, the better off you'll be. **Length: at least 4 pages.**

(This is optional, and only if your subject gives you permission: take some photographs of this person, or gather up some that you already have, and bring them to class to show the class as we read and discuss your interview.)

Assignment 2.2
Primary Assignment

Go back to this person and conduct a second interview. Let this be your opportunity not only to ask new questions but also to go back to the person's earlier responses in order to get more information and further clarification. As before, you can either stick to the interview format or assemble the results of your interview into a narrative. **Length: at least another 4 pages.**

Assignment 2.3
Primary Assignment

Conduct one final interview with your person. By this time some of your classmates will have told you where they'd like to hear more about the person you're interviewing. In this last interview ask questions that might get the interviewee to supply more anecdotes and insights. Also, ask the interviewee what he or she would like to talk about and why. Let him or her play a role in selecting the topics discussed.

After this final interview, look at all the information you've collected and put together a brief oral history of this person. The end result can look like an interview, or you can assemble the material into a narrative. As you put together this assignment, ask yourself: What information should I include, and why? What might get edited, and why? How might I rearrange this material for better effect? Are there any themes I find running throughout this person's life? What exactly makes this person's history worth recording? Don't just attach all three assignments together; think about ordering and arranging them to make a more finished, coherent product.

It would be a good idea to write an introduction to your interview and maybe even conclude it with an afterword in which you provide some additional information about the person you're interviewing: why you chose this person, any details about your relationship with him or her, any closing thoughts you have about this person and what you learned from these interviews, and so on. It's okay—preferable, really—to let the introduction and/or conclusion be fairly long.

Also, if you wish, you can interject commentary throughout the interview, inserting your comments in parentheses or italics to differentiate it from the main narrative. For example, in the past, some writers have indicated stuff like: "At this point we moved into the living room; my mom put her feet up on the coffee table, obviously exhausted from having worked in the bakery for thirteen hours that day. I started asking a few more questions. . . ." **Length: at least 6 pages.**

For examples of how others have conducted oral histories, see the following: Cowan and Cowan, *Our Parents' Lives: Jewish Assimilation and Everyday Life*; Davis, *Mexican Voices/American Dreams: An Oral History of Mexican Immigration to the United States*; Dolci, *Sicilian Lives*; Frommer and Frommer, *Growing Up Jewish in America: An Oral History*; Hurmence, *My Folks Don't Want Me to Talk about Slavery: Twenty-One Oral Histories of Former North Carolina Slaves*; McMahan and Rogers, *Interactive Oral History Interviewing*; Tenhula, *Voices from Southeast Asia: The Refugee Experience in the United States*; Terkel, *Race: How Blacks and Whites Think and Feel about the American Obsession*.

Tribe
Introduction

Just as we are shaped by the places in which we live, so too are we constructed by various cultural communities. This assignment sequence gives you a chance to describe in detail a particular culture or "tribe" that you either belong to or have had an opportunity to observe. Like the oral history preservation project, this assignment will provide an opportunity to preserve elements of the chosen culture for others to read. This sequence might be particularly appealing to students interested in anthropology, cultural studies, history, and sociology.

Here are a few examples of topics that past students have chosen to write about when doing this assignment: life as a girl in a small Mexican village, the significance of dim sum in Chinatown, traveling with the Grateful Dead, Goth culture, snowboarders, botanicas, Carneval, the politics of clubbing, Sioux humor, Rrriot Grrrls, Dungeons and Dragons, Santeria, Trekkie culture, queer zines, changing Guyanese values, local amateur wrestling tournaments, and so on.

The culture you choose to write about might be your own ethnic heritage. Or it could be a "subculture" that you're a part of. It might be a culture that you don't belong to but that you're close to (maybe your significant other belongs to an orienteering club, and you want to write about that). In the past some students have even written about gangs that they have belonged to. There are numerous possibilities.

Make sure you do not pick a group that is too large to be dealt with in one short essay. Unless the cultural group you're writing about is particularly small, chances are you'll want to zero in on a particular aspect of that culture—say, the presence of machismo in a certain Latin American community, and how women in that community accept certain characteristics of this machismo while rejecting others. In other words, don't try to write about "African American culture" or "Chinese culture" since there are so many diverse cultural groupings that can be lumped under such umbrellas. Instead, be as specific as possible— say, a specific Haitian community in Brooklyn, or a look at the belief in ghosts within a Chinese family. As always, make an appointment with me if you want some help with focusing your topic.

Your job in this assignment sequence will be to introduce readers to your chosen culture, showing them its inner workings, its layers of complexity. You're going to want to help make this culture come alive for them, showing them why it's important, why it matters.

Assignment 2.1
<u>Reading Response</u>

Read Clifford Geertz's essay "Deep Play: Notes on the Balinese Cockfight" (you can skip the fourth and fifth sections of this essay, "Odds and Even Money" and "Playing with Fire," which get a little too detailed for our purposes here). As you read this famous essay, look at how, with each section, Geertz goes deeper and deeper in trying to get a handle on what, exactly, this cultural ritual is all about. One thing anthropologists like Geertz do is remind us of just how complex and multilayered even simple cultural rituals are. Chances are, the more we investigate them, the richer and deeper they become, full of additional meaning. Also pay attention to the end of the essay, where Geertz practically comes out and says that his interpretive analysis here is closer to a performance: he isn't really arriving at any "fact" or "truth," but ultimately telling a story. All we can do, he almost seems to say, is tell stories about what we observe. After reading Geertz's essay, write a response to it. What are your thoughts about Geertz's method? Does his approach give you any ideas about how you might write about or investigate your own cultural group or tribe? **Length: 2 pages.** (Optional: if you're particularly interested in this business of culture, look at the introductory passage I have on reserve from Roy Wagner's book *The Invention of Culture.* E-mail me any thoughts you have about this text, and it'll count for extra credit.)

Primary Assignment

Write a piece that introduces your readers to the cultural group or tribe that you've chosen to write about. Is this a tribe you have belonged to since birth? Or one that you joined later on? Are you a "member" of this group or an outsider looking in? If the latter, how did you come to know this group? Let your reader understand the circumstances surrounding your relationship to this tribe.

Next, describe this tribe in as much detail as you can. Remember, if the "tribe" you're writing about is very large and complex, this might mean focusing on a specific feature of it: for example, dating rituals within a traditional Ecuadorian family, or the Hong Kong gangs your uncle belonged to. As you write about this tribe, give your reader as many details as you can. Who are the people you're writing about? Where do they come from? What do they do, and how do they interact with each other in ways different from those who don't belong to this tribe? What stands out about this culture? Why is it important that this culture be preserved in writing? **Length: at least 3 pages.**

If you can, take some pictures of some of the people, places, or objects associated with this culture, and bring them to class.

Assignment 2.2
Primary Assignment

Continue writing about your tribe in response to any feedback you've received. As you write, imagine that you are preserving this culture for posterity: your words will, to some extent, make this culture, this group of people with their distinct lives and practices, enter the imaginations of other people. Why is this significant? What's to be gained from this? Why does it matter to preserve this cultural group? How would you respond to someone who might say, "That's nice, but I'm not really interested in this culture you're writing about." Let these questions help you continue to expand upon this piece of writing. As you do so, think about any feedback from peers that indicates a desire for more information. What else can you add? What do you think members of this particular "tribe" might want other readers to know? **Length: at least 3 pages.**

Reading Response

Read Maxine Hong Kingston's "No Name Woman" (in *The Woman Warrior*), in which Kingston tries to imagine the circumstances surrounding the death of an aunt she never knew. Among other things, this work of imaginative nonfiction is about reconstruction and preservation: how to reconstruct a person's life that was in danger of disappearing forever, and preserve it in writing. To what extent are you too engaging in an act of cultural construction or preservation? What are some of the implications of writing about this tribe, "capturing" it for others to encounter, via your writing? As part of your response, let me know what you thought about the Kingston piece as well. **Length: 2 pages.**

Assignment 2.3
Primary Assignment

Write an essay in which you introduce your readers to certain elements of the culture or "tribe" you've been writing about for this phase. As you write the essay, think about the kinds of images and ideas you will want to leave in the minds of your readers. This will be a continuation of the thinking and writing you have done during the previous two weeks. Be sure that the title for this essay is as specific as possible: try to zero in on a particular aspect of the culture or subculture you're focusing on. **Length: at least 5 pages.**

If you have photographs, incorporate them within your final piece of writing.

Eutopia
(utopia = the perfect place; eutopia = the good place)

Introduction

If you're someone with an interest in architecture, planning, urban studies, community revitalization, or environmental studies, then you might be interested in this sequence. It will give you a chance to further reflect upon what you think should be done about the places in which we live. It will offer you a chance to investigate what James Howard Kunstler calls "the art of making good places." This assignment sequence extends the thinking you did when you wrote about place in phase 1.

Assignment 2.1
Primary Assignment & Reading Response Combined
    Read *one* of the following chapters from Jane Jacobs's classic book *The Death and Life of Great American Cities*:

> "The Uses of Sidewalks: Safety" (you might look at this chapter if you're concerned about safety in your neighborhood);

> "The Uses of Sidewalks: Contact" (you might pick this chapter if you feel that it's hard getting to know the people in your neighborhood);

> "The Uses of Sidewalks: Assimilating Children" (look at this chapter if you're concerned about the impact of your neighborhood on the children in your community);

> "The Uses of Neighborhood Parks" (look at this chapter if you have concerns about the absence of parks or the condition of existing parks in your neighborhood);

> "The Need for Mixed Primary Uses" (this chapter explains the idea behind "mixed use"—having a mixture of businesses, schools, residences, etc. all within walking distance—and why this is important);

> "The Need for Small Blocks" (this chapter gets us thinking about how the shape and size of our blocks affects, for better or worse, how we feel about our neighborhoods)

> Then, read Hiss's "The 'Sacred Sites' That Make a Neighborhood Work." As you read one of Jacobs's chapters and this one newspaper article, think about a neighborhood, community,

or town you would like to improve (it's okay—in fact, desirable—that you focus on the community you wrote about in phase 1, or the general area in which you now live). What could be improved about this place? How does your impression of what is wrong about this place compare to conclusions in the assigned readings? Write a response to the two readings, making sure to relate some of the ideas in these texts to the place you want to write about. **Length: at least 3 pages.**

Assignment 2.2
Primary Assignment & Reading Response Combined

Read pages 15–38 of Calthorpe's *The Next American Metropolis: Ecology, Community, and the American Dream*, Roseland's "Dimensions of the Future: An Eco-city Overview," and Moe and Wilkie's "Preservation in the Age of Sprawl" (Chapter 7) from *Changing Places: Rebuilding Community in the Age of Sprawl*. All of these writers investigate alternatives for designing and planning contemporary American towns and cities. Write a response to these texts in which you explain which of the authors' claims you agree with, which you disagree with, and why. As always, as you reflect upon the ideas circulating in these texts, draw upon your own knowledge of one or more neighborhoods that you're familiar with, and reflect upon how your knowledge of these places supports or contradicts any of the findings in the texts you've read. **Length: at least 3 pages.**

Assignment 2.3
Primary Assignment & Reading Response Combined

Write an essay in which you describe for your readers what a "eutopia" would be—in other words, a truly "good" place (not a perfect place, which is what the word "utopia" implies). What would such a place have to have? Would it be anything like the visions described and reported on in the writings by Jacobs, Hiss, Calthorpe, Roseland, and Kunstler? Or would you design it entirely differently? Do you think such eutopias are still possible? Or not? Or maybe they already exist—in which case, let a significant piece of your essay be a depiction of some particular place you know of that fulfills many of your requirements for a eutopia. **Length: at least 5 pages.**

Service-Learning Project
Introduction

"Service-learning" is when students learn more about a particular subject matter by helping or serving others, often (but not always) through an organization or agency. It's not necessarily all that different from doing volunteer work, but one difference is that the work you do must be related to the course you're taking. Also, implicit within service-learning is that you reflect upon the nature of the work you're doing. While there are various models of service-learning, the one I'm using here is where students pick a neighborhood or community they'd like to work in (usually where they live) and find an organization they'd like to work with for a total of ten to fifteen hours during the semester. Throughout this service-learning project you'll keep a journal to document your activities. (Keep in mind that even if you pick the service-learning project for this second phase, you might end up "serving" your agency or organization throughout the rest of the semester. In other words, while you are required to conduct ten to fifteen hours of service, those hours could be spent all in one week or spread across any number of weeks between now and the end of the semester.)

Instead of breaking down the service-learning project into a three-week assignment sequence, read all of the following now, and then meet with me to discuss a possible schedule for fulfilling the rest of this assignment.

1. First, think of a neighborhood or community that matters to you. Make sure this is a place you can get to relatively easily. Then make two lists: (1) some of the things that bother you about this place and that should be changed for the better, and (2) some of the good things about this place that should be preserved and/ or enhanced. If you could wave a magic wand, what would you do to this place to make it better? What would you do in relation to traffic? Graffiti? Idle kids? Parks and streets? Child care? Schools? Senior citizens? Local businesses? Litter? Note: Make sure the place you choose to focus on is not too big and is somewhat public in nature. It can be just about anything—a street corner, a park, the street in front of your house, a group of stores

Sustainability in a Composition Course

you hang out in front of, and so on; but don't let it be so large as all of, say, Flushing, or so private as to be your backyard.

2. There are lots of different types of community work. Make an appointment with me so the two of us can take five minutes to look over the following categories, and determine which ones seem most interesting to you [these categories have been taken from Popple, with paraphrased versions of his descriptions]:

Community care: social networks and voluntary services aimed at helping the welfare of especially young, old, and disabled residents.

Community organizations: organizations directed toward improving coordination between various welfare agencies, such as councils for voluntary service, racial equity councils, and settlements.

Community development: helping groups get the skills and confidence to improve the quality of life of their members; self-help through community groups, education, literacy, substance abuse counseling.

Social/community planning: agencies and services that analyze local social conditions, community programs, services, and resources and set goals and priorities accordingly.

Community education: building relationships between education and community: community schools; homeschooling organizations; preschool centers; adult education.

Community action: community residents and stakeholders using conflict and direct action to influence power holders on specific issues, usually class-based: welfare rights movement; resistance against development; squatters; tenants' action.

Feminist community work: women's rights, equality, health, welfare issues addressed at a local level: women's health groups, therapy centers, clinics.

Cultural preservation community work: antidiscrimination and antiracism organizations, social justice groups, preservation of nonmainstream cultures, languages, and ethnicities.

Community arts and sciences: promotion of groups supporting local artists, writers, musicians, and performers; science and literacy programs.

After I get an idea of which area you're interested in, I'll contact the Service-Learning Office to help identify some agencies in or near the geographic area where you'd like to work. After we identify some organizations, we'll contact them to see which one(s) might be right for you.

3. After we've found a site where you can do your service work, you'll work out a schedule with someone at that site. As you conduct your hours of service—whether you do it all in one week or distribute those hours across the rest of the semester—you'll keep an informal journal of your experiences during this project, which you'll submit throughout the course of your service-learning project.

Your Choice

I realize that not all of these assignment sequences will be appealing to everyone. So, if none of the options thrill you, you can spend this phase writing whatever you wish: for example, short fiction, memoir, poetry, editorials, a journal, or the beginnings of a novel or screenplay. You just have to see me at least a week before the first assignment is due to talk about what you'd like to pursue. Whatever you choose, I'll most likely give you some assigned readings to go along with it.

Phase 3

For Phase 3 you can choose from the following options: work, education, consciousness, service-learning, or a project of your design. The first three of these are described below. The service-learning and self-designed options are described in the section on phase 2. Read through all of the choices before you decide which one you want to pick.

Work
Introduction

This sequence might be of particular interest to those of you who are in the College of Business Administration, since much of this sequence is as much about business as it is about work. After all, all work is connected in some way to business.

If you are like most people, for the next four or five decades you're going to be working. And if you're like most students, getting the job or career you want is a major reason you're in college in the first place. (For many people it's the only reason.) We might say, then, that for many people college is an elaborate (and certainly expensive) job prep ritual: in other words, you need to "go through" college to get your degree, which is a necessary prerequisite for many of the jobs students desire.

It is interesting, however, that students don't necessarily have much opportunity in their college courses to investigate the nature and philosophy of work, or to critique the work environments they already know or will be entering. How can we get a better idea of what work holds for us in the next few decades? How might we articulate what is problematic about work, and how work might be improved? And if it's within our reach, how might we make work synonymous with joy, exuberance, play, and even spiritual fulfillment? These are key questions for this sequence, which is designed around three assumptions: that work as we know it can be much improved; that there might be fewer opportunities for good work in the future; and that there is value in significantly reimagining the concept of work.

Assignment 3.1
<u>Primary Assignment</u>

Find two people who are currently working. Try to pick one person who really likes his or her job and one who doesn't. Talk to both at length and try to figure out what it is exactly that makes their work so great or awful. If the person who loves his or her job suddenly won the lottery, would he or she keep on working there? For as many hours? Why or why not? As for the person who hates his or her work, find out why, exactly, it's so miserable. Based on your interviews, see if you can make a list of the characteristics that make great jobs great and awful jobs awful.

To help you in your interviews, use the "Spirituality of Work Questionnaire" taken from Matthew Fox's *The Reinvention of Work*. (If you can't find a person who loves his or her job, talk instead to two people who hate their jobs—or at least two people who, if they won the lottery, would quit their jobs immediately and never look back.) **Length: at least 3 pages.**

Reading Response

Read Bob Black's "The Abolition of Work" and Al Gini's "Work, Identity, and Self: How We Are Formed by the Work We Do." While reading Bob Black's essay, make a list of all the reasons he hates work. Make a list too of what he would like to see us do instead of work. While reading Gini's essay, make a list of all the ways he thinks work forms our identities. Bring your lists to class and be prepared to talk about them.

Assignment 3.2

Primary Assignment and Reading Response Combined

Read three of the six articles below (you pick which ones) and write a response about some of what you consider to be the major ideas circulating in each. (For extra credit, read all of them. Keep in mind that the more you read, the more information you'll have to think about as you write your essay next week.) **Length: at least 3 pages.**

> Paul Hawken, "Preface" and "A Teasing Irony" (Chapter 1) from *The Ecology of Commerce: A Declaration of Sustainability* (xi–xvi, 1–17). Hawken believes that our entire concept of business must be changed, radically. Business can no longer be all about making a profit; instead, it must mean working towards a sustainable economy. (By "sustainable," he means, in part, a business that replenishes resources as it uses them.) For Hawken, anything less than this is unethical and maybe even suicidal. Do you agree with his argument? If not, why not? If so, do you think it's feasible?

> Robert Goodland, "The Case That the World has Reached Limits." Goodland argues that our economy has grown too big too fast, and that we've already reached the point where

we can no longer replenish limited resources. Goodland's point of view is very different from many of the pro-growth arguments one hears in the media. What do you think of his position? What are the implications of his argument?

Jeremy Rifkin, "New Technology and the End of Jobs." Rifkin has argued that in the near future there will be less good work available because technology will have made so many jobs obsolete. What are the implications of this argument?

Robert Alan Sessions, "Ecofeminism and Work." Taken from the collection *Ecofeminism: Women, Culture, Nature* (edited by Karen J. Warren), this essay by Sessions critiques the idea of work from an ecofeminist perspective. He argues that today's job systems are environmentally, socially, and economically dysfunctional and need to be redesigned according to ecofeminist perspectives.

Jerry Mander, "The Rules of Corporate Behavior," or Greider, "'Citizen' GE," or Mander and Boston, "Wal-Mart: Global Retailer." All three of these articles (each one counts as a selection for this assignment), taken from the same collection of essays, paint a very negative picture of large corporations. What are some of the arguments in each essay? Where do you find yourself agreeing or disagreeing with the authors?

Barbara Brandt, "Less Is More: A Call for Shorter Work Hours." Brandt, along with writers like Jeremy Rifkin and Bob Black, argue that the forty-hour workweek is unethical and unnecessary. They want us to be more like other countries where the workweek is shorter, so that people will have more time to devote to themselves and their families. What are your thoughts about this argument?

Assignment 3.3
Primary Assignment
(Choose A or B. **Length for either: at least 5 pages.**)
   A. Imagine that you are the owner of a small business. You want your employees to love their jobs so much that, even if they

won the lottery, they would still want to work for you. How would you design your workplace to make it the best it could possibly be for your employees? Be as detailed as you can: How many hours would you make people work? How much flexibility would there be? What would the workplace look and feel like? What would your company make or do? And so on.

As you write this essay think about the previous two assignments. What makes some peoples' work experiences miserable? Why do some people love their jobs? What insights did you pick up from reading last week's articles? Let all of this information assist you in designing your version of the ideal workplace. Keep in mind that what you are doing here is not just creating a short piece of fiction but laying the groundwork for your own philosophy of work.

OR

B. Write an essay in which you articulate your philosophy of what work is, and what work should be. Let your reader know what you think about this phenomenon called work. If you have a fairly negative view of work, let your reader know why. Let your reader know what work should be instead and whether you think your alternative vision is plausible or just a fantasy. Or, if you are more or less content with the way work is now, use this essay as an opportunity to argue with people like Bob Black and the other authors of the pieces you read last week, all of whom severely critique, from various angles, our current concepts of work. Somewhere in this essay you might want to describe what you think your own future work experience will be like, whether good or bad.

Reading Response
Explore the Sustainable Business Network, which is located at www.sustainablebusiness.com. Write one to two pages describing what you found there, and what you think of this Web site.

Education
Introduction
This sequence will obviously appeal to those of you who are thinking about becoming teachers at some point in the future—

which might include a number of you, since in the next ten years approximately two million teachers are going to have to be hired in this country to replace retiring faculty and to handle a growing population of students.

In your life, you have spent more hours going to school than doing anything else, with the exception of sleeping. This makes you something of an expert on education. This sequence gives you a chance to examine various critiques of education and create your working philosophy of what education should be all about. At the end of this sequence you can focus on primary, secondary, or higher education, whichever is more relevant to your own concerns and interests.

Assignment 3.1
Primary Assignment

Think back on the years you've spent in school. What teachers or classes stand out as positive or negative? Write a response in which you give examples of both good and bad teachers and/ or classes you have had at any point in your educational career. As you present these memories to us, try to explain what it was exactly that made these experiences good or bad: What were the teachers doing? What did they believe in? How would you describe their educational philosophies? **Length: at least 3 pages.**

Reading Response

Read Gatto's "The Seven-Lesson Schoolteacher" (pages 1–21 from *Dumbing Us Down: The Hidden Curriculum of Compulsory Schooling*), and pages 111–17 from Longstreet and Shane's *Curriculum for a New Millennium*. In the first reading, Gatto argues that, as a high school teacher, he can't do his job—in other words, be a good teacher—because high school demands that he teach seven (bad) lessons. In the past, some students who read this essay misunderstood Gatto's sarcastic tone and thought that he was actually advocating for these seven lessons. He isn't, of course: he's saying that these seven lessons he is forced to teach are hateful and wrong, but because of the educational system he works in, they are unavoidable. His essay is a condemnation of the way high school teachers are forced to teach. The second reading is an excerpt from a textbook describing the differences between four distinct educational philosophies, which we'll spend one class period talking about in some detail.

As you read Gatto's article, be sure you understand what these seven negative lessons are that, according to him, teachers are forced to teach to students due to the nature of our very problematic educational system. Does your experience as a student confirm anything that Gatto has written? If so, what exactly have you experienced that makes you agree or disagree with some of what Gatto says? As you read the second text, try to understand the differences between the four curricular philosophies. Which theory makes the most sense to you? Which one best describes the system you're part of now? Be prepared to talk about this in class. **Length: at least 3 pages.**

Assignment 3.2
Reading Response

Read two of the three excerpts below (or all three, for extra credit) and write a response about the major ideas circulating in each selection. What are the authors' main arguments? Are they sensible or unrealistic? How feasible are they? Most of all, to what extent do you agree or disagree with what they're saying? **Length: at least 3 pages.**

> David Orr, "What Is Education For?" in *Earth in Mind: On Education, Environment, and the Human Prospect* (7–15). All education, says Orr, should be "environmental education," and this chapter explains why he says this. To what extent do you agree with him?

> Michael Blitz and C. Mark Hurlbert, "Strangers," Chapter 1 from *Letters for the Living: Teaching Writing in a Violent Age* (1–18). Blitz and Hurlbert both teach undergraduate writing courses to students just like you—Blitz especially, since he teaches students at John Jay College in Manhattan. Together they have found that the majority of their students experience violence directly or indirectly in their lives, and that consequently they share a desire to encounter peace. Blitz and Hurlbert argue that when teachers, especially those teaching composition, design their courses, they must take into

account the needs, fears, and hopes of their students. What are your thoughts after reading this passage?

Ted Trainer, "Education," in *The Conserver Society: Alternatives for Sustainability* (166–77). Trainer argues that, if we're to survive, humans must create a "conserver economy." In this chapter he explains how the educational system as we know it works against a conserver economy. He also offers an alternative vision of what education should be. Do you agree with his ideas? Do you think it is possible to implement his vision for a different kind of educational institution?

Assignment 3.3
Primary Assignment
(Choose A or B. **Length for either: at least 5 pages.**)
    A. Write an essay in which you reinvent the curricular policies and/or educational objectives of your own major. Before you write, think about your educational philosophy (refer to the four types you read about two weeks ago). How would this shape what you think should or shouldn't be done in the classroom? To what extent would you agree or disagree with what Orr, Blitz and Hurlbert, or Trainer say education should and shouldn't be? Use the articles you've read, your responses, and our discussions in class to articulate a plan to improve upon and reform the current requirements for your own major. Keep in mind that what you are doing here is not just creating a short piece of fiction, but laying the groundwork for your own philosophy of education. (If you are for the most part satisfied with the requirements for your major, then use this as an opportunity to argue against the stated or implied objectives of the arguments presented by Orr, Trainer, or Blitz and Hurlbert.)

OR

    B. Write an essay in which you articulate your philosophy of what school (whether primary, secondary, or college) should be. You might begin by letting your reader know what you think about this phenomenon called education, based on your own experiences. If you have a fairly negative view of school, let your reader know why. Let your reader know what education should be instead and whether you think your alternative vision is plausible or just a fantasy. Or, if you are more or less content with the way school is now, use this essay as an opportunity to argue with people like David Orr and Ted Trainer, both of whom severely critique the current state of higher education. If you want, write this in the form of an extended college mission statement (see the St. John's mission statement at the beginning of your college catalog for an example). Be sure your reader understands to what degree contemporary higher education does or does not conform to your vision.

Consciousness
Introduction

What is consciousness? We "do" consciousness all the time—or maybe it's better to say that our consciousness constructs each of us—and yet most of us don't spend any time actively thinking about what this most intimate of experiences is all about. After all, nothing, it would seem, is closer to us than our own consciousness. And yet for many of us it's hard to even talk about this—What? A thing? An act? An event? A performance?—for very long, or with any kind of authority or confidence.

This sequence is not intended to be an introduction to consciousness or "enlightenment" in any way that would satisfy, say, your psychology or philosophy or theology professors (although, if you are majoring in any of these areas, this sequence should interest you). But it is a chance to look at several readings designed to get us thinking more about this phenomenon called consciousness. John Taylor Gatto (people doing the education sequence are reading an essay by him) says that in school we have far too few opportunities to experience solitude and quiet reflection, or what might be called "contemplative practice." Some think that much of the pain we encounter on a daily basis might be prevented if we had more time to reflect upon who we are, where we're going, what we need (as opposed to what we desire). Or maybe some of us just need time to meditate on nothing at all: to consciously "clear" consciousness from our minds.

In this sequence, I've put together some reading assignments, but you and I will have to meet to determine what exactly you'll write during this phase. For example, you might try to meditate three or four times a week for this entire phase, keeping a journal of that experience along the way. Or you might keep a "dream journal" and think about what your mind is doing while you're unconscious. You might work toward an essay in which you wrestle with your own spiritual convictions in relation to some of the information in these texts. You might write a "metalogue" with one or more of your inner personae. Those of you who are drawn to this sequence should see me right away so we can, together, create the additional assignments for this sequence.

Assignment 3.1
<u>Reading Response</u>
Read and write a response to the following. **Length: 3 pages.**

Joseph Goldstein, excerpts from *The Experience of Insight: A Simple and Direct Guide to Buddhist Meditation* (pages 7–16).

Thich Nhat Hanh. Chapter 1 ("The Essential Discipline") and Chapter 2 ("The Miracle Is to Walk on Earth") from *The Miracle of Mindfulness: A Manual of Meditation* (pages 1–8, 11–24).

Chan Master Cijiao of Changlu, "Models for Sitting Meditation," in Thomas Cleary's *Minding Mind: A Course in Basic Meditation* (pages 16–19).

<u>Primary Assignment</u>
To be determined individually. Make an appointment with me to discuss this.

Assignment 3.2
<u>Reading Response</u>
Read and write a response to the following. **Length: 3 pages.**

Sogyal Rinpoche, Chapter 1 ("In the Mirror of Death") and Chapter 2 ("Impermanence") from *The Tibetan Book of Living and Dying* (pages 3–14, 15–27).

Marvin Minsky, "The Society of Mind," "One Self or Many?" "The Soul," "Consciousness," "Thinking without Thinking," "Momentary Mental State," all from *The Society of Mind* (pages 20, 40, 41, 56, 63, 151).

Primary Assignment

To be determined individually. Make an appointment with me to discuss this.

Assignment 3.3
Primary Assignment

To be determined individually. Make an appointment with me to discuss this.

Phase 4

Future
Introduction

What will the future be like? Not the distant future, but life twenty-five years from now? What kind of world will the next generation grow up in? None of us has a crystal ball, and those who claim the art of prophecy usually end up embarrassing themselves. On the other hand, we have more access to information than ever before, information that might lead us to make educated guesses about likely future scenarios. This phase gives you the opportunity to let people know what you think is on the horizon, for better or worse (or both).

Assignment 4.1
Primary Assignment & Reading Response Combined

The following four texts give a spectrum of views about the future. Peter Schwartz is optimistic; so are Bill Gates and the "prophets of boom" interviewed in Kevin Kelly's article. Eugene Linden, on the other hand, anticipates a very bleak future. Hartmut Bossel thinks we're poised to go in either direction, and Robert Yaro and Tony Hiss paint both positive and negative scenarios about the immediate future of the New York City region. Read all of these selections and write a response in which you make it clear which scenarios (if any) make sense to you, which (if any) don't, and why. **Length: at least 4 pages.**

Peter Schwartz, Chapter 9 ("The World in 2005: Three Scenarios") from *The Art of the Long View*.

Kevin Kelly, "Prophets of Boom: Five Champions of the Endless Upswing."

Bill Gates, *The Road Ahead*, pages 9–11.

Eugene Linden, Chapter 15 ("New York City: Advertising Adapts") from *The Future in Plain Sight: Nine Clues to the Coming Instability*.

Robert D. Yaro and Tony Hiss, "Appendix: Envisioning Two Futures" from *A Region at Risk: The Third Regional Plan for the New York–New Jersey–Connecticut Metropolitan Area*.

Hartmut Bossel. *Earth at a Crossroads: Paths to a Sustainable Future*, pages 1–18.

Assignment 4.2
<u>Primary Assignment & Reading Response Combined</u>
This week's assignment will be the same as last week's, only with different readings. First, look at the excerpts from the November-December 1999 issue of MIT's *Technology Review,* which features a number of tiny articles under the heading "100 young innovators predict the future of computing, biotech, the Web and nanotech" ("Technology Review 100"). Then read Paul and Anne Ehrlich's article, in which they express concern about overpopulation. The third selection is by David Ehrenfeld, who looks at mass extinctions. In the fourth and fifth readings, researchers at the Worldwatch Institute document various trends that are shaping our future, some good, many of them bad. Next, Jim Motavalli looks at several future possibilities: "Fortress World," "Ecotopia," and "The Planet in Peril." Finally, Hawken, Lovins, and Lovins argue that we are on the verge of a new industrial revolution structured around "natural capitalism." **Length: at least 4 pages.**

"The Technology Review 100," *Technology Review,* November-December 1999: pages 73–74, 76, 80–83, 86–87, 90, 92, 94–99, 102, 104, 106–111, 116, 118, 120–125, 128, 130, 133–135. Even though this is a lot of pages, keep in mind that these are not articles but just captions for each of the 100 "innovators" selected by the magazine's editors. Your goal here is not to "know" all of this material inside and out, but rather to constructively skim (remember our class discussions on this) through each of the five sections in the article—"software," "biotech," "World Wide Web," "materials," and "hardware"—and identify a small handful of the innovators represented within each section whose ideas or comments stand out to you, for whatever reason.

Paul R. and Anne H. Ehrlich, "Why Isn't Everyone as Scared as We Are?"

David Ehrenfeld, "Life in the Next Millennium: Who Will Be Left in the Earth's Community?"

Lester R. Brown et al., *Vital Signs 1997: The Environmental Trends That Are Shaping Our Future* (selected excerpts).

Lester R. Brown et al., *Vital Signs 1999: The Environmental Trends That Are Shaping Our Future* (selected excerpts).

Jim Motavalli, "2000: Planet Earth at the Crossroads."

Paul Hawken, Amory Lovins, and L. Hunter Lovins, *Natural Capitalism: Creating the Next Industrial Revolution*, pages 1–11 and Chapter 2, "Reinventing the Wheels."

Assignment 4.3
Primary Assignment
In the past two weeks we've been reading various future scenarios, ranging from grim to great. And in class we've been discussing our own best guesses about what we think is on the horizon and why. Write an essay in which you tell your readers what *you* expect to see in the next twenty-five years, for better or

for worse. This is not an essay about what you hope to see, but rather what you think will *probably* come about. Obviously, no one knows exactly what the future will bring; but there is value in making educated guesses about the future. If you are worried about the future, tell your readers about your fears—what they are, and why you have them. If you have high hopes about the future, tell us what they are, and why you have a positive outlook. **Length: at least 6 pages.**

Snapshot of an Environmental Footprint

How a disposable camera comes into being; from Richard Powers's *Gain* (New York: Farrar, Straus and Giroux, 1998), 345–48.

It all starts in sun. The cardboard case, the instantly pitched packaging: a sunny upland stand of southern yellow pines. A thing that once lived for light.

Somewhere on the coast of British Columbia, machines receive these trees. Pulper, bleacher, recovery plant, and mill synchronize a staggering ballet, juggling inventory from calcium hypochlorite to nitrogen tetroxide, substances ranging from Georgia clays to the South Pacific guano.

Timber, scrap, and straw cook together in the maws of enormous chemical vats. Black liquors and white liquors—spent and new infusions of caustic soda and sodium sulfide—swirl the raw chips downward into the continuous digesters. Screened and washed of sodium brews, the pulp proceeds to beating. Microadjustable blades tease out the fibers. Into this smooth mash mix sizers and fillers and dyes. Calcium carbonate, aluminum sulfate, aluminum silicate, titanium dioxide, hydrated silica, hydrated alumina, talc, barium sulfate, calcium sulfate, zinc sulfide, zinc oxide, cationic starch, polyacrylamide resins, locust bean gum, guar gum, and asbestos combine to make any kind of paper the world wants made.

As the creamed blend dries, subatomic van der Waals forces assert a new mat of tentative filaments. A Fourdrinier machine forms the wet stock, presses the draining sheets between felts, and carries them through a series of high-energy furnaces and dryers. Every pound of paper takes sixty pounds of heated air just to drive off the birthing fluid. The sandwich of myriad paperboard layers paste together to a thickness just under one millimeter.

The outermost layer is manila-coated and impregnated, by thermoplastic extruder, with an invisible skin of polyethylene plastic. Molten resin flows through a heated cylinder under high pressure. A die heats the resin to a precise temperature and viscosity, squeezing it into a film of absurdly controlled thickness. Hot film slips onto the rolling stream of paper so perfectly that paper and plastic bond permanently into a weird, third thing that, within the last few years, has become another universal given.

All this for the box, the throwaway. The product's one-piece pup tent is also a self-contained sales-rack display. A series of machines cut, fold, and glue the cast around the finished camera. Powdered glue for sealing the carton arrives at an assembly plant in Guangzhou in whole railway cars, by the metric ton. The double crucifix of cardboard still bears the kerf of the complex jigsaw that cut this continuous contour. Parallel paper mold marks run down its inside surface, invisible except in slant light. A person could go to her grave not knowing that blank cardboard is so striated.

The thing that Canada ships to Guangzhou for gluing is already an orchestral score. The chipboard must be perfect, to hold the vibrant stripes and bursts of look-at-me words that promise a life that will not fade prior to expiration date. The product calls itself after a youthful West Coast city. The trademark scrawls across package front in a childish rainbow of noisy graffiti. Variegated promises of well-behaved euphoria dance on a white background. The inks and resins smell musty and antiseptic, like an obstetrician's waiting room.

Dyes stain the front with a photographic transfer of the enclosed camera, itself ensleeved in a dye-transfer rainbow re-creating the design of the outside box. Down one side, text identifies each machine feature with an arrow. A golden star bursts above the scene, reading: "New: With Eye-Glare Elimination. Ultra-thin profile. Drop in your pocket!"

Stamped onto the bottom, a disclaimer states:

> Liability for any product found to be defective in manufacture, packing, or shipping will be limited to replacement. As color dyes

will change over time, this film bears no warranty for accuracy or fidelity, either implied or expressed. Not responsible for any damages consequent upon the use, misuse, failure to use, or inability to use this product.

Next to these words stands a broken-toothed comb of bar codes, precise enough to be read by wands the world over. Next to that, the "Recycled" triangle and the words "Develop Before 12-99." Ten more digits hide under a folded flap: GB72-020-001. The number means something to someone. At the bottom, in the smallest of fonts that will not smear, the manufacturer discloses its address: a town in a state where people assemble things made elsewhere.

The high-tech paperboard encloses a vacuum-packed camera-in-a-bag. Hermetic foil pouching extends the thing's shelf life, as if it were a slow-ripening fruit. The bag is part aluminum alloy, part plastic, part space-age oilskin. Inside, the camera itself: "Thinner than 'n inch." On its inner cardboard wrap, the camera wears its own unlosable instructions. Explanatory icons lighten the labor of reading. All across the intricate machine, pointers identify the salient features: the electric flash, the ready light, the film counter window and ratcheted thumb wheel, the pressed lenses more exact than whole workshops of Dutch Golden Age scientists could hope to grind.

The smooth, black plastic of the camera's right side is impressed with a dimple the size and depth of the median human thumb: a composite grip averaged from several thousand hands by painstaking research. Another research team orchestrates the eyepiece, a third the flash. An army of chemical engineers, fresh from school, selects ingredients for the plastic casing. Perhaps management has a grasp of the general theory, a cartoon notion of what you'd need to rig up color film from scratch. But when the strained chains of infrastructure next crack, history will return to those long centuries after the Empire packed up, when a farmer's scythe falling down a well meant permanent farewell to iron.

Plastic happens; that is all we need to know on earth. History heads steadily for a place where things need not be grasped to be used. At a shutter click, a bite-sized battery dispatches a blast through a quartz tube filled with halogens. Excited electrons, falling back down the staircase of available energy states, flash for a second, to dissipate the boost that lifted them briefly into rarefied orbitals. This waste energy bounces off the lines of a grieving face and back down the hole of the aperture, momentarily opened. Inside, reflected light ruffles the waiting film emulsion like a child's hand impressing a birthday cake. Years from now, metal from the flash battery will leach into runoff and gather in the fat of fish, then the bigger fish that eat them.

The camera jacket says: "Made In China With Film From Italy Or Germany." The film itself accretes from more places on the map than emulsion can cover. Silver halide, metal salts, dye couplers, bleach fixatives, ingredients gathered from Russia, Arizona, Brazil, and underwater seabeds, before being decanted in the former DDR. Camera in a pouch, the true multinational: trees from the Pacific Northwest and the southeastern coastal plain. Straw and recovered wood scrap from Canada. Synthetic adhesive from Korea. Bauxite from Australia, Jamaica, Guinea. Oil from the Gulf of Mexico or North Sea Brent Blend, turned to plastic in the Republic of China before being shipped to its mortal enemies on the Mainland for molding. Cinnabar from Spain. Nickel and titanium from South Africa. Flash elements stamped in Malaysia, electronics in Singapore. Design and color transfers drawn up in New York. Assembled and shipped from that address in California by a merchant fleet beyond description, completing the most heavily choreographed conference in existence.

On the label, the manufacturer warns: "To avoid possible shock, do not open or disassemble." And still they will be sued, by someone, somewhere. These words hide a feat of master engineering under the hood too complex for any user to follow. What makes the sale is transparency. Set to go, right out of the package, and ready to disappear when used. No anything required.

. . . Labor, materials, assembly, shipping, sales markups and overheads, insurance, international tariffs—the whole prodigious creation costs less than ten dollars. The world sells to us at a loss, until we learn to afford it.

Such a wonder has to be cheap enough to jettison. You cannot have a single-use camera except at a repeatable price. Buy it; shoot it; toss it. As mundane as any breakthrough that seemed our whole salvation once. A disposable miracle, no less than the least of us.

NOTES

Chapter One

1. For a critique of the "whiteness" of ecocriticism, see Carl Anthony's interview with Theodore Roszak, in which Anthony critiques the Eurocentric biases embedded in the assumptions of some deep ecologists. In responding to Aldo Leopold's claim that people think like mountains, Anthony responds, "Why is it so easy for these [white] people to think like mountains and not be able to think like people of color?" (Anthony 273)

2. This is not to say that one should infer any inherent connection between winning a Nobel Prize and having a clue about environmental stewardship. In her attempt to find out what the world's most famous economists have to say regarding the environment, Carla Ravaioli reveals a stunning lack of environmental awareness among many internationally famous economists. In particular, see part of an interview with Milton Friedman (Ravaioli 63–65).

3. As of this writing, both groups can be found at http://groups.yahoo.com/.

4. See too Edward Flattau's *Tracking the Charlatans: An Environmental Columnist's Refutational Handbook for the Propaganda Wars.*

5. Unfortunately, writers like Ray and Guzzo find their way into "green readers" used in writing courses. Consider how, even though the collection clearly seeks to instill a strong environmentalist ethic in students, the editor of *Reading the Environment* (Walker) has seen fit to insert among her otherwise "green" selections two irresponsibly deceptive pieces of propaganda: William Booth's "So What If It's Getting Hot?" and Ray and Guzzo's "Environmentalism and the Future." The former is a brief editorial that dismisses global warming as a lie perpetuated by "eco-technocrats" and argues that even if the temperature does rise, humans will be the better for it. The latter is typical of Ray and Guzzo's method of arguing without evidence: they claim that "environmentalism" "incorporates a strongly negative element of anti-development,

anti-progress, anti-technological, anti-business, anti-established institutions, and, above all, anti-capitalism. Its positive side, if that is what it can be called, is that it seeks development of a society totally devoid of industry and technology" (qtd. in Walker 531–32). It's not so much that the editor of this reader has chosen to include such examples of wrongheaded writing within the anthology, but that students who encounter these texts have no immediate way to gauge the degree to which these authors are manipulating readers through the distortion and absence of evidence. No questions accompany these two selections; their presence in the anthology implicitly casts them as neither more nor less authoritative than the other selections. An example of a reader where similar texts are presented within a more critical context is Anderson and Runciman's *A Forest of Voices,* in which the editors encourage readers to actively question the claims raised in an article by Dixy Lee Ray and "be aware of the political orientation of the publications you look at": "In the end, draw some tentative conclusions about the nature of 'scientific fact' and the relationship of facts and politics" (567). Jenseth and Lotto take a similar tack in including P.J. O'Rourke's "The Greenhouse Affect" in their reader *Constructing Nature*: "Even though we may not agree with the message behind some humor, often the humor itself allows us to understand a different perspective" (426).

6. Gelbspan's harsh criticism of the greenhouse skeptics is supported by Paul Epstein of the Center for Health and the Global Environment at Harvard Medical School, whose research explores the relationship between global climatic changes and the rise of new infectious diseases (Patz et al.; Epstein "Ecosystem"). Epstein states that there are about six scientists left who seriously debate the reality of global warming, only one or two of whom are able to publish in refereed journals (Epstein "Emerging"). Similarly, Gail E. Christianson writes, "Few of [the greenhouse skeptics'] papers have been placed in respected scientific journals, where all articles are subject to intense peer review. Instead, they pen short books that are published by the ideologically driven think tanks to which they belong."

Chapter Two

1. Peter Sloep calls attention to how the introduction of sustainability has changed environmental science from a multidisciplinary field (i.e., limited to a handful of related disciplines) to an "interdiscipline" or an "interfield." One could also say that writing across the curriculum and cultural studies have helped composition and English studies to metamorphose into interfields. As "fields," English and composition studies are undeniably rich—wide enough to embrace and be transformed by

cultural and postcolonial studies, science, pop culture, architecture, visual studies, multimedia, and so on. But until sustainability surfaces within composition and English studies in a substantive way, the cross-disciplinary reach that characterizes these fields can go only so far.

2. Lyons, Moore, and Smith further define intergenerational justice as a combination of "*intragenerational equity*—justice and fairness in society today, along with *intergenerational equity*—a fair treatment for future generations" (243). My own treatment of sustainability throughout this work focuses more on intergenerational than on intragenerational equity, a fact pointed out to me by Sean Southey of the United Nations Development Programme. A logical follow-up to this book would be a more extensive inquiry into sustainability from an intragenerational framework, within which more attention is paid to local service-learning initiatives and to communication between American undergraduates and members of poor and Third World communities.

3. An important overview of ecological economics can be found in Krishnan, Harris, and Goodwin's *A Survey of Ecological Economics*. However, the ninety-five "frontier essays" included in this collection are not reprints of the original articles but detailed summaries of those articles by the three editors. Consequently, whenever I refer to an article summarized in this collection, readers should keep in mind that in these cases I have not consulted the primary texts but have relied upon the editors' summaries of those publications.

4. True sustainability, Greider writes, would mean "a factory [that] . . . cleans up its own mess and uses the materials over and over again. Consumers who do not throw things away, but send them back to the factory as raw materials for conversion into new products. Workers who merge their skills with robotic machines to do the dirty, dangerous work of saving the earth" (450).

5. Engel's emphasis on the "whole community of life on Earth" and Clugston's "circuits of aliveness" require clarification, as both hint at a "deep ecology" position which views humans as equal to all other living entities. I think Herman Daly and John Cobb articulate an ecologically more supportable position:

> We believe there is more intrinsic value in a human being than in a mosquito or a virus. We also believe that there is more intrinsic value in a chimpanzee or a porpoise than in an earthworm or a bacterium. This judgment of intrinsic value is quite different from the judgment of the importance of a species to the interrelated whole. The interrelated whole would probably survive the extinction of chimpanzees with little damage, but it

would be seriously disturbed by the extinction of some species of bacteria. We believe that distinctions of this sort are important as guides to practical life and economic policy and that the insistence that a deep ecologist refuse to make them is an invitation to deep irrelevance. (Daly and Cobb 378)

6. Lyons, Moore, and Smith point out that Ted Trainer goes beyond Daly and Cobb's argument for "a market economy, a model of small-scale decentralized communitarian capitalism" (252). Trainer argues for de-development, living simply—not just "zero-growth economy, but relative to contemporary capitalist society . . . *de-development*": "De-development will produce more simple and less expensive lifestyles and self-sufficiency at the national, local and household levels. 'Barren suburbs' will be converted into local economies with local farms and cottage industries" (qtd. in Lyons, Moore, and Smith 252). Nevertheless, Lyons, Moore, and Smith refer to both Daly and Trainer as promoters of "deep sustainability." For more on the distinction between "desirable" and "undesirable" growth, see John Peet's chapter "The Physics and Morality of Growth" in *Energy and the Ecological Economics of Sustainability* (100–113).

7. In her essay "Development Beyond Economism: Local Paths to Sustainable Development," Hazel Henderson reminds us that the economic indicators GNP and GDP "were developed for military mobilization purposes in Britain and the United States" and therefore "their materialistic view of progress cannot guide humanity beyond consumerism toward moral growth and sustainable development" (94).

8. Not only did "we" benefit from the Exxon Valdez oil spill, we are responsible for causing it in the first place, as Thomashow points out:

> To what extent are all American citizens, including environmentalists, responsible for the *Exxon Valdez*? Exxon should be held accountable for their actions, but that doesn't relieve "distant observers" of their responsibility or their connection to the disaster. For example, after the oil spill, some analysts, many of whom were environmentalists, called attention to the type of economy and the cultural orientation that allows such dangerous ships to be built in the first place. Perhaps the whole culture is at fault and all people who drive cars to some extent share the responsibility. What are the historical, economic, and political conditions that contribute to the *Exxon Valdez*? (156)

9. See Peterson for an extended argument for interpreting sustainable development as a key for negotiating the gap between ecocentric and anthropocentric views.

Chapter Three

1. In *Letters for the Living: Teaching Writing in a Violent Age*, Michael Blitz and C. Mark Hurlbert paraphrase J. Elspeth Stuckey, who

> noted that teachers do a lot of talking about the way things ought to be, but that we rarely talk candidly about who we really are, where we really come from, what we've really done in our "secret lives" away from, and before we ever got to, our schools, colleges, and universities. She wondered out loud whether we all thought these "private" matters weren't relevant to our everyday work as educators. In other words, she was suggesting that we might all be pretending. (2)

2. Because of the confusing mélange of towns and villages overlapping one another across the island, coupled with the absence of village centers, Long Islanders often identify themselves according to the exit on the Long Island Expressway nearest their home. When people ask me where I live, all I need to say is "near exit 60." For many Long Islanders, our sense of place is often determined by commuting distance—to Manhattan, to work, or to family in the area.

3. In the 1999 film *200 Cigarettes* two teenagers from Ronkonkoma (Christina Ricci and Gaby Hoffman) spend New Year's Eve on the Lower East Side. One of the film's recurring jokes is that no one can understand where exactly the two young women come from or what they say, given the odd name of their town and their impenetrable "Lawn Guyland" accents.

4. This active KKK presence is, sadly, less surprising when one considers that during the 1700s roughly 20 percent of Long Island's population consisted of slaves, mostly Black but also American Indian. One historian (amazingly) equates ownership of slaves with Long Island's contemporary car culture: "Slaveholding was to colonial status on Long Island what car-owning is to contemporary status: prosperous families owned fourteen or more slaves, while poorer residents could afford only one or two" (Bookbinder 39). An insensitive comparison for obvious reasons—car owners around here spend considerable money "detailing" their machines, not torturing, raping, and murdering them—the analogy is also backwards: to live in suburban sprawl means to be a slave to one's car, or, rather, to the planners who built these communities designed around automobile transportation.

5. "The influence of the Cold War was profound. In the 1950s, the civil Defense Committee of AASHTO, the American Association of State

Highway Transportation Officials, was a dominant force in the determination of street design criteria. Its prescription was straightforward: street design must facilitate evacuation before, and cleanup after, a major 'nuclear event'" (Duany et al. 65). Ironically, fear of the bomb is what drew so many "come-outers" to the suburbs in the first place, away from urban centers that had become atomic bomb targets (Stilgoe 301).

6. Portions of this wooded lot have since been bulldozed to make way for a road widening project; the rest is up for sale.

7. "Two-thirds of all freight shipped to and from the five boroughs is moved by trucks . . . but in Queens, 84 percent of freight moves in trucks." Furthermore, "New York is one of the few major cities where most goods are shipped by trucks, clogging roads, polluting the air and driving up shipping costs for businesses. . . . Adding to the problem is [the fact] that many trucks move off designated routes and illegally drive through residential areas" (Bazzi).

Chapter Four

1. From Jack Forbes's book *Columbus and Other Cannibals*:

> The truth of the matter is that Harvard or Yale graduates, for example, are quite capable of lobbying for a "concession" of territory in Brazil, or Colombia, or Bolivia, the development of which will mean the utter annihilation of thousands of Native Americans. Of course, the refined gentlemen will not personally order the liquidation of the Indians, but they will set in motion a chain of events leading inevitably (under conditions current in South America) to the enslavement, removal, and death of the indigenous tribes. (12)

2. The appeal of this badly drawn comic lies in its depictions of workplace idiocy, slacker cubicle-dwellers, and idiotic managers—with many of the comic strip ideas coming from disgruntled employees who send Adams his three hundred daily e-mail messages. The comic strip is so well known that it might be the one thing all American corporations have in common—it is hard to imagine an office building that does not have at least one *Dilbert* comic push-pinned to a cubicle partition or taped near the photocopy machine. The irony, as Norman Solomon argues in detail in *The Trouble with Dilbert: How Corporate Culture Gets the Last Laugh,* is that *Dilbert* itself is loaded with a sort of stealth

version of Adams's own unabashed and fairly heinous pro-corporate views. (Thanks to Tom Tiller for bringing Solomon's book to my attention.)

3. Forms of employment like telemarketing can be thought of as workpain viruses in that the employee's workpain—in this case, the phone salesperson forced to sound happy and helpful for hours each day—spills into the consciousness of people who are home, away from work, thus temporarily infecting that otherwise work-free environment.

Chapter Five

1. At that time, four New York City police officers were on trial for violating the civil rights of Haitian immigrant Abner Louima, who was beaten and tortured by police in a 70th Precinct station bathroom. About the same time, another four New York City police officers were indicted on second-degree murder charges for killing Amadou Diallo, an unarmed West African immigrant. The quoted headline refers to New York City Police Commissioner Howard Safir's statements that the demonstrations mounted in response to the Diallo killing were using the incident to stir up racial unrest.

Chapter Six

1. While not writing specifically about English studies, C. A. Bowers has long argued that "contributing to the long-term sustainability of ecosystems, and thus to the survival of cultures, should become one of the criteria now missing from current educational thinking" (*Educating* 15). Although this 1995 title has received very little recognition, Bowers's *Educating for an Ecologically Sustainable Culture: Rethinking Moral Education, Creativity, Intelligence, and Other Modern Orthodoxies* is an essential volume for cultural theorists and curriculum reformers.

2. Schwitter's coinage of the term "merz" (which he sometimes rendered as "Merz" or "MERZ") came from tearing apart the word "kommerz" to liberate the second syllable. Merz was not a personal style or theory but his entire field of vision: "Later on I expanded this name 'MERZ' to include my poetry . . . and finally all my relevant activities. Now I call myself MERZ" (Schmalenbach 93).

3. In *Curriculum for a New Millennium*, Longstreet and Shane add a fifth philosophical perspective, existentialism, which "places its emphasis on

the self as a primary source of knowledge about life and its meaning," and in which the student's perspective remains the "primary source of knowledge, independent . . . of any social grouping to which she or he may belong, and without specific reference to other-worldly or earth-centered authority" (118). But I find their educational existentialism to consist largely of Christian humanism inspired by nineteenth-century romanticism, reminiscent of composition's liberal expressivist turn throughout the 1970s.

WORKS CITED

Adcock, Sylvia. "A Look at Delays to Come." *Newsday* 3 May 1998: A3.

Adler, Jonathan H. *Environmentalism at the Crossroads: Green Activism in America.* Washington, DC: Capital Research Center, 1995.

Anderson, Charles M., and Marian M. MacCurdy. *Writing and Healing: Toward an Informed Practice.* Urbana, IL: NCTE, 2000.

Anderson, Chris, and Lex Runciman, eds. *A Forest of Voices: Reading and Writing the Environment.* Mountain View, CA: Mayfield, 1995.

Anthony, Carl. "Ecopsychology and the Deconstruction of Whiteness." *Ecopsychology: Restoring the Earth, Healing the Mind.* Ed. Theodore Roszak, Mary E. Gomes, and Allen D. Kanner. San Francisco: Sierra Club, 1995. 263–78.

Arakawa, and Madeline Gins. *Architectural Body.* Unpublished manuscript, 2000.

———. "Architectural Body." *Reversible Destiny: Arakawa/Gins.* Organized by Michael Govan. New York: Guggenheim, 1997. 168–87.

———. *Architecture: Sites of Reversible Destiny (Architectural Experiments After Auschwitz-Hiroshima).* London: Academy Editions, 1994.

Arcosanti 1997 Construction Workshops. Brochure. Mayer, AZ: Cosanti Foundation/Arcosanti.

"Arctic Ozone in Jeopardy." Discover.com News. 25 May 2000. Alreem Environmental Site. <http://www.alreem.com/news58a.htm>. Accessed 14 June 2001.

Aronowitz, Stanley, and William DiFazio. *The Jobless Future: Sci-Tech and the Dogma of Work.* Minneapolis: U of Minnesota P, 1994.

Aronowitz, Stanley, et al. "The Post-Work Manifesto." *Post-Work: The Wages of Cybernation.* Ed. Stanley Aronowitz and Jonathan Cutler. New York: Routledge, 1998. 31–80.

"Asia Faces Looming Environmental Disasters." Discover.com News. 19 June 2000. <http://www.discovery.com/news/briefs/20000619/ea_asia.html>. Accessed 3 July 2000.

AtKisson, Alan. *Believing Cassandra: An Optimist Looks at a Pessimist's World.* White River Junction, VT: Chelsea Green, 1999.

Auping, Michael. *Jess: A Grand Collage, 1951–1993.* With essays by Michael Auping, Robert J. Bertholf, Michael Palmer, and an interview with Jess. Buffalo: Buffalo Fine Arts Academy, 1993.

Ayres, Ed. *God's Last Offer: Negotiating for a Sustainable Future.* New York: Four Walls Eight Windows, 1999.

Bartlett, Albert A. "Reflections on Sustainability, Population Growth, and the Environment—Revisited." *Renewable Resources Journal* 15 (Winter 1997–98): 6–23.

Bateson, Gregory. *Mind and Nature: A Necessary Unity.* New York: Dutton, 1979.

Bazzi, Mohamad. "Rumblings Over Truck Routes." *Newsday* 7 April 1999: A6.

Beardsley, John. *Gardens of Revelation: Environments by Visionary Artists.* New York: Abbeville, 1995.

Beatley, Timothy, and Kristy Manning. *The Ecology of Place: Planning for Environment, Economy, and Community.* Washington, DC: Island, 1997.

Beitz, Charles R., and Michael Washburn. *Creating the Future: A Guide to Living and Working for Social Change.* New York: Bantam, 1974.

Bell, Wendell. *Foundations of Futures Studies: Human Science for a New Era.* New Brunswick, NJ: Transaction, 1997.

Berlin, James. *Rhetorics, Poetics, and Cultures: Refiguring College English Studies.* Urbana, IL: NCTE, 1996.

Berry, Wendell. *The Unsettling of America: Culture and Agriculture.* New York: Avon Books, 1977.

Birkerts, Sven. "Place: A Fragment." *The Sacred Theory of the Earth.* Ed. Thomas Frick. Berkeley, CA: North Atlantic Books, 1986. 53–55.

Black, Bob. "The Abolition of Work." *Semiotext(e) USA* (Vol. 13). Ed. Jim Fleming and Peter Lamborn Wilson. Brooklyn: Autonomedia, 1987. 15–26.

Blitz, Michael, and C. Mark Hurlbert. *Letters for the Living: Teaching Writing in a Violent Age*. Urbana, IL: NCTE, 1998.

Blumenfeld, Yorick. *2099: A Eutopia*. Prospects for Tomorrow. London: Thames & Hudson, 2000.

Bodley, John. *Victims of Progress*. Mountainview, CA: Mayfield, 1999.

Bookbinder, Bernie. *Long Island: People and Places, Past and Present*. New York: Abrams, 1983.

Bossel, Hartmut. *Earth at a Crossroads: Paths to a Sustainable Future*. New York: Cambridge UP, 1998.

Bowers, C. A. *Educating for an Ecologically Sustainable Culture: Rethinking Moral Education, Creativity, Intelligence, and Other Modern Orthodoxies*. Albany: State U of New York P, 1995.

———. *Education, Cultural Myths, and the Ecological Crisis: Toward Deep Changes*. Albany: State U of New York P, 1993.

Boyer, Ernest L., and Lee D. Mitgang. *Building Community: A New Future for Architecture Education and Practice*. Princeton, NJ: The Carnegie Foundation for the Advancement of Teaching, 1996.

Brameld, Theodore. *Philosophies of Education in Cultural Perspective*. New York: Holt, Rinehart and Winston, 1955.

Brandt, Barbara. "Less Is More: A Call for Shorter Work Hours." *Transitions: Lives in America*. Ed. Irina L. Raicu and Gregory Grewell. Mountain View, CA: Mayfield, 1997. 300–307.

Brock-Utne, Birgit. *Educating for Peace: A Feminist Perspective*. New York: Pergamon, 1985.

Brown, Cynthia Stokes. *Like It Was: A Complete Guide to Writing Oral History*. New York: Teachers and Writers Collaborative, 1988.

Brown, Lester R. "The Battle for the Planet: A Status Report." *Environment in Peril*. Ed. Anthony B. Wolbarst. Washington, DC: Smithsonian Institution P, 1991: 154–87.

———. *Building a Sustainable Society*. New York: Norton, 1981.

———. "Population Growth Sentencing Millions to Hydrological Poverty." Worldwatch Issue Alert. 21 June 2000. <http://www.worldwatch.org/chairman/issue/000621.html>. Accessed 30 June 2000.

Brown, Lester, et al. *State of the World 1989*. New York: Norton, 1989.

Brown, Lester, et al. *State of the World: 1997*. New York: Norton, 1997.

Brown, Lester R., Michael Renner, Brian Halweil, et al. *Vital Signs 1999: The Environmental Trends That Are Shaping Our Future.* New York: Norton, 1999.

Brown, Lester R., Michael Renner, Christopher Flavin, et al. *Vital Signs 1997: The Environmental Trends That Are Shaping Our Future.* New York: Norton, 1997.

Brown, Stephen Gilbert. "Composing the Eco Wars: Toward a Literacy of Resistance." *JAC: A Journal of Composition Theory* 19 (1999): 215–39.

Bryant, Adam. "Looking for Purpose in a Paycheck." *New York Times* 21 June 1998: 4:1.

Butterfield, Fox. "As Inmate Population Grows, So Does a Focus on Children." *New York Times* 7 April 1999: A1+.

Byrd, Don. *The Poetics of the Common Knowledge.* Albany: State U of New York P, 1994.

Cage, John. "Conversation with Joan Retallack." *Aerial 6/7.* Ed. Rod Smith. Washington, D.C.: Edge Books, 1991. 97–130.

———. *A Year from Monday.* Middletown, CT: Wesleyan UP, 1967.

Calthorpe, Peter. *The Next American Metropolis: Ecology, Community, and the American Dream.* New York: Princeton Architectural, 1993.

Campbell, Colin J. *The Coming Oil Crisis.* Brentwood, Essex: Multi-Science Publishing Company and Petroconsultants, 1997.

Campbell, Colin J., and Jean H. Laherrère. "The End of Cheap Oil." From *Scientific American,* March 1998. <www.dieoff.org/page140.htm>. Accessed 10 Feb. 1999.

Cantrill, James G., and Christine L. Oravec, eds. *The Symbolic Earth: Discourse and Our Creation of the Environment.* Lexington: UP of Kentucky, 1996.

Caro, Robert A. "The City-Shaper." *The New Yorker* 5 Jan. 1998: 38–50, 52–55.

———. *The Power Broker: Robert Moses and the Fall of New York.* New York: Vintage, 1974.

Chianese, Robert. "Sustainability." *Living in America: A Popular Culture Reader.* Ed. Patricia Y. Murray and Scott F. Covell. Mountain View, CA: Mayfield, 1998. 528–31.

Christianson, Gale E. "Naysayers, Thriving in the Heat." *New York Times* 8 July 1999: A27.

"City Living Looks Gloomy in Future." National Geographic.com. 12 June 2000. <http://www.ngnews.com/news/2000/06/06202000/cityliving_2782.asp>. Accessed 30 June 2000.

Clark, Mary E. "Rethinking Ecological and Economic Education: A Gestalt Shift." Krishnan et al. 73–76.

Cleary, Thomas, trans. *Minding Mind: A Course in Basic Meditation.* Boston: Shambhala, 1995.

Clugston, Richard M., and Thomas Rogers. "The Earth Charter." Tufts Environmental Literacy Institute. Fletcher School of Law and Diplomacy. Tufts University, Medford, MA. 11 June 1997.

Costanza, Robert. "Escaping the Overspecialization Trap: Creating Incentives for a Transdisciplinary Synthesis." *Rethinking the Curriculum: Toward an Integrated, Interdisciplinary College Education.* Ed. Mary E. Clark and Sandra A. Wawrytko. New York: Greenwood, 1990. 95–106.

Costanza, Robert, and Herman E. Daly. "Toward an Ecological Economics." Krishnan et al. 55–58.

Cowan, Neil M., and Ruth Schwartz Cowan. *Our Parents' Lives: Jewish Assimilation and Everyday Life.* New Brunswick, NJ: Rutgers UP, 1996.

Creighton, Sarah Hammond. *Greening the Ivory Tower: Improving the Environmental Track Record of Universities, Colleges, and Other Institutions.* Cambridge, MA: MIT P, 1998.

Crosbie, Liz, and Ken Knight. *Strategy for Sustainable Business: Environmental Opportunity and Strategic Choice.* New York: McGraw, 1995.

Crossette, Barbara. "Half-Hearted Global Warming Conference Closes Gloomily." *New York Times* 28 June 1997: A3.

Curtis, Ann Farnum. *Three Waves: The Story of Lake Ronkonkoma.* Ronkonkoma, New York: Review Publishing. 1993.

Cushman, Ellen. "The Rhetorician as an Agent of Social Change." *College Composition and Communication* 47 (February 1996): 7–28.

Daily, Gretchen C., Anne H. Ehrlich, and Paul R. Ehrlich. "Optimum Human Population Size." *Population and Environment: A Journal of Interdisciplinary Studies* 15 (July 1994). <www.dieoff.org/page99.htm>. Accessed 11 March 1999.

Daly, Herman E. "The Economic Growth Debate: What Some Economists Have Learned But Many Have Not." Krishnan et al. 125–28.

————. "Postscript: Some Common Misunderstandings and Further Issues Concerning a Steady-State Economy." Daly and Townsend 365–82.

————. "The Steady-State Economy: Toward a Political Economy of Biophysical Equilibrium and Moral Growth." Daly and Townsend 325–63.

————. "Sustainable Growth: An Impossibility Theorem." Daly and Townsend 267–73.

Daly, Herman E., and John B. Cobb, Jr., with contributions by Clifford W. Cobb. *For the Common Good: Redirecting the Economy toward Community, the Environment, and a Sustainable Future.* Boston: Beacon, 1989.

Daly, Herman E., and Kenneth N. Townsend, eds. *Valuing the Earth: Economics, Ecology, Ethics.* Cambridge, MA: MIT P, 1993.

Davis, John. *Greening Business: Managing for Sustainable Development.* Cambridge, MA: Basil Blackwell, 1991.

Davis, Marilyn P. *Mexican Voices/American Dreams: An Oral History of Mexican Immigration to the United States.* New York: Holt, 1990.

Demoretcky, Tom. "Crime in the Suburbs: A Deadly Parade of Violence Brings Pain to Peaceful Neighborhoods." *Newsday* 21 June 1998: H16.

Dewey, John. The Child and the Curriculum, and The School and Society. Chicago: U of Chicago P, 1956.

Diamond, Jared. "Easter's End." *Discover* August 1995: 63–69.

Dixon, John A., and Louise A. Fallon. "The Concept of Sustainability: Origins, Extensions, and Usefulness for Policy." Krishnan et al. 93–96.

Dobrin, Sidney I., and Christian Weisser, eds. *Ecocomposition: Theoretical and Pedagogical Approaches.* Albany: State U of New York P: 2001.

————. *Natural Discourse: Toward Ecocomposition.* Albany: State U of New York P: Forthcoming 2001.

Dobrin, Sidney I., and Christopher J. Keller. *The Nature of Writing.* Albany: State U of New York P: Forthcoming 2001.

Dolci, Danilo. *Sicilian Lives.* New York: Pantheon, 1981.

Dolnick, Edward. "Less Is More." *Utne Reader* 69 (May-June 1995): 65.

Dorman, Peter. *Markets and Mortality: Economics, Dangerous Work, and the Value of Human Life.* New York: Cambridge UP, 1996.

Dowie, Mark. *Losing Ground: American Environmentalism at the Close of the Twentieth Century.* Cambridge, MA: MIT P, 1997.

Duany, Andres, Elizabeth Plater-Zyberk, and Jeff Speck. *Suburban Nation: The Rise of Sprawl and the Decline of the American Dream.* New York: North Point, 2000.

Durning, Alan Thein. *How Much Is Enough? The Consumer Society and the Future of the Earth.* New York: Norton, 1992.

Durning, Alan Thein, and Ed Ayres. "The History of a Cup of Coffee." *World Watch* September/October 1994: 20–22.

Dutton, Thomas A. "Cultural Studies and Critical Pedagogy: Cultural Pedagogy and Architecture." *Reconstructing Architecture: Critical Discourses and Social Practices.* Ed. Thomas A. Dutton and Lian Hurst Mann. Minneapolis: U of Minnesota P, 1996. 158-201.

Eagan, David, and David Orr, eds. *The Campus and Environmental Responsibility.* San Francisco: Jossey-Bass, 1992.

Egan, Timothy. "Less Crime, More Criminals." *New York Times* 7 March 1999: WK1+.

———. "Urban Sprawl Strains Western States." *New York Times* 29 December 1996: A1+.

———. "War on Crack Retreats, Still Taking Prisoners." *New York Times* 28 February 1999: A1+.

Ehrenfeld, David. "Life in the Next Millennium: Who Will Be Left in the Earth's Community?" *The Last Extinction.* Ed. Les Kaufman and Kenneth Mallory. Cambridge, MA: MIT P, 1987. 167–86.

Ehrlich, Paul R., and Anne H. Ehrlich. *Betrayal of Science and Reason: How Anti-Environmental Rhetoric Threatens Our Future.* Washington, DC: Island, 1996.

———. "Why Isn't Everyone as Scared as We Are?" Daly and Townsend 55–67.

Engel, J. Ronald. "Introduction: The Ethics of Sustainable Development." Engel and Engel 1–23.

Epstein, Paul R. "Ecosystem Health/Human Health: An Integrative Framework." Tufts Environmental Literacy Institute. Fletcher School of Law and Diplomacy. Tufts University, Medford, MA. 10 June 1997.

———. "Emerging Diseases and Ecosystem Instability: New Threats to Public Health." *American Journal of Public Health* 85:2 (February 1995): 168–72.

Fagin, Dan. "A No-Win Situation: In Backyards Islandwide, the Nightmare Next Door." *Newsday* 23 August 1998: A6+.

———. "Trouble on the Rise: Global Warming Is Real, and Threatens Dramatic Changes to Our Shoreline, Water Supply and Weather." *Newsday* 4 April 1999: A18–19, 43–46.

"Federal Report on Global Warming Predicts Widespread Impact on U.S." CNN.com. 12 June 2000. <www.cnn.com/2000/NATURE/06/12/climate.changes/>. Accessed 14 June 2001.

Feigenbaum, Randi. "Short on Thrift: Savings Rates Have Plunged to Near Zero." *Newsday* 21 February 1999: F8–F10.

Flattau, Edward. *Tracking the Charlatans: An Environmental Columnist's Refutational Handbook for the Propaganda Wars.* Washington, DC: Global Horizons, 1998.

Flavin, Christopher. "Global Temperature Goes Off the Chart." Brown, Renner, Halweil 58–59.

Fleay, Brian J. "Oil Supply: The Crunch Has Arrived!" 13 March 2000. <www.hubbertpeak.com/fleay/crunch.htm>. Accessed 16 March 2000.

Forbes, Jack D. *Columbus and Other Cannibals: The Wétiko Disease of Exploitation, Imperialism and Terrorism.* Brooklyn: Autonomedia, 1992.

Fox, Matthew. *The Reinvention of Work: A New Vision of Livelihood for Our Time.* San Francisco: HarperSanFrancisco, 1994.

Frank, Robert H., and Philip J. Cook. *The Winner-Take-All Society: How More and More Americans Compete for Ever Fewer and Bigger Prizes, Encouraging Economic Waste, Income Inequality, and an Impoverished Cultural Life.* New York: Free, 1995.

Frommer, Myrna, and Harvey Frommer. *Growing Up Jewish in America: An Oral History.* New York: Harcourt, 1995.

Fuller, R. Buckminster, with Eric A. Walker and James R. Killian Jr. *Approaching the Benign Environment.* New York: Collier, 1970.

Gallagher, Winifred. *The Power of Place: How Our Surroundings Shape Our Thoughts, Emotions, and Actions.* New York: Poseidon, 1993.

Gamst, Frederick C. "Considerations of Work." *Meanings of Work: Considerations for the Twenty-First Century.* Ed. Frederick C. Gamst. Albany: State U of New York P, 1995. 1–45.

Garay, Mary Sue, and Stephen A. Bernhardt, eds. *Expanding Literacies: English Teaching and the New Workplace.* Albany: State U of New York P, 1998.

Gardner, Gary. "People Everywhere Eating More Fast Food." Brown, Renner, and Halweil 150–51.

Gates, Bill, with Nathan Myhrvold and Peter Rinearson. *The Road Ahead.* New York: Viking, 1995.

Gatto, John Taylor. *Dumbing Us Down: The Hidden Curriculum of Compulsory Schooling.* Philadelphia: New Society, 1992.

Gazzaniga, Michael S. "How to Change the University." *Science* 282 (9 October 1998): 237.

Geertz, Clifford. "Deep Play: Notes on the Balinese Cockfight." *The Interpretation of Cultures.* New York: Basic, 1973. 412–53.

Gelbspan, Ross. *The Heat Is On: The High Stakes Battle over Earth's Threatened Climate.* Reading, MA: Addison, 1997.

Gilpin, Alan. *Dictionary of Environment and Sustainable Development.* New York: Wiley, 1996.

Gini, Al. *Work, Identity and Self: How We Are Formed by the Work We Do.* Unpublished manuscript, 1997.

Glotfelty, Cheryll, and Harold Fromm. *The Ecocriticism Reader: Landmarks in Literary Ecology.* Athens: U of Georgia P, 1996.

Goldsmith, Edward. *The Way: An Ecological World-View.* Athens: U of Georgia P, 1998.

Goldsmith, James. "The Winners and the Losers." *The Case Against the Global Economy.* Mander and Goldsmith 171–79.

Goldstein, Joseph. *The Experience of Insight: A Simple and Direct Guide to Buddhist Meditation.* Boston: Shambhala, 1983.

Goodland, Robert. "The Case That the World Has Reached Limits: More Precisely That Current Throughput Growth in the Global Economy Cannot Be Sustained." *Environmentally Sustainable Economic*

Development: Building on Brundtland. Ed. Robert Goodland, Herman Daly, Salah El Serafy, Bernd Von Droste. Belgium: UNESCO, 1992. 15–27.

Gordon, Anita, and David Suzuki. *It's a Matter of Survival.* Cambridge, MA: Harvard UP, 1991.

Greenhouse, Steven. "So Much Work, So Little Time." *New York Times* 5 September 1999: WK1+.

Greider, William. "'Citizen' GE." Mander and Goldsmith 323–34.

———. *One World, Ready or Not: The Manic Logic of Global Capitalism.* New York: Simon, 1997.

Gross, Jane. "Poor Without Cars Find Trek to Work Is Now a Job." *New York Times* 18 November 1997: A1+.

Halbfinger, David M. "I've Been Sleeping on the Rail Road." *New York Times* 15 September 1999: B1+.

———. "Scandal in Brookhaven: The Reaction Is Ho-Hum: Extortion Charges Are Latest on a Long List." *New York Times* 16 December 1998: B1+.

Hamilton, William L. "How Suburban Design Is Failing Teen-Agers." *New York Times* 6 May 1999: F1+.

Hanson, Jay. *dieoff.* 1997. dieoff.org. 2 May 2001 <http://www.dieoff.org>.

Haraway, Donna. *Modest_Witness@ Second_Millennium.FemaleMan©_Meets_OncoMouse™: Feminism and Technoscience.* New York: Routledge, 1997.

Harris, Jonathan M. "Theoretical Frameworks and Techniques: Overview Essay." Krishnan, Harris, and Goodwin 97–105.

Hartley, Jean, et al. *Job Insecurity: Coping with Jobs at Risk.* London: SAGE, 1991.

Hasselstrom, Linda M. "Addicted to Work." Vitek and Jackson 66–75.

Hawken, Paul. *The Ecology of Commerce: A Declaration of Sustainability.* New York: HarperBusiness, 1993.

Hawken, Paul, Amory Lovins, and L. Hunter Lovins. *Natural Capitalism: Creating the Next Industrial Revolution.* Boston: Little, 1999.

Healy, Seán Desmond. *Boredom, Self, and Culture.* Rutherford: Associated University Presses, 1984.

Henderson, Caspar. "Coral Reef Scientists Call for Climate Change Action." 27 October 2000. <www.oneworld.net/news/reports/corals_oct00.html>. Accessed 14 June 2001.

Henderson, Hazel. *Creating Alternative Futures: The End of Economics.* West Hartford, CT: Kumarian, 1996.

———. "Development Beyond Economism: Local Paths to Sustainable Development." *People, Land, and Community: Collected E. F. Schumacher Society Lectures.* Ed. Hildegarde Hannum. New Haven, CT: Yale UP, 1997. 89–104.

Henderson, Linda Dalrymple. *The Fourth Dimension and Non-Euclidean Geometry in Modern Art.* Princeton: Princeton UP, 1983.

Herndl, Carl G., and Stuart C. Brown. *Green Culture: Environmental Rhetoric in Contemporary America.* Madison: U of Wisconsin P, 1996.

Hiss, Tony. *The Experience of Place.* New York: Vintage, 1990.

———. "The 'Sacred Sites' That Make a Neighborhood Work." *New York Times* 12 March 1995: LI 7.

Hochschild, Arlie Russell. "There's No Place Like Work." *New York Times* 20 April 1997, sec. 6: 51+.

Hoegh-Guldberg, Ove. "Coral Bleaching: Physical Factors, Genetic Variability and Symbiotic Dysfunction." American Coral Reef Society 1998 Scientific Programme. 17 October 1998.

Holmberg, Johan, and Richard Sandbrook. "Sustainable Development: What Is to Be Done?" Krishnan, Harris, and Goodwin 91–93.

Horridge, Adrian. "Bee Vision of Pattern and 3D." *BioEssays* 16 (12 December 1994): 877–84.

The Hubbert Peak of Oil Production. 1994. EcoSystems (Ecotopia). 2 May 2001. <http://www.hubbertpeak.com>. Accessed 1 July 2000.

Huber, Peter. *Hard Green: Saving the Environment from the Environmentalists: A Conservative Manifesto.* New York: Basic, 2000.

Hunnicutt, Benjamin Kline. *Kellogg's Six-Hour Day.* Philadelphia: Temple UP, 1996.

Hurmence, Belinda, ed. *My Folks Don't Want Me to Talk about Slavery: Twenty-One Oral Histories of Former North Carolina Slaves.* Winston-Salem, NC: Blair, 1984.

Illich, Ivan. *Deschooling Society.* New York: Harper, 1970.

"Information Economy Boom Obscuring Earth's Decline." Worldwatch News Release. 15 January 2000 <http://www.worldwatch.org/alerts/000115.html>. Accessed 30 June 2000.

Isachsen, Y. W., et al., , eds. *Geology of New York: A Simplified Account.* Albany: New York State Museum/Geological Survey, State Education Department, State U of New York, 1991.

Jacobs, Jane. *The Death and Life of Great American Cities.* New York: Modern Library, 1993.

Jensen, Bill. "A True-Crime Tour." *Long Island Voice* 15–21 October 1998: 16–18.

Jenseth, Richard, and Edward E. Lotto, eds. *Constructing Nature: Readings from the American Experience.* Upper Saddle River, NJ: Prentice, 1996.

Jones, Libby Falk. "Creating Partnerships for Literacy in the College Workplace." Garay and Bernhardt 299–313.

Joss, Molly W. "A New World Order: The Digital Revolution Comes to Prepress and Printing. Are You with It?" *Long Island Computer User* April 1999: 1+.

Kane, Hal. "Half of Languages Becoming Extinct." Brown et al., *Vital Signs 1997* 130–31.

Kaplan, Robert. *The Coming Anarchy: Shattering the Dreams of the Post Cold War.* New York: Random, 2000.

Kelly, Kevin. "Prophets of Boom: Five Champions of the Endless Upswing." *Wired* September 1999: 156–64.

Keniry, Julian. *Ecodemia: Campus Environmental Stewardship at the Turn of the Twenty-first Century.* Washington, DC: National Wildlife Federation, 1995.

Killingsworth, M. Jimmie, and Jacqueline S. Palmer. *Ecospeak: Rhetoric and Environmental Politics in America.* Carbondale and Edwardsville, IL: Southern Illinois UP, 1992.

Kingston, Maxine Hong. *The Woman Warrior: Memoirs of a Girlhood Among Ghosts.* New York: Vintage, 1989.

Kirby, Alex. "Climate Change Risk from TV." BBC News Online. 16 May 2000. <http://news.bbc.co.uk/hi/english/sci/tech/newsid_750000/750700.stm>. Accessed 2 June 2000.

————. "Dawn of a Thirsty Century." BBC News Online. 2 June 2000. <http://news.bbc.co.uk/hi/english/sci/tech/newsid_755000/755497. stm>. Accessed 3 July 2000.

————. "Pollution Hits Poor Hardest." BBC News Online Network. 23 September 1999. <news.bbc.co.uk/hi/english/sci/tech/newsid_454000/ 454586.stm>. Accessed 29 Sept. 1999.

Knoblauch, C. H., and Lil Brannon. *Critical Teaching and the Idea of Literacy*. Portsmouth, NH: Boynton/Cook, 1993.

————. *Rhetorical Traditions and the Teaching of Writing*. Upper Montclair, NJ: Boynton/Cook, 1984.

Kolodny, Annette. *Failing the Future: A Dean Looks at Higher Education in the Twenty-First Century*. Durham, NC: Duke UP, 1998.

Krech, Shepard. *The Ecological Indian: Myth and History*. New York: Norton, 1999.

Krishnan, Rajaram, Jonathan M. Harris, and Neva R. Goodwin, eds. *A Survey of Ecological Economics*. Washington, DC: Island, 1995.

Kristof, Nicholas D. "Asian Pollution Is Widening Its Deadly Reach." *New York Times* 29 November 1997: A1+.

Kroeber, Karl. *Ecological Literary Criticism: Romantic Imagining and the Biology of Mind*. New York: Columbia UP, 1994.

Kroll, Lucien. *An Architecture of Complexity*. Trans. Peter Blundell-Jones. Cambridge, MA: MIT P, 1987.

Kunstler, James Howard. *The Geography of Nowhere: The Rise and Decline of America's Man-Made Landscape*. New York: Simon, 1993.

Kurson, Ken. Compiler of statistics for *New York Times* issue on "Money on the Mind." 7 June 1998: 61+.

Lafargue, Paul. *The Right to be Lazy*. Trans. Charles H. Kerr. Chicago: Kerr, 1989.

Lambert, Bruce. "The Father of Parks, and Traffic." *New York Times* 31 October 1999: 14:1+

Leakey, Richard, and Roger Lewin. *The Sixth Extinction: Patterns of Life and the Future of Humankind*. New York: Doubleday, 1995.

Leal Filho, Walter, ed. *Sustainability and University Life*. New York: Lang, 1999.

Linden, Eugene. *The Future in Plain Sight: Nine Clues to the Coming Instability.* New York: Simon, 1998.

Livingston, John A. "Other Selves." Vitek and Jackson 132–39.

Longstreet, Wilma S., and Harold G. Shane. *Curriculum for a New Millennium.* Boston: Allyn, 1993.

Lyons, Graham, Evonne Moore, and Joseph Wayne Smith. *Is the End Nigh? Internationalism, Global Chaos and the Destruction of the Earth.* Aldershot, England: Avebury, 1995

Madrick, Jeffrey. *The End of Affluence: The Causes and Consequences of America's Economic Dilemma.* New York: Random, 1995.

Mander, Jerry. "The Rules of Corporate Behavior." Mander and Goldsmith 309–22.

Mander, Jerry, and Edward Goldsmith, eds. *The Case Against the Global Economy: And for a Turn Toward the Local.* San Francisco: Sierra Club, 1996.

Mander, Kia, and Alex Boston. "Wal-Mart: Global Retailer." Mander and Goldsmith 335–43.

Markandya, Anil, and David W. Pearce. "Development, the Environment, and the Social Rate of Discount." Krishnan et al. 266–71.

Martin, Elizabeth. "*y*-Condition." *Architecture as a Translation of Music.* Ed. Elizabeth Martin. Pamphlet Architecture 16. New York: Princeton Architectural P, 1994: 16–25.

Mastny, Lisa. "Melting of Earth's Ice Cover Reaches New High." Worldwatch News Brief. 6 March 2000. <http://www.worldwatch.org/alerts/000306.html>. Accessed 30 June 2000.

Matlin, David. Telephone interview. 1999.

Maturana, Humberto R., and Francisco J. Varela. *The Tree of Knowledge: The Biological Roots of Human Understanding.* Boston: New Science Library/Shambhala, 1987.

McAndrew, Donald A. "Ecofeminism and the Teaching of Literacy." *College Composition and Communication* 47 (1996): 367–82.

McComiskey, Bruce. *Teaching Composition as a Social Process.* Logan: Utah State University Press, 2000.

McKibben, Bill. "The Earth Does a Slow Burn." *New York Times* 3 May 1997: A23.

———. *The End of Nature.* New York: Random, 1989.

McMahan, Eva M., and Kim Lacy Rogers, eds. *Interactive Oral History Interviewing.* Hillsdale, NJ: Erlbaum, 1994.

Meadows, Donella H., Dennis L. Meadows, Jorgen Randers, and William H. Behrens III. *The Limits to Growth.* 2nd ed. New York: Potomac Associates/Universe, 1974.

Merchant, Carolyn. *Radical Ecology: The Search for a Livable World.* New York: Routledge, 1992.

Michael, Donald N. *The Unprepared Society: Planning for a Precarious Future.* New York: Basic, 1968.

Minsky, Marvin. *The Society of Mind.* New York: Simon, 1986.

Moe, Richard, and Carter Wilkie. *Changing Places: Rebuilding Community in the Age of Sprawl.* New York: Holt, 1997.

Moore, Michael. *Downsize This!* New York: Crowne, 1996.

"More Than Any Other Democracy." *The Economist* 20 March 1999: 30–31.

"More U.S. Drought, Floods as Climate Warms—Report." EnviroLink News Service. 26 May 2000. <http://www.envirolink.org/environews/reuters/articles/Environment/05_25_2000.reute-story-bcweather droughtfarmers.html>. Accessed 8 July 2000.

Motavalli, Jim. "2000: Planet Earth at the Crossroads." *The Global Ecology.* Ed. Edward Moran. New York: Wilson, 1999. 14–24.

Mydans, Seth. "Its Mood Dark as the Haze, Southeast Asia Aches." *New York Times* 26 October 1997: 3.

Myers, Norman, and Julian L. Simon. *Scarcity or Abundance: A Debate on the Environment.* New York: Norton, 1994.

Myerson, George, and Yvonne Rydin. *The Language of Environment: A New Rhetoric.* London: UCL P, 1996.

Naisbitt, John. *Megatrends: Ten New Directions Transforming Our Lives.* New York: Warner, 1984.

Nasar, Sylvia. "Economic Growth in Last Part of '98 Was Robust 6.1%." *New York Times* 27 February 1999: A1+.

National Council of Teachers of English. *Trends and Issues in Postsecondary English Studies.* Urbana, IL: NCTE, 2000.

Nelson, Erik. "Why You Have to Own Up to Your Mess, Mr. Wizard." *Long Island Voice* 11–17 February 1999: 9.

"New Analysis of World's Ecosystems Reveals Widespread Decline." World Resources Institute. 19 June 2000. <http://www.wri.org/wri/press/wr2000_hannover.html>. Accessed 30 June 2000.

"New York Incomes Decline, Report Says." *New York Times* 7 September 1999: B7.

Nhat Hanh, Thich. *The Miracle of Mindfulness: A Manual on Meditation.* Trans. Mobi Ho. Boston: Beacon, 1975.

Nordheimer, Jon. "One Day's Death Toll on the Job: Despite Years of Progress on Safety, 13 Lives Are Cut Short." *New York Times* 22 December 1996: C:1

North, Stephen M., with Barbara A. Chepaitis, David Coogan, Lâle Davison, Ron MacLean, Cindy L. Parrish, Jonathan Post, and Beth Weatherby. *Refiguring the Ph.D. in English Studies: Writing, Doctoral Education, and the Fusion-Based Curriculum.* Urbana, IL: NCTE, 2000.

Oldenburg, Ray. *The Great Good Place: Cafés, Coffee Shops, Bookstores, Bars, Hair Salons, and Other Hangouts at the Heart of a Community.* New York: Marlowe, 1989.

O'Meara, Molly. "Urban Air Taking Lives." Brown, Renner, Halweil 128–29.

"One in 8 Birds Faces Extinction in Next 100 Years." Yahoo! News, Science Headlines. 14 October 1999. <http://forests.org/archive/general/envibird.htm>. Accessed 14 June 2001.

O'Reilley, Mary Rose. *The Peaceable Classroom.* Portsmouth, NH: Boynton/Cook, 1993.

Orr, David W. *Earth in Mind: On Education, Environment, and the Human Prospect.* Washington, DC: Island, 1994.

———. *Ecological Literacy: Education and the Transition to a Postmodern World.* Albany, New York: State U of New York P, 1992.

Owens, Derek. *Resisting Writings (and the Boundaries of Composition).* Dallas: Southern Methodist UP, 1994.

Park, Robert L. "Scientists and Their Political Passions." *New York Times* 2 May 1998: A15.

Patz, Jonathan A., et al. "Global Climate Change and Emerging Infectious Diseases. *JAMA* 275:3 (17 January 1996): 217–23.

Payne, Daniel G. *Voices in the Wilderness: American Nature Writing and Environmental Politics.* Hanover, NH: UP of New England, 1996.

Pearce, David. "Foundations of an Ecological Economics." Krishnan et al. 58–61.

Peet, John. *Energy and the Ecological Economics of Sustainability.* Washington, DC: Island, 1992.

Peterson, Tarla Rai. *Sharing the Earth: The Rhetoric of Sustainable Development.* Columbia: U of South Carolina P, 1997.

"Polar Regions Show Signs of Heating Up." *USA Today.* 9 September 1997: 6D.

Popple, Keith. *Analysing Community Work: Its Theory and Practice.* Buckingham: Open UP, 1995.

Powers, Richard. *Gain.* New York: Farrar, 1998.

———. *The Gold Bug Variations.* New York: HarperPerennial, 1991.

President's Council on Sustainable Development. "From Classroom to Community and Beyond: Educating for a Sustainable Future." Feb. 1997. <http://clinton4.nara.gov/PCSD/Publications/TF_Reports/linkage-top.html>. Accessed 14 June 2001.

Preston, Julia. "A Fatal Case of Fatalism: Mexico City's Air." *New York Times* 14 February 1999: WK3.

Prugh, Thomas, with Robert Costanza et al. *Natural Capital and Human Economic Survival.* Solomons, MD: International Society for Ecological Economics P, 1995.

Randers, Jørgen. "The Quest for a Sustainable Society—A Global Perspective." Skirbekk 17–27.

Rasula, Jed. *The American Poetry Wax Museum: Reality Effects, 1940–1990.* Urbana, IL: NCTE, 1996.

Rather, John. "Babies' Teeth and Radiation's Path." *New York Times* 6 June 1999: LI 1+.

———. "Contaminant from Gas Is Found in Water." *New York Times* 29 August 1999: LI 1+.

Ravaioli, Carla. *Economists and the Environment.* Trans. Richard Bates. With a contribution by Paul Elkins. London: Zed, 1995.

Ray, Dixy Lee, with Lou Guzzo. *Environmental Overkill: Whatever Happened to Common Sense?* New York: HarperCollins, 1993.

Readings, Bill. *The University in Ruins.* Cambridge, MA: Harvard UP, 1996.

Relph, E. *Place and Placelessness.* London: Pion, 1976.

Revkin, Andrew C. "A Shift in Stance on Global Warming Theory." *New York Times* 26 Oct. 2000: A22.

———. "Struggling to Scare a Contented World." *New York Times* 28 September 1997: WK5.

Rifkin, Jeremy. *The End of Work: The Decline of the Global Labor Force and the Dawn of the Post-Market Era.* New York: Putnam's, 1995.

———. "New Technology and the End of Jobs." Mander and Goldsmith 108–21.

Rinpoche, Sogyal. *The Tibetan Book of Living and Dying.* San Francisco: HarperSanFrancisco, 1993.

Roorda, Randall. *Dramas of Solitude: Narratives of Retreat in American Nature Writing.* Albany: State U of New York P, 1998.

———. "Sites and Senses of Writing in Nature." *College English* 59 (1997): 385–407.

Roseland, Mark. "Dimensions of the Future: An Eco-city Overview." *Eco-City Dimensions: Healthy Communities Healthy Planet.* Ed. Mark Roseland. Gabriola Island, BC, Canada: New Society, 1997. 1–12.

Rosenbaum, Ron. "Long Island, Babylon." *The Secret Parts of Fortune: Three Decades of Intense Investigations and Edgy Enthusiasms.* New York: Random, 2000: 612–628.

Roy, Rob. *Mortgage-Free! Radical Strategies for Home Ownership.* White River Junction, VT: Chelsea Green, 1998.

Ryan, Paul. *Earthscore for Educators: A Method of Creating Curriculum for Sustainability.* Unpublished manuscript, 1998.

———. *Video Mind, Earth Mind: Art, Communications and Ecology.* New York: Lang, 1993.

Sale, Kirkpatrick. "The Columbian Legacy and the Ecosterian Response." *People, Land, and Community: Collected E. F. Schumacher Society Lectures.* Ed. Hildegarde Hannum. New Haven: Yale UP, 1997. 13–21.

Sanera, Michael, and Jane S. Shaw. *Facts, Not Fear: A Parent's Guide to Teaching Children about the Environment.* Washington, DC: Regnery, 1996.

Savage, Mary C. "Writing as a Neighborly Act: An Antidote for Academentia." *ADE Bulletin* 92 (Spring 1989): 13–19.

Schmalenbach, Werner. *Kurt Schwitters.* New York: Abrams, 1970.

Scholes, Robert. *The Rise and Fall of English: Reconstructing English as a Discipline.* New Haven: Yale UP, 1998.

Schor, Juliet B. *The Overspent American: Upscaling, Downshifting, and the New Consumer.* New York: Basic, 1998.

———. *The Overworked American: The Unexpected Decline of Leisure.* New York: Basic, 1991.

Schwartz, Peter. *The Art of the Long View: Planning for the Future in an Uncertain World.* Chichester: Wiley, 1998.

Sessions, Robert Alan. "Ecofeminism and Work." *Ecofeminism: Women, Culture, Nature.* Ed. Karen J. Warren. Bloomington: Indiana UP, 1997. 176–92.

Shrader-Frechette, Kristin. "Sustainability and Environmental Ethics." Skirbekk 57–78.

Shrivastava, Paul. *Greening Business: Profiting the Corporation and the Environment.* Cincinnati: Thomson Executive, 1996.

Simon, Paul. "Are We Running Dry?" *Parade Magazine* (23 August 1998): 4–6.

Sivaraksa, Sulak. *Seeds of Peace: A Buddhist Vision for Renewing Society.* Ed. Tom Ginsburg. Berkeley: Parallax, 1992.

Skirbekk, Gunnar, ed. *The Notion of Sustainability and Its Normative Implications.* Oslo: Scandinavian UP, 1994.

Sledd, James. *Eloquent Dissent: The Writings of James Sledd.* Ed. Richard D. Freed. Portsmouth, NH: Boynton/Cook Heinemann, 1996.

Sloep, Peter B. "The Impact of 'Sustainability' on the Field of Environmental Science." Skirbekk 29–55.

Sloterdijk, Peter. *Critique of Cynical Reason*. Trans. Michael Eldred. Minneapolis: U of Minnesota P, 1987.

Smith, April A., and the Student Environmental Action Coalition. *Campus Ecology: A Guide to Assessing Environmental Quality and Creating Strategies for Change*. Venice, CA: Living Planet, 1993.

Smith, Gregory A. *Education and the Environment: Learning to Live with Limits*. Albany: State U of New York P, 1992.

Smith, Joseph Wayne, Graham Lyons, and Evonne Moore. *Global Anarchy in the Third Millennium? Race, Place, and Power at the End of the Modern Age*. New York: St. Martin's, 2000.

Smithson, Robert. *Robert Smithson: The Collected Writings*. Ed. Jack Flam. Berkeley: U of California P, 1996.

Solomon, Norman. *The Trouble with Dilbert: How Corporate Culture Gets the Last Laugh*. Monroe, ME: Common Courage, 1997.

Spilka, Rachel. "Influencing Workplace Practice: A Challenge for Professional Writing Specialists in Academia." Spilka 207–19.

————, ed. *Writing in the Workplace: New Research Perspectives*. Carbondale and Edwardsville, IL: Southern Illinois UP, 1993.

"Spills of the Island." *Newsday* 23 August 1998: A44.

Stead, W. Edward, and Jean Garner Stead. *Management for a Small Planet: Strategic Decision Making and the Environment*. 2nd ed. Thousand Oaks, CA: SAGE, 1996.

Stein, Gertrude. *Gertrude Stein's America*. Ed. Gilbert A. Harrison. New York: Liveright, 1965.

Stella, Frank. *Working Space*. Cambridge, MA: Harvard UP, 1986.

Sterngold, James. "Song of the Millennium: Cool Prelude and a Fiery Coda." *New York Times* 9 March 1999: F5.

Stevens, William. "Oceans Absorb Much of Global Warming, Study Confirms." *New York Times* 2 March 2000: A16.

Stilgoe, John R. *Borderland: Origins of the American Suburb, 1820–1939*. New Haven: Yale UP, 1988.

"Study: Brazilian Rain Forest Fading Fast." *Newsday* 8 April 1999: A26.

"Study: North America Pollution Rises." Discover.com News. 31 May 2000. <http://www.discovery.com/news/briefs/20000531/enviro_pollute.html>. Accessed 30 June 2000.

"Sustain." *Oxford English Dictionary.* 2nd ed. 1989.

Taylor, Jim, Watts Wacker, and Howard Means. *The 500-Year Delta: What Happens After What Comes Next.* New York: HarperBusiness, 1998.

"The Technology Review 100." *Technology Review* November-December 1999: 73+.

Tenhula, John. *Voices from Southeast Asia: The Refugee Experience in the United States.* New York: Holmes, 1991.

Terkel, Studs. *Race: How Blacks and Whites Think and Feel about the American Obsession.* New York: New, 1992.

————. *Working.* New York: Avon, 1975.

Thomashow, Mitchell. *Ecological Identity: Becoming a Reflective Environmentalist.* Cambridge, MA: MIT P, 1995.

Thomson, Bruce. "Convince Sheet: The Oil Crash and You." 12 December 2000. <http://groups.yahoo.com/group/runningonempty/files/>. Accessed 14 June 2001.

Toffler, Alvin. *Future Shock.* New York: Random, 1970.

Tokar, Brian. *Earth for Sale: Reclaiming Ecology in the Age of Corporate Greenwash.* Boston, MA: South End, 1997.

Trainer, Ted. *The Conserver Society: Alternatives for Sustainability.* London: Zed, 1995.

Uchitelle, Louis. "Global Good Times, Meet the Global Glut." *New York Times* 16 November 1997: WK3.

————. "Keeping Up With the Gateses? Life Styles of the Rich, Sought by the Middle Class." *New York Times* 3 May 1998: BU12.

————. "More Work, Less Play Make Jack Look Better Off." *New York Times* 5 October 1997: WK:4.

Union of Concerned Scientists. 18 November 1992. "World Scientists' Warning to Humanity." 19 July 1997 <http://www.earthportals.com/Earthportals/ucs.html>. Accessed 13 May 1998.

United Nations Environment Programme. *GEO-1*. Global State of the Environment Report 1997. 1997. <http://www.unep.org/unep/eia/geo1/index.htm>. Accessed 1 June 2001.

Varela, Francisco. "Laying Down a Path in Walking." *Gaia, a Way of Knowing: Political Implications of the New Biology*. Ed. William Irwin Thompson. Great Barrington, MA: Lindisfarne, 1987. 48–64.

Verhovek, Sam Howe. "Fighting Sprawl, Oregon County Makes Deal with Intel to Limit Job Growth." *New York Times* 9 June 1999: A1.

Vitek, William, and Wes Jackson, eds. *Rooted in the Land: Essays on Community and Place*. New Haven, CT: Yale UP, 1996.

Wacker, Bob. "Why Living Here Can Be Murder." *Long Island Voice* 15–21 October 1998: 15+.

Wagner, Roy. *The Invention of Culture*. Chicago: U of Chicago P, 1981.

Walker, Melissa, ed. *Reading the Environment*. New York: Norton, 1994.

Wallulis, Jerald. *The New Insecurity: The End of the Standard Job and Family*. Albany: State U of New York P, 1998.

"West's Pollution Blamed for World Disasters." Guardian Unlimited Network. 15 May 2000. <http://www.guardianunlimited.co.uk/Archive/Article/0,4273,4018224,00.html>. Accessed 30 June 2000.

"Where Bacteria Meet the Beach." Environmental News Network. 11 June 2000. <http://www.enn.com/enn-subsciber-news-archive/2000/06/06112000/ap_bacteria_13815.asp>. Accessed 14 June 2001.

Winkler, Karen J. "Inventing a New Field: The Study of Literature About the Environment." *Chronicle of Higher Education* (9 August 1996): A8+.

Wolbarst, Anthony B., ed. *Environment in Peril*. Washington: Smithsonian Institution, 1991.

World Commission on Environment and Development. *Our Common Future*. Oxford: Oxford UP, 1987.

Yaro, Robert D., and Tony Hiss (Regional Plan Association). *A Region at Risk: The Third Regional Plan for the New York-New Jersey-Connecticut Metropolitan Area*. Washington, DC: Island, 1996.

Yoon, Carol Kaesuk. "A 'Dead Zone' Grows in the Gulf of Mexico." *New York Times* 20 January 1998: F1+.

————. "Study Jolts Views on Recovery from Extinctions." *New York Times* 9 March 2000: A20.

Youngblood, Gene. *Expanded Cinema*. Introduction by R. Buckminster Fuller. New York: Dutton, 1970.

Youngquist, Walter. *GeoDestinies: The Inevitable Control of Earth Resources Over Nations and Individuals*. Portland, OR: National Book, 1997.

Zeldin, David. *The Educational Ideas of Charles Fourier, 1772–1837*. New York: Kelley, 1969.

Zencey, Eric. "The Rootless Professors." Vitek and Jackson 15–19.

INDEX

AUTHOR

Derek Owens lives on Long Island, New York, with his wife Teresa Hewitt and son Ryan. He is associate professor of English and director of the Writing Center at St. John's University in Queens, New York City. Owens is pictured with Ryan in the family's backyard vegetable garden.

This book was typeset in Sabon by Electronic Imaging.
The typeface used on the cover was Futura.
Cover calligraphy was done by Barbara Yale-Read.
The book was printed on 60-lb. Lynx Opaque Recycled
by Versa Press, Inc.